WB-BS6-541

Thrift Score

Thrift Score

AL HOFF

HarperCollins*Publishers*

HarperCollins books may be purchased for educational, business, or sales promotional use. For information please write: Special Markets Department, HarperCollins Publishers, Inc., 10 East 53rd Street, New York, NY 10022.

FIRST EDITION

Designed by Jessica Shatan

Library of Congress Cataloging-in-Publication Data

Hoff, Al, 1964–
    Thrift score / Al Hoff. — 1st ed.
      p. cm.
    Includes bibliographical references.
    ISBN 0-06-095209-1
    1. Thrift shops. 2. Secondhand trade.   I. Title.
  HF5482.4.H64   1997
  381'.19—dc21   97-25713

97 98 99 00 01 ❖/RRD 10 9 8 7 6 5 4 3 2

This book is dedicated to everyone who ever laughed at me

Contents

Acknowledgments

This book grew out of my zine about thrifting—*ThriftSCORE*—and I owe an enormous debt to all the readers, contributors, reviewers, and distributors of that zine. Without your constant stream of letters, kind words, and dollar bills, I could never have pursued this project. Thanks to all of you for validating my obsession with thrifting and sharing your many thrifting tales. Thrift on and on!

Many people patiently answered inane questions and volunteered information. Your expertise is appreciated: Bill Hallquist, Matt Householder, Jay Rosenthal, Kim Cooper, Chip Rowe, Jim Morton, Mary Driscoll, Kelly Patterson, Vernon Stoltz, Russ Forster, Matthew Tinkcom, Joy Van Fuqua, Amy Villarejo, Alison Franks, James Stockstill, Peter Huestis, Pagan Kennedy, Paul Lukas, Barbara Plotz, and Dave Nuttycombe.

Thanks to tattooed Sassy Boys and other staff at the Carnegie Library of Pittsburgh who dug out millions of dusty periodicals for me.

Tisha Parti, Randy Reeves, Candi Strecker, Lynn Peril, and John Marr, thank you for sharing your writing and holding my hand a lot. Big thanks to Hoblitzelle, Paul Wilson, Nick Fetterick, and Jim Shaw for allowing me to poke around in their thrifting habits. I am grateful to the following people who supplied artwork: Jim Brennan, Julie Peasley, Orson, Matthew Veltkamp, Sergio de la Torre, Paul Wilson, Michelle Gienow, Gordon Simpson, and especially Vanessa Domico.

Big thanks to my editor Kate Ekrem at HarperCollins for first envisioning this book and helping to massage it into shape. To Kim Witherspoon and Maria Massie at Witherspoon Associates, thank you for all your work on my behalf.

I owe a big debt of gratitude to my parents, Bob and Elizabeth Hoff, for training me early in the glories of thrifting, among many other things. And finally, my husband, Pat Clark, who deserves first credit for suggesting I write about thrifting and last credit for having to put up with me doing so.

Introduction

"*Where* did you get that incredible thing?!" people demand of me. "What thing?" I ask, scanning my pad. The beer-can hat? The bowling-ball bar? The two-tone vinyl rocker that looks like the missing link between a '61 Bel Air and a living room? If it's fantastic and I have it, it came from a thrift store. Some folks figure thrift stores are filled with useless garbage. They'd be wrong. Just because something gets dumped at the thrifts doesn't mean it's worthless—it only needs to be rescued, reclaimed, and loved again.

PHOTO BY VANESSA DOMICO

So, this book is not about tightwadding or buying *less* stuff. It's a look at thrifting as obsession, what's out there for sale and what fun you can have with the stuff you drag home. *Thrift Score* is as varied as a thrift store itself, a grab bag of cultural history, fact, anecdote, helpful hints, and trivia. We begin with a brief discussion of Big Thrift Issues that thrifters continually confront (either consciously or not): disposable culture, value, "collectible mania." Once you are familiar with the larger issues that create and affect the thrift marketplace, we move on to address some hard mechanics of thrifting.

Since nearly everything you might buy in a thrift store becomes part of your home, I have chosen a House Tour as the structure of this book. You are under no obligation to store your dishes in your Dining Room, but I put them there to facilitate easy lookup. Also, this Thrift Dream Home is a pretty fanciful and spacious construction. We should all be so lucky to have libraries and separate entertainment areas, but it'd be tough reading if I had to adhere to real life and dump everything into one chapter—"Studio Apartment."

Naturally, this book can't cover *everything* available for sale in a thrift but I tried to write about cool things you could reasonably expect to find in *any* thrift store. And you have my word of honor: Everything mentioned or photographed in this book is guaranteed to have been *thrifted* (OK, a couple of things might have come from a yard sale or flea market . . .) or *seen in a thrift store.*

Thrifting *is* becoming more popular. There's grumbling within the thrifting community that this is the Beginning of the End and soon there'll be no "good stuff" left. Well, you can never go back to the "good old days"—whenever that was—when you were the only person in the universe into Hawaiian shirts, Martin Denny discs, Franciscan dishware, or whatever. Time marches on, with or without you. On the other hand, it's good to see that other people are busting out of the retail loop and discovering the thrills of second-hand.

And really, of a hundred shoppers in a thrift store, only one or two might even be looking for the same things you are. If you see somebody buying the *exact* same twelve things as you, you should probably ask them out. People shop in thrift stores for a zillion different reasons. For those who scour the thrifts looking for cultural debris and kooky clothes, the real danger doesn't come from the many looking-for-cheap-office-clothes converts, but from the scary guy who's trolling for the collectible or retro clothing store.

So what if all the "good stuff" is gone? There's plenty more to come! Given the correct brain-training, *any* object in a thrift—today or in the future—can be appreciated. We must learn to find delight in things because they *are* or because they have some attractive quality of their own, *not* because somebody else has made them "collectible" or they are what everybody else wants. I hope that this book shakes your mind up and inspires you to go out, find, buy, and wonder on your own. Read on, then thrift on!

Thrift Score

1 Why?

WHY THRIFT STORES?

Why thrift stores? What about flea markets, garage sales, yard sales, church bazaars, junk stores, auctions, dumpsters, and the curb on garbage pickup day? This book focuses on thrift stores because, while I have shopped all types of secondhand venues, thrift stores have always intrigued me the most. A few key things distinguish thrift stores from other used-goods marketplaces.

The Stigma

Traditionally, thrift shopping has been associated with the poor. The stigma of "used" has fallen away from the flea market, garage sale, and consignment stores, but it still clings to the thrifts. Have you ever met those people who think garage saling is great fun and filled with bargains, but think thrift shopping is gross? This stigma is still so pervasive that some thrift stores are working overtime to freshen up their images in an attempt to reach middle-class shoppers. The downside for us culture-junkers is that "fancier" thrifts now jettison a lot of the schlocky donated merchandise in favor of sure-sellers like office blouses donated by retail stores. The Goodwill chain is especially guilty of this upscaling, stocking large areas of the store with cheap new $1–$4 plastic merchandise. Hey, Goodwill! If I wanted to go to the Dollar Store, I would! I come here for the chipped teapots and rotary phones!

The Anonymity

While we've all been bothered by chatty thrifters, and these conversations run from the reasonable ("Hon, do you like this sweater on me?") to the bizarre ("Steal anything good lately?"), thrifts are where you can shop in peace and anonymity. Other shoppers are fixated just like you on buzzing about the store and snaring the bargains. There's a pleasant intensity to it—you've got thirty people in a small confined area, all semi-frantic that the other twenty-nine are going to find the good thing first. Timing is critical in thrifts, and most shoppers won't give it up to chitchat about the weather.

Sellers in small junk stores, flea markets, and yard sales have a vested interest in getting rid of their stuff—it's taking up valuable space in their store or they don't want to load it back in the van. (Thrift-store employees could care less if the merchandise sits and gathers dusts.) Such sellers are apt to be bored from sitting all day watching their junk age. They can be eager to talk you into a sale either by being friendly or by helpfully pointing out the frying pan that matches your shirt. Now, unless you enjoy being rude, you're trapped into responding, and the worst is when they hard-sell some awful thing you have no interest in buying. Some people *love* the chattiness of fleas and yard sales. Nothing wrong with that, but it ain't my scene.

Comeback City

With flea markets or yard sales, even though it may be junk to the sellers, they're still motivated enough to drag it out and hopefully make back a few bucks. However, the thrift donor has no financial motive. Thrift merchandise has traveled so very close to the bottom. Somebody was a wee bit considerate and gave the junk to the thrift stores rather than just pitching it in the trash. I like knowing that an item in the thrift just barely escaped death and, pending a purchase, will get a second shot at life.

"But . . . I Love Garage Sales!"

All that said, let me stress that there is no reason *not* to shop at garage sales and flea markets, drop into any odd store that looks dark and quirky, or root around the trash cans in your neighborhood. I do—and much of the information in this book will certainly enhance your shopping pleasure at these other secondhand markets. It's about finding *what* you want and for the *price* you love! Wherever. Hell, if Macy's marked everything down to 99 cents tomorrow, I'd be first in line.

WHY THRIFT?

Save Money!

Thrifting sure will save you money. Lots of money. New stuff is rarely cheap, and used goods are sold for a fraction of the original cost while still remaining functional. You'll save mountains of money, if—and here's the catch—*if* you can control your impulses and only buy stuff you need. You don't *need* eight identical statuettes that say "I Love You This Much." If you can't help being a frivolous shopper and a spendaholic, you're still better off at the thrifts. Simple math says that for $10 you can score one thing at the mall or a dozen items at the thrift.

PHOTO BY VANESSA DOMICO

If you already know you're a compulsive thrift shopper—or you begin to realize you might be— here's some free advice: By all means, keeping buying. It's good for the economy, it keeps forlorn objects out of the landfill, and it makes you feel good. I don't recommend trying to keep track of just how much you do spend at thrifts. I did this once. It evolved out of an argument with my husband about who was spending more money on useless items. I wrote an elaborate database for tracking purchases by buyer, store, and item bought. At the end of three months (a fiscal quarter), I tallied up the numbers. Never mind who spent more—I couldn't see the trees for the forest! I was so shocked by the amount we had spent on crap in a mere three months that I deleted the entire database and decided ignorance is bliss. Better to consider items individually, as in "This only cost 79 cents."

Saved from the Trash!

The other obvious plus of thrifting is ecological. By rescuing items from the thrift store and reusing them, you're keeping them from the growing garbage heaps. Scads of perfectly decent stuff gets thrown away, and it's a higher calling to maximize the use of these items until they die a natural death. Pure capitalists may tear at their hair and wail that you're upsetting the delicate balance of the whole national economy. That's nonsense. We'd all be in better shape if we weren't so wasteful as a culture. Besides, you're just as apt to spend the money you save on something new you need, like beer, so the real-world economy keeps rolling along.

Ad? What Ad?

You're out of the advertising loop. There are fashions in how we live our lives (dress this way, decorate that way), all conveyed to us through advertising. The manufacturers constantly change the requirements so they can sell more goods. Because nothing currently advertised is in the thrifts (though it *will* be one day!), you can ignore all advertising.

The Never-Ending Treasure Hunt

Thrift shopping is way more fun than retail shopping. Besides the thrill of a bargain, there's the excitement of the treasure hunt. Rule No. 1: You *never* know what you're going to find. For thrifters, it's a variation on the classic all-night chicken-or-egg argument as to whether it's more exciting to finally score something you've been seeking for years or to unearth something fabulous you never even knew you wanted! Doesn't matter—like chickens and eggs, both are good. Thrifters are drawn again and again to the stores. "Maybe this will be the day I find my '50s chenille bathrobe?" Who can't help but shiver with anticipation and delight when the doors to the thrift swing open and you catch your first whiff of dusty merchandise? But the other possibility is just as exciting. What fantastic thing that I'm not even aware of yet am I going to find?! When I *do* find it, I'll know that I was unconsciously searching for it all these years!

I believe that everything can end up at a thrift store, from originals of the Declaration of Independence tucked behind a bad watercolor, to brand new 1930s men's shoes, to that one weird-sized screwdriver you've been looking for. Of course, it's pure chance where these items end up—whether it's at a thrift near you and on the day you choose to go—but thrifters are *ever* hopeful. It's like the lottery—somebody's gotta win. Someone *will* buy that bathrobe or whatever it is you covet. It just might be you and it just might be today!

It's All About Me

If retail shopping is taking home what *they* want you to buy, then thrift shopping is picking up what *you alone* want to buy (well, you and your two friends who *really* think that purple fun-fur chair is the best!). The thrifts present you with a completely random and rotating selection of goods, and you make the call. There are no rules; it's just about buying things you like. If you decorate out of thrift shops, there's no way anyone else in the whole universe can have the same room as you! When guests admire your new chartreuse easy chair and ask where you got it, you smugly say, "The thrift store." See their disappointment as they realize they can never buy one like it.

"Renting" Items

Thrifting is the perfect way to acquire goods you know you'll only *temporarily* need or want. Maybe you need a few "decent" looking garments for that office temp job between acting gigs, something crazy to wear to a costume party, or thermal underwear for your once-a-decade trip to the slopes. Clothing required for specific activities, events, or climes is the obvious temporary purchase, but occasionally you might need a temporary housewares item, like an ashtray for a smoking guest, a towel to dye your hair, or a wash basin to flea-dip the cat. Thrifters who are less inclined to amass may find many of their purchases to be temporary or "rentals." Use a few times and redonate. No big cash outlay; no big commitment.

WHY <u>NOT</u> TO THRIFT?

In your life, you'll have to deal with the nonbelievers, those who don't understand something as "icky" as thrifting. Some shoppers downplay the fact that they thrift, and you're under no obligation to reveal where or how you got good stuff. I take the opposite tack. I don't wait two seconds to say I thrifted something. I'm proud of every piece of crap I've bought. Also, life is short. I like to weed out the nose-wrinklers early on.

We're clear on why we *want* to thrift, but look at these silly reasons other people give us *not* to thrift: "Thrifts smell." Big whoop, lots of life smells funny. Next. "Thrifts are full of weirdos." Weirdos are everywhere. "Thrifts are in bad neighborhoods." Some are, but most aren't. "Thrifts are noisy." So's the mall. Such reasons are easily dismissed. Two other common complaints from nonthrifters may initiate more discussion: "used clothing and thrifts are for needy people."

Dead Men's Clothes

"What if somebody *died* in those clothes?" antithrifters ask. I always counter with "What if somebody *famous* died in these clothes?" Really, of all the clothes people have, they only die in one or two garments. They're not wearing everything they own when they go, so the odds are on your side. Anyway, this is a non-argument for me. If the person is repulsed by secondhand clothing in general, then I can't change their mind. I'm amused by the common misperception that used clothes from strangers might have been subjected to more disgusting activities and lifestyles than used clothes from family members. Can you really be sure about what your big brother did in those jeans?

And let's not leave class out of it! I know people who buy used clothing from "nice" secondhand sources like the Junior League but express horror that I would wear something from the Salvation Army. The underlying implication is that well-to-do people lead clean and circumspect lives (a myth, by the way) while the poor die lingering contagious deaths in their clothing, which is then given unwashed to Goodwill. While more poor people may shop at the Salvation Army than at the Junior League, the clothing donations come from all walks of life.

This is probably what bothers a lot of antithrifters and frankly is where a lot of thrifters *do* draw the line
PHOTO BY MICHELLE GIENOW

These persnickety types are bothered by the unanswered questions posed by secondhand clothes, but a lot of us are fascinated by the mystery. Where was the garment bought? How did this great Hawaiian shirt end up in Cleveland? Was there really a woman this big who wore an op-art patterned housedress? Was this dress bought for a special occasion? Thrifters pore over their finds looking for tiny clues to past lives. The label may say at what store and city the garment was purchased. We might know enough about fashion history to guess a manufacturing date. Men's suits often have tailoring labels with the date of alteration and sometimes the buyer's name. The pockets are carefully checked. I've turned up photographs, money, grocery lists, ticket stubs, newspaper clippings, stray bits of tobacco, and matchbooks. Sometimes I just wonder where a garment has been all these years. I bought a man's basic wool overcoat once. Clearly, it had never been worn—not a speck on it, the lining as crisp as the day it had been sewed in. The tailor's label said G. LEWIS, APRIL 1933. 1933!? Where had this coat *been* all this time, and what kept it so beautifully preserved? Mr. Lewis had never worn it. Why not? Did the donor know how old it was when he or she gave it to Goodwill? I'll never know.

Thrift Stores Are for Poor People

Some people ask me, "What about poor people? Thrift stores are for them—and you don't *need* to shop there and you're taking stuff away from them." I usually bite my tongue and refrain from asking, "So what have *you* done for poor people lately?" because it's a fair question. Fair to ask, at least. I'm not sure there is a right answer, but here's a handful of justifications you may ponder or use, some of which are no doubt pretty self-serving.

1. The big giant one is simply that as a culture we already tolerate poverty. If we didn't, perhaps it wouldn't exist. But it does and for hundreds of tangible and intangible reasons. I have yet to find the logic path that proves my shopping at a thrift store alters this situation. It doesn't make a person poorer if I buy something, nor can it be proven that if I didn't buy object X and he did, his situation would improve.

2. By shopping thrift stores, we are directing funds towards charitable causes, many of which are designed to benefit the poor. Thrifts may already have a surplus of usable items (housewares, clothes) that can be given to the needy, and the cash collected at the register is more useful. Before you use this argument, make sure you understand just how the thrifts you patronize use the cash they get. Some

Like the sign says, "Shop Here—Help Others"
PHOTO BY AUTHOR

thrifts are run for profit or donate only a small percentage of the cash to a charity. Ask. They're obligated to explain their exact involvement with a charity. The Big Three—Salvation Army, Goodwill, and St. Vincent de Paul (plus Deseret Industries out west)—are all safe for-charity bets.

3. Some big thrifts seem more interested in attracting middle-class shoppers than they do the needy. Recently, the big thrift chains have been closing their inner city locations and relocating to the suburbs. The suburban locations are clean, bright, and well-aisled; have dressing rooms and bathrooms; accept credit cards; and have acres of parking. These thrifts heavily promote the concept that it's "smart" or "fashion-

able" to shop at thrifts. ("My fashion secret? I got it at Goodwill.") Ironically, thrifts never advertise to attract the rabid impulse-buyers like myself who drop zillions of bucks in their coffers. "Come in! We have six dumpsters overflowing with weird-looking stuff!"

4. There's no shortage of goods available. This argument depends on the bounty of thrifts in your areas. Some shoppers can legitimately claim that there is so much merchandise and that it is being restocked with such rapidity that it's a fair playing field no matter who's shopping. Other thrifts are more stagnant and may only see a few nice items a week.

5. "I give as much as I buy." I can't claim this one, but some people can. Seems pretty fair to me—you're providing usable goods for free, *plus* spending cash in the store.

If these issues are really odious to you, you can choose not to shop at thrift stores. Or temper your compulsive shopping with some good deeds. Maybe you don't care at all. Whatever. I'm not your conscience. Do I feel bad? Sure, sometimes I really do. Occasionally, I'll be in a thrift store where I am clearly the only middle-class person, and there I am smirking over polyester shirts or something. Some of the St. Vincent de Pauls in the Midwest are set up strictly to provide clothing to the poor—pretty much all they have is clothes, and everything is usually a quarter. I was in a St. Vinnie's in Jackson, Michigan, one bitter winter day, when the cashier announced that all sweaters were free, as many as you wanted. I already had a sweater in hand that I liked. When I went to pay for it, the lady said, "They're free." I insisted, and she made me feel worse by explaining the obvious, that all sweaters were free because it was such a cold day. I finally got her to grudgingly accept a dollar "donation," but I felt pretty low.

2 Big Thrift Issues

DRAWING FROM THE DISCARD PILE

The past fifty years of prosperity, invention, and self-conscious class anxiety set up patterns of household spending that laid the foundation of the consumer culture we all know and love today, but it also initiated the never-ending disposal of goods that accounts for today's staggering piles of thrift merchandise. This incredible stockpile of perfectly functional discarded items is created when old objects are swapped for this year's new objects. Casual disposal relies on surplus, that you already own more than you need. Without the bounty of clothing sitting in our closets, we couldn't nonchalantly discard perfectly wearable garments. The poor have no such luxury—they must eke every last bit of function out of an item. And how easily we throw perfectly good things away! "I'm bored with it." "It looks ugly now." "I only wore it once." (While this is offered as an good excuse for why it *should* be thrown away, the logic is completely twisted. Shouldn't you have worn it a lot more times before you ditched it?) It takes a nation of capricious mass-consumers to sustain our thrifting hobby!

We are all trained to consume and enjoy it. Folks aren't joking when they list shopping as a hobby. And what is this thrifting? Why, nothing more than mass-consumption at another venue! I've had visitors to my packed-to-the-rafters house admire how "political" and "antisystem" I am for rejecting consumer culture. *Au contraire*, I say. I shop a lot. I probably shop more than the average

American. And guess what: I hardly *need* any of it! I'm the worst kind of overconsumer. Just because I'm buying from the discard pile doesn't mean I've rejected the evil pleasure of acquisition.

Why Is Something Valuable at the Mall and Not at the Thrift?

But what happens to an item's value once it gets ditched at the thrift store? Thrifts are the Limbo of Value—goods are temporarily suspended between discard and worthiness. Objects begin life at Full Value (new), go to No Value when disposed of and then to Semi-Value at the thrifts. Occasionally they do make it back to Re-Value if they become "collectibles." Most stuff in the thrifts is hovering in the No Value to Semi-Value zone. Like the "real" afterlife, once the item enters Limbo, it doesn't ever fall into Hell (the landfill), but it's a toss-up between Heaven (happy purchase) and Someplace Else (the rag rug factory or a boat to the Third World.)

How Low Can You Go?

Most thrifters also employ another value system, a complete inversion of the price tag. Thrifters reject the traditional value marker, which is high cost (whether the item is new or used) and redefine value based on *low cost* and lack of desirability. "You won't believe how little this cost!" While mall shoppers may also trumpet this, they're happy about a reasonable reduction in the cost of the item— say 30 percent off. The thrifter, on the other hand, loves the fact that the chair was only a dollar. It's a good price to pay for a chair, but he also relishes *the complete dismissal and unworthiness* of this chair by all, as reflected in the ridiculous $1 price tag.

The pleasure is twofold: the cost savings, plus scoring off of other people's ignorance of the item's "true" value. It may be a traditionally expensive item such a cashmere blazer for $3, an odd item that has high value in a specific marketplace such as a collectible record, or something that only has special meaning to the shopper. The less valued the item, the bigger the score. Price is your primary indicator of the value the thrift assigned it, but sometimes you'll get a bigger thrill if you learn how many other shoppers overlooked this treasure, too. The clerk who says "I can't believe somebody *finally* bought this" should be rewarded with a big smile. You'll be dining out on that quote later.

Thrifters can be just as petty and immature as the expensive item bragger. Thrifters occasionally *lie* when relating the Big Score and deliberately fudge the price or knock a few dollars off. Of course, if some real-world shopper is bragging about how much something he bought cost, you should leap right in to point out that he got ripped off and that you just thrifted a nearly identical item. Feel free to drop a few dollars off the price, just for good measure. Reverse snobbery is the power trip we thrifters feed on.

ON BEYOND THRIFTING PROFILE NO. 1

This is the first of four On Beyond Thrifting Profiles. These thrifters were selected because of their ability to take thrifting beyond the simple acquisition of goods.
Who: Hoblitzelle (a pseudonym), an Oakland, California, artist.
Thrifting Origins: Began thrifting sophomore year in high school for cool clothes. Now he thrifts primarily to support his Thrift Store Art Project, but, like all thrifters, he is not averse to picking up the occasional swell garment or knickknack.

• • •

Hoblitzelle doesn't just buy art at the thrifts. Inverting all known laws of the art world and consumer culture, for the past two years he's been sneaking his own art into the thrift. The project begins with a thrift-store purchase. Hoblitzelle buys aluminum housewares (coffeepots and storage ware) or picture frames and takes them home. There, the housewares are etched and anodized (color dyes are affixed to the aluminum through electricity and an acid bath process) and the frames are matched to his own collection of drawings or prints. All the images depict scenes from his family life or personal history.

Originally, each new piece of artwork (thrift purchase + new art) was assigned a number and recorded (date and location purchased, price paid, what piece it is, and when or where it was placed). Later, he began including a self-addressed stamped envelope with the piece (usually visible) and occasionally he also added an artist statement, additional artwork, or cash, all intended to facilitate a response from the buyer. He keeps the original thrift price tag on or adds a new low price of his own before it goes back to the thrift store.

"Then, guerrilla-style, I walk into the thrift store in a determined fashion with the completed art. Once inside, the employees assume that I've picked up the piece in there and that I am still browsing. I go to the art or housewares section, place the object, and then walk around for a bit. I return to where I placed the item and photograph it. I stay in the thrift for a bit to watch how people respond to it.

Sometimes they do, sometimes they don't. I take off. Sometimes I come back the next day and the piece is gone. Only once did I see two women buy one of my framed prints."

Hoblitzelle places the artwork ("Cough-Fee") in an Oakland, California, thrift.
PHOTO BY SERGIO DE LA TORRE

How on earth does an artist get the idea to give his art away in the thrift stores? Quite simply, he went to art school! "I was walking around the painting department thinking to myself, 'This stuff is such crap.' It could easily be in a thrift store, given the assumption by many that artwork in thrift stores is shit. Why don't I just speed up the process and just debase my artwork by putting it in a thrift store? This is antithetical to art or going to art school. You go to art school to make all this money off of your artwork. You know, to be the lone famous artist. By putting my artwork in the thrift store, automatically it's seen as secondhand or that somebody didn't want it. So, people are buying it, or are turned on to it because they *aesthetically* like it, not for status or predetermined 'art' value as it might be viewed in a gallery. In the case of housewares, they might need it for something and it has the added bonus of 'art' on the piece.

"I put my art in the thrifts to broaden my audience. My artwork is not just in galleries, but in thrift stores throughout California and the country. Not as many people go to art galleries, but a couple hundred people of all sorts a day might see my piece in a thrift store. It takes the control out of my hands as to who views and chooses to buy my art. Artwork *should* be really cheap, which is again why I put it in thrift stores."

The photos taken in the thrift stores are then professionally printed, framed, editioned, and sent to art galleries. "If people buy the photo from the art gallery, they are buying a potential history of this piece if the original art is bought at the thrifts and the buyer responds. The photo of my anodized coffeepot is in an art museum. The *actual* coffeepot went to a thrift store. The roles are reversed. Now these fancy gallery-goers or museum-goers get the fake (which is usually what everybody gets) and the thrift store-goers—whoever they might be—get the original for cheaper than the photograph. The photo is $100, but I priced the pot at $2.95.

"My work is intended to be a catalyst for interaction. What's important to me is the interaction with these people who do take the time out of their life and have the courage to write. That, to me, is what's rewarding. It's important to find out something about people and their lives, to perhaps initiate a dialog about art and life, like to find out where they hang the piece or what it's doing in their lives."

Of the approximately one hundred pieces of art Hoblitzelle has left in the thrifts, he has had four and a half responses: three letters from Los Angeles (one guy sent some of his own art in the form of a CD) and one from Kansas, and an individual in New York City who kept the frame, but returned the artwork with no further comment.

Still fascinated by art and value, Hoblitzelle, along with friend and fellow thrifter Mike Pare, recently recreated a thrift store within an art gallery. He and his pals gathered typical thrift merchandise (the stuff was donated, thrifted, or just rounded up around the house.) "We priced it ourselves comparable to thrift-store prices. We got to play thrift-store manager where we placed our own value on seemingly random items. Stuff that was sentimental to us we priced high." The merchandise (or was it "art"?) was for sale. "The best was, everything that didn't sell . . . at the end of the show, we just called the Salvation Army and they took the show away!"

Despite the low response, Hoblitzelle is committed to continuing his guerrilla thrift art. "It's all about communication and value and thumbing my nose at the art world because I think it's full of shit. At the very least, it's like reverse shoplifting. The thrifts are making double the money selling the frame or tea canister twice!"

● ● ●

WELCOME TO THE PAST

As our culture changes, bits and pieces of forgotten fads, fashions, and ways of life can now be retrieved from the secondhand realm. The thrifts are superb repositories of "lost" items. Because people keep some things for a long time—for continued use, for sentiment, or because they plumb forgot they had it—donations to the thrift can range from last week's free sports bottle to Dad's old ties from the 1940s. The sheer volume of goods in each thrift usually guarantees a selection from several decades.

Museums may preserve the "important" stuff, but it's the thrifts that hold the secrets of past *everyday* lives. Every object in the thrift store has already "lived" somewhere before. Every time you enter a thrift store, you're on your own little archaeology mission. It's a free historical exercise gliding down aisles and somehow accounting for all those jumbled-up forlorn objects. It's no museum time capsule, where each item is laid out and labeled by some benevolent brainiac who has typed up little cards placing each item into context for you. *You* get to make the historical connections, if any. You can disregard the item's history or treasure it as an artifact and eke out the lost meaning. (Some items lend themselves to easy historical study. For instance, read a few thrifted housewife manuals from the 1950s and suddenly the last forty years of women's social history is right in context!) Especially motivated thrift archaeologists can even use these items to live vicariously in the past. (See On Beyond Thrifting Profile #2 in Chapter 7.)

Dead Fads Are Fun!

Nothing amuses me more about digging through the past via thrifting than unearthing dead fads. America is delightfully fad-obsessed, and fads provide a great peek into our collective culture. A fad happens when some item or activity suddenly resonates with everybody. They may occur when a new item, like designer jeans, hits the marketplace or when an existing item, like CB radios, is suddenly rediscovered and heralded. Other fads, like fondue, exist on their own weird energy. The media helps to sustain many fads, and the more products that can be exploited through a fad, the bigger buzz there'll be. But often, as quickly as they spring up, fads wither and fade away.

Look for the Dead Fad marker

Where would we be without those backlashes? Each new dying fad brings another wave of crap ashore in thriftland. Thrifters get to scavenge among the remains, marvel at past folly, pick out what we wish to keep, and perhaps even use it for another round of fun. Thrifters can use the fad as a framework to search out various items singly that can then be compiled in your home as a cultural unit. A fad will often cast its merchandising net across many spheres. The CB radio fad gave us clothing, books, records, glassware, and toys. In the thrift store, each of those items would be found in its own distinct area, but in your home, you can assemble them on a shelf or in a corner and get the big wide-screen image of the fad.

Several dead fads will be spotlighted in this book. The fad will be placed in some context so you can understand how it might have arisen, what impact it had on our culture at the time, and then, most important, what debris it left behind when it died. Hopefully, by examining a few representative dead fads, you'll be prepared to spot the next live one. See it on the street, then wait for it to hit the thrift!

COLLECTIBLES AND THE COLLECTIBLES MARKET

There is nothing wrong with collecting things. People like certain objects, and having several similar items adds to the enjoyment. Every hard-core thrifter understands that six is better than one. My complaint is with "collectibles," used items from the secondhand markets that have become revalued and fiercely desired. This is a recently created category of merchandise distinct from antiques, which have been a source of amusement and investment for rich people for centuries. The antiques market is not without its inflated value problems but is of little concern to us thrifters.

Let's just assume for the sake of argument that antiques do have real value. There aren't many Louis XIV chairs around, they are really old, and they're beautifully made pieces of handcrafted furniture. Some antiques are like works of singular art that can never be duplicated—remnants of a truly lost time and skill. But this argument doesn't work for the current collectibles market. Current "hot" collectibles include dishware, pottery, toys, 1950s kitsch items, and it seems nearly anything else twenty years old! Most of this desired stuff was mass produced, and plenty of

It's estimated that Americans shell out $5 billion a year for collectibles.[1] That's $25 for each man, woman, and child, or one Six Million Dollar Man trash can each at current rates.
PHOTO BY VANESSA DOMICO

today's high-priced collectibles were pretty darn inexpensive when new—souvenir tablecloths, McCoy pottery (I've thrifted McCoy pottery that still had the original drugstore sticker on it: 69 cents), costume jewelry, plastic toys, etc.

Ordinarily I could care less if a bunch of people with too much money to spend are running around obsessing over Star Wars figures or cookie jars. But we can no longer ignore the very real effect this new collectibles mania is having on thrifts. The last few years have seen one previously junky item after another move from the back shelves to the front counter. Often the information about collectibles that has trickled down to the thrifts is spotty or misunderstood. Some thrifts seem to mark up anything more than ten years old as

THE LUNCH BOX INCIDENT

"Three years ago I wanted to get a marketing monopoly on a collectible and hit all the angles," said Scott Bruce in 1988.[2] Bruce decided on metal lunch boxes—average purchase price, he says, $10 each. He reckoned they'd be easily exploitable as a collectible commodity because metal lunch boxes weren't manufactured anymore and they hit right at the heart of the baby boomer nostalgia market (1950–1970) with the added bonus of TV/movie tie-ins. After boning up in the lunch box makers' archives, he began to publish a collectors' newsletter, *Hot Boxing*. Then came the coffee table book and the price guide (both essentially covering his collection). What happened next? The price of lunch boxes went through the roof! What is so scary about the lunch box plot is how well it worked. A man simply inflated the prices on the objects he owned, making a profit by deliberately creating a market. And every single one of us who's been thrifting within the past ten years has seen the effect.

What does it all mean? (1) Scott Bruce will probably never go hungry in a consumer-driven society. (2) Collectibles markets are capable of being artificially created. (3) The trickle-down effect of these prefab markets is devastating to thrifters and more casual accumulators of stuff—those driven by the pure pleasure of owning, not by any perceived monetary or investment value.

Who doesn't like a metal lunch box? Hardly a *bad* item—lunch boxes are a great shape and a handy carrying or storage case. Most of us hold our own nostalgia for the metal lunch box we once had. They're great popular culture markers, a fun item, and a good buy *for a couple of bucks!* They're not made of gold. They were cheap, mass-produced items, and I mean, MASS-produced. (An estimated 120 million were made between 1950 and 1970.)

Back in the 1980s, I would buy lunch boxes I liked the picture on. My limit was $2. By 1990, I saw lunch boxes priced at $5 and up (and up!) at flea markets and retro stores. About this time, I came across Scott Bruce's lunch-box book and was flabbergasted! Gradually, the lunch boxes in the thrifts started migrating from the back wall near the hockey masks up to the front counter. I stuck by my price limits, but even I was affected by the lunch-box collectible mania in an odd reverse way. Whereas I used to buy only the images I liked, now if I saw a lunch box that was under my price limit, I'd buy it regardless of the image (Strawberry Shortcake—blech) *just* to keep it out of the hands of evil collectors. Even if they piled up underappreciated in some corner of my house, at least the lunch box was still only worth $2 and hadn't been snapped up at the thrift by some speculator who was now negotiating a four-digit figure for its release.

Now, there's hardly a thrift store in the most remote area of the U.S. that doesn't know lunch boxes are supposed to be expensive. Some even keep *plastic* lunch boxes behind the counter. Most of the lunch boxes I currently see in thrifts are $10 to $30. I don't know how that compares to the "collectibles market" (and I refuse to care), but I walk on by. Let somebody else be a sucker. Just recently I got a nice plaid lunch box in Ohio for 65 cents, so maybe things are returning to normal . . .

collectible. You'll see a Herb Alpert record behind the counter marked "vintage vinyl" or a stack of recent grubby comic books for five bucks each. One local thrift has had a box of "antique" (1940s) airmail envelopes behind the counter for ages. Still another thrift has been trying to sell a repro lava lamp from the 1990s for $25!

Thrift stores are interested in recouping more money for certain items. They're in the business not just to provide items at low cost but also to raise cash. But since the thrift store has long been distinguished as a place outside the established value system of consumer culture, this new collectibles frenzy undermines what makes thrifts so attractive—everything in them is discarded junk. Now they're hardly different from a retro shop exploiting collectibles mania. I shop at thrifts for the delight of finding a treasure amongst the dreck, "treasure" being defined as something *I* value, not something the thrift has learned is collectible.

Junk to Jewel—Collectibles Alchemy

Doesn't it seem odd that some crap from the recent past is collectible and other stuff is not? Certain items are junk one year, "hot collectibles" the next. It seems random but it's not. Markets for collectibles are created by those who have a personal interest in profiting from them. (See p. 16 on lunch boxes for a very illustrative story.)

Daily papers, decorating guides, women's magazines, financial periodicals, and news weeklies all regularly run excited stories about collectibles. The story usually covers a rise in value (though this rise may be based only on the word of one big dealer or someone's new book) or when there is an anticipated rise in an item's value (e.g. the interest in past O. J. Simpson memorabilia after his arrest). It's always a rags-to-riches story—how some ordinary thing has become extraordinary. There is no news value in reporting on a stable market or worse, acknowledging the truth that our culture is packed with discarded and worthless crud.

The Urban Legend—Finding Treasures in Your Attic

Many of these recent collectibles articles pose the question, "What treasures could be hiding in your attic?" (Each article usually gets in the dig that the reader may have *already* thrown this item away [!] before they were educated about its value. Human nature is pretty predictable. If you *used* to have something that is now considered valuable, you are likely to want to repossess it. We don't need Freud to tell us that this desire is compounded one hundredfold if it was your mother who threw this item out.) "Unearthing treasures" is one of the most powerful engines of collectibles allure. Articles simultaneously play up the "ordinariness" of an item and the banal place it was found, but they never fail to deliver the money shot—what's it's *really* worth!! These tales become like urban legends, eagerly retold "Did you hear about . . . ?" tales. Finding the Green Hornet decoder ring could happen to anybody!

The fallacy with the "treasures in your attic" argument is that, while you may have a shiny Brady Bunch lunch box in your attic and the media tells you it's worth $200, that doesn't mean *you* can actually sell it for $200. That price represents the high end, what a Greenwich Village retro shop could get from a big-bucks individual well versed in the current market for lunch boxes. Also what may be limited in one area can be commonplace in another. *Metropolitan Home* says souvenir tablecloths are hot and gives New York City prices that make you drool. You drag your grandma's (never used!) tablecloths out for the yard sale and can't get a buck for them. What you do get is a lot of other shoppers telling you that *their* grandmother has a bunch of those old tablecloths too! So you pack 'em up muttering to yourself, "In New York, I could get hundreds for these tablecloths." Maybe you could, but you ain't there, baby, and there're too many old tablecloths in your 'hood.

The Thrifter's Meager Battle Plan

There is no reason not to collect things or even not to want those now-collectible things. I gnash my teeth with envy over people's spectacular collectibles so beautifully photographed in a book or magazine. The difference is what I'm willing to pay for them. What can the low-budget thrifter do? You can't defeat capitalism (all experiments have failed . . .), but it is a market-driven economy and you can fight back with your pocketbook by *not* paying the inflated prices. Set your own price limits—*what is it worth to you?* Maybe if enough people refuse to buy into the increased pricing schemes, prices will be reconsidered and low-

Somebody at my local thrift heard old Hawaiian shirts are worth big bucks and put this shirt out on the racks with a $50 price tag. When I saw it in the store, I guffawed loudly and said, "They'll *never* get that! Who do they think shops here?!" A month later, I bought it. The tag was down to $3.95, but it was last week's tag, so I only paid half.
PHOTO BY AUTHOR

ered. Probably not, but at the very least, you have the small satisfaction of remaining pure and not being part of the problem. I'm no great prognosticator of economic trends, but there is the possibility that this hypercollectible market will not hold up. After much hoo-ha and wild financial speculation, the interest in lunch boxes or Franciscan dishware will wane and prices will drop. They may not drop to precollectible levels, but it might temper the inflation on the next round of "hot items."

THE BICENTENNIAL REVISITED: PUT DOWN YOUR MUSKET, MY COUNTRYMAN, AND MEET ME AT THE MALL

No need to reprise what the Bicentennial was or what it commemorated; everybody learned this in high school. And we're not interested in the birth of democracy or U.S. history. We're interested in the stuff. And *stuff* there was, an unprecedented amount of commemorative items from expensive guaranteed-to-be-collectible *objets* like a $55,000 14K gold bust of George Washington (classy!) to the red, white, and blue-ing of the most mundane and inappropriate items (garbage bags!).

DEAD ·FAD·

A gazillion articles were written about the Bicentennial—rehashes of history, guides to festivities, sociohistorical essays—but the best source of information about Bicentennial goods are the "horror" pieces about how commercialized the entire event was becoming. While every one of these writers decried the overuse of the Bicentennial logo, the three-man Revolutionary Band, and the stars and stripes, a separate overuse award could go to these reporters for the very unimaginative and repeated use of the term "BUY-centennial." Each story sought to outdo the other in isolating the "worst" Bicentennial items. The toilet seat! No, a bar of soap shaped like Uncle Sam's head! The cake mold shaped like George Washington's head! No no no—the Spirit of '76 coffin!! OK, you win.

The Bicentennial event was created to be exploited, and it was inescapable—the message, the meaning, the logo, the stuff was forced on Americans at every turn. You succumbed because there was little choice. (I bought a pair of Bicentennial shorts at Sears. I chose them less because I was into celebrating the Bicentennial than because there probably wasn't much else on the racks that summer.) There weren't just manufactured commemorative items that you could consciously decide *not* to buy, but there were everyday things you couldn't avoid that got the Bicentennial spin: laundry bags, garbage trucks, fire hydrants, fast-food restaurant napkins, sugar packets, etc. Unfortunately, a lot of that everyday stuff is lost to us now (how I wish I hadn't had such a bad attitude about the whole affair at the time and had been smart enough to stockpile the crassest products!), but there's no shortage of Bicentennial merchandise still for sale at the thrifts.

And Anyhow, It's What Made This Country Go Zowee

Democracy? . . . whatever. The Bicentennial was really about the triumph of capitalism and consumer culture. The occasional person got it. "I see no harm in these Bicentennial products," said Robert Williams, executive secretary of the New York chapter of the Sons of the Revolution. "There's nothing wrong with making a buck. Free enterprise is the thing that has made this country go zowee."[3]

Of course, everybody knew the Bicentennial was being overcommercialized, but who wasn't a little cynical anymore about American history? Vietnam and Watergate were fresh memories that had sucked a lot of air out of the "America is great" and "the government is good" balloons. Yes, the Declaration of Independence reproduced on toilet paper trivialized and devalued American history, but Americans were already in the process of relinquishing naive symbolism. The Bicentennial was a benign way to participate in patriotism without the unpleasant associations of foreign war or jingoism.

And listen, it's not like the Feds took the high road! The American Revolution Bicentennial Administration licensed at least 120 companies to place the "official" logo (the red, white, and blue curvy star) on their products. (They covered their butts, though. The money went to fund public Bicentennial events.) And no less a source than the official government publication, *Bicentennial Times*, said "Buying souvenirs is as American as apple pie."[4] Amen brother—and pass the pie.

It's Party Time!

Throughout this book, you will find several theme party ideas. Look for the Party Marker! The thrifts are your best source for cheap party fun, whether it's a tiki party or an '80s retro affair. The most important thing is planning. You can't decide Tuesday that you're gonna have a tiki party Saturday and run out to the thrift on Friday to stock up. Thrifting the right ingredients for your theme party takes time. Pick a party idea in this book (or think up your own), and jot down the items you might need. Also, don't be afraid to enlist the help of your thrifting friends. After all, they'll be coming to the party too, so

Look for the
Party marker

group effort adds to everyone's enjoyment. If it's a party where you'd like your guests to come in particular dress, it's polite to give them as much lead time as possible to thrift just the right outfit.

Tonight We're Gonna Party Like It's 1976!

The good thing about stocking up for a Bicentennial party is that not only are future commemorations soon upon us (2001—the 25th anniversary!), but you can drag this stuff out every year on the Fourth of July. Or rattle convention entirely by staging your Bicentennial party on a weekend in October.

Clothing: At the very minimum guests should come attired in red, white, and blue. Extra points will be awarded to those who arrive in '76-era Bicentennial clothing (T-shirts, ties, shorts, dresses, hats, belt buckles, socks, scarves, pants—hardly any item escaped Bicentennialification). A grand prize should go to anyone who can thrift a replica Revolutionary War costume! Live recreations of key historical events were very popular with civic groups and schools.

PHOTO BY AUTHOR

Food: If you can't get the aforementioned cake mold shaped like George Washington's head, look for other more common molds like eagles, bells, or the flag. These are good for gelatin desserts, too. At the very least, make one of those sheet cakes you see pictured every summer in *Ladies Home Journal*—the Cool Whip–covered one with blueberries and strawberries arranged like the American flag. The ingredients to make red, white, and blue food are fairly limited. A trick is to make whatever you like but give it some high-falutin' Bicentennial name like Liberty Bell Peppers with Valley Forge Dip, Yankee Doodle Noodles, or Paul Revere Two-If-By-Sea Pizza. While tending bar (or, should I say, while presiding over your tavern), drive your guests nuts by repeatedly declaring "I regret that I have but one drink to give to my country!"

Prize: You can set aside a particularly good piece of Bicentennial schlock to be awarded as a prize, perhaps for the best outfit, the most clever invention of a Bicentennial-themed recipe or cocktail, or if you're really in the spirit, give a pop quiz on the actual historical events of 1776.

Entertainment: This will not be your hippest party aurally. Unfortunately, they didn't have much rockin' music back in 1776. Commemorative records for the Bicentennial were released, mostly of has-been entertainers and choirs singing patriotic songs interspersed with oral recitations of Revolutionary speeches or "what my country means to me." The camp value of these recordings may wear thin quickly. You can substitute recordings of patriotic songs as performed by "hipper" people like Elvis Presley, Ray Charles, and Jimi Hendrix. A cheating rock alternative would be to only play songs from the summer of '76. The number one song the week of July Fourth was "Love Hangover" by Betsy—uh, I mean—Diana Ross. *The* album that summer was *Frampton Comes Alive,* but remember Peter Frampton was British and British people were a big no-no in 1776.

What Goodies Are out There?

Some of this merchandise will be even more yummy for the crass overlapping of promotion. Lots of companies got in on the act and did their civic duty by giving away Bicentennial stuff that also had their name on it. I thrifted a stemmed coffee mug that says "1776–1976 Bicentenary" on one side. The other side says "Winchester Safety Award—5 million hours—August 1974–September 1975." You can ponder two hundred years of history or, if you're not so reflective, turn the mug around and contemplate a mere year of rifle safety.

When party planning, don't overlook standard patriotic stuff that can be incorporated: anything with images of U.S. flags, stars and stripes, the Revolutionary War, American eagles, and leftover decorations from Fourth of July parties. The last few years have seen a surge of Bicentennial products donated to the thrifts as people have grown weary of keeping them. ("Honey, why do we still have these Bicentennial beer glasses?"). To the untrained eye, this stuff does look pretty silly and out of place in the 1990s. More for us.

The following items are all fairly common in thrift stores.

- Coffee mugs: glass, ceramic, stemmed, and plastic
- Drinking glasses. Buy them as you see them. You'll be able to put a set together quickly, but there's nothing wrong with a little variety.
- Beer steins: pewter, fake pewter, ceramic, plastic, and glass
- Beer goblets
- Trays
- Place mats
- Wall hangings
- Candles
- Art/paintings. Look for special Bicentennial paint-by-numbers!

- Colonial-style fabric. This was actually popular decades earlier—think of the "early American" living room with colonial-style curtains and the eagle lamp base—but it's dead useful for party decorations.

These items are not as common but do turn up:

- Liquor decanters
- Clothing: T-shirts, denim, polyester prints, scarves, hats, belt buckles, ties
- Commemorative records
- Books like *The Revolution to Mixed Drinks*, a Spirit of '76 bar guide

And finally, from the Why-Oh-Why-Can't-I-Find-This? dream item category. . .

One of the best pieces of thrifted Bicentennial merchandise I ever saw was a small Zenith kitchen TV. It had woodgrain sides with signatories to the Declaration of Independence on it! The sheer brilliance of merging the Declaration of Independence with a TV is staggering. We can only hope there will be such a *creative* time in American culture again! See you in 2076!

3 Let's Go Thrifting

SOME BASIC STRATEGIES

You're going thrifting today? Remember this: you're probably *not* going to find what you're looking for in the thrift store. Not today anyway. But I bet you find something else you want. Oh, and sooner or later, you will find that thing you were looking for. But that's not important. It's the *want* that matters. Therein lies the essence of obsessive thrift shopping—the continual desire, quest, and unfulfilled need that keeps us all dashing into thrifts at any spare moment.

There is probably a neophyte thrifting stage we've all passed through and repressed, when we thought logically, but foolishly, "Gee, I need a cool raincoat, think I'll go out to the thrift and get one." We returned empty-handed and disappointed, because there were no cool raincoats. Maybe some of you even went to the mall! But the dedicated thrifters persevered. We returned to the thrift, this time looking for a laundry hamper *and* a raincoat. Still another time we returned—now in search of laundry hamper, raincoat, and Hawaiian music. Didn't find any, but left with great amateur painting of a tree on fire. And still we kept going. The "needs" now include raincoat, laundry hamper, Hawaiian music, and thrift-store paintings. See a pattern? Are you shaking your head in bemusement remembering that simpler time when you only had *four* items (not forty) on your "need list"?

If I had one piece of advice to pass on, it would be to *keep that list*. Keep it in your head or write it down if you have to. The list represents a mature and even logical approach to the completely random nature of what merchandise is available in a thrift store at any given moment. There is no guarantee of what may turn up, so it's foolish to keep your list too low. Let it spiral out of control! Who wants the heartache of coming home empty-handed? People who thrift with me for the first time are always stunned at how much stuff I find. My secret is not in my commonsense thrifting skills. No, my method is in my madness—I have a list a mile long. Essentially, I "need" everything (except miniblinds). My cart is always full, and some desire is therefore always sated.

The more you want, the more you'll find! The more you desire, the more you'll thrift! The more you thrift, the more you'll see and add to your list! If it sounds like some sort of self-perpetuating self-delusional justification for filling your home with society's flotsam and jetsam—well, it is. So what? Let other people worry about your mental health and what a fire hazard your pad is. You've got stuff to buy.

Searching Out the Thrifts

Let your fingers do the walking. Look in the phone book. It's that simple. In the Yellow Pages, look under *Thrift Stores, Secondhand, Used Goods, Used Furniture,* and *Consignment.* And doublecheck

When driving around, be alert for the word "thrift." Go mad at the number of Thrift Bakeries there are!
PHOTO BY AUTHOR

the White Pages: look up the names of the biggies—Salvation Army, Goodwill, St. Vincent de Paul, Thrift whatever, Value whatever, and any other thrift chains in your area. (Occasionally, the thrift will be listed in the White Pages and not the Yellow Pages.) If it's your hometown, figure out where they are and get over there pronto.

When planning a road trip, your library may have other cities' phonebooks. In an out-of-town thrift chain, check to see if they have any signs or fliers that list other store locations. Ask the employees if there's other thrifts in town or nearby. Thrifts can come grouped in one area and they'll know that the other store is just down the street behind the donut shop. Try asking other shoppers, too. Don't worry about looking foolish or "green"— you don't even live here! Make a note of other thrifts or pick up fliers even if you don't have time to visit them that day.

Some people get concerned that thrift stores will be in bad neighborhoods. It's been my personal experience that most aren't in the worst neighborhoods. Nonetheless, use your good judgment. If it's an area you're unfamiliar with and you don't feel comfortable, you can keep driving.

Shop Alone or with Friends?

The number one problem with shopping with your thrifting pals is competition. You're all friends for a reason, and it's likely that your tastes are similar. It can be a little tense. I know that feeling of imperceptibly picking up my pace as we all cross the parking lot toward the door—who's gonna go in first? Is Biff going to the dishes? Binky to the records? It's an unwritten rule: once in the door, everybody scatters and heads off to "private territories." In theory, everybody gets first crack at one section.

Two exceptions come to mind: (1) There's been a previous intention stated that has merit. "The cat puked all over my bed this morning," says Barney. Barney should be given first go at linens. (2) You are entertaining a visitor. Visiting thrifters should always be given first priority in your town. After all, you live there and will return to this thrift. It's their one shot, and why not maximize the pleasure of their visit? You'd expect nothing less from them when you cruise through their turf another time. The emphasis is on *visiting*. If the "visit" becomes extended or the visitor starts putting down roots, it's every man for himself. Ditto for first-time thrifters.

I'll back off the first time, but after that they better be ready to race me for the golf sweaters.

The basic rule is whoever sees it first gets it. If you're really mercenary, this can mean whoever *grabs* it first gets it. That's the way of the jungle and it's ugly. But *do* consider your friends. I'll relinquish some item if a friend can make a good case for it (like it's the fourth glass they need for a set). The whine "I wish *I'd* seen that first" is not a good case. It's not a bad idea to establish a pattern of generosity among your thrift friends. Hopefully, you can rely on reciprocal behavior when they score the thing you really want. Hopefully. If you perceive a one-sided "giving" situation, you may want to just get ugly and hunker down for battle. It is OK to make a little noise about how you wanted something they got. You want them to remember you when they get bored with that item and ditch it. Also, most hard-core thrifters with too much stuff are guilty of "home-shopping." When called upon to provide a present for some occasion, they just walk about the house till something catches their eye that seems appropriate. Friends that initially scored the cool thing

ADVANTAGES TO SHOPPING ALONE:

1. There's more room in the car for stuff.

2. No competition from your friends.

3. You can buy gifts for your friends for 49 cents and they'll never know.

4. If you go way over some price limit (you get caught in a buying frenzy and pay $20 for something you know shouldn't go for more than $5), there's nobody to see. You can lie about it later.

5. Your friends can't talk you into buying that idiotic thing.

DISADVANTAGES TO SHOPPING ALONE:

1. Lonely.

2. No free advice on whether clothing looks good on or if that item is cool.

3. No one to help carry that chair to the car (or worse, on the bus!).

4. Possible feelings of shame for not inviting your thrifting pal who you know is probably watching Nickelodeon reruns at home.

5. You lose the "SWAT team" maneuver. Successfully executed, you and your pals swarm out across the store—one cases the glassware, another the records—snatching up all the good stuff simultaneously so you can reconnoiter later and divvy it up.

6. No one to share the score with, at the store and later in the post-game, spread-out-all-over-the-floor, detagging wrap-up.

have eventually presented it to me as a gift. (How easy for them—they *knew* I wanted it!)

Thrifting with nonthrifting friends can be fun or frustrating. It can be a delight to see their eyes pop out when they realize the *plus* of thrifting. "Hey look look look, I've been searching for a book bag and look look look this one's only $3—I *can't* believe it." Smile benevolently—we've all had our first thrill once. It can be a chore, though, if they don't get it immediately and you have to hand-hold them through the whole store while other people are bagging all the good stuff over in the book aisle. And nothing is worse than shopping with the nonthrifter who just *refuses* to deal and stands sulking and whining to leave.

Why even thrift with nonthrifters? Sometimes it helps to promote a better understanding of yourself to another party, be they a good friend, potential lover, or family member. If you're a hard-core thrifter, it shows. It sneaks into every aspect of your life, from the clothes you wear to the crap you keep on your desk at work. This can baffle and confuse people: "I don't understand why you have so much weird stuff and why you spend every waking minute trying to buy more." A thrift visit can (though not always) help them "get" who you are and put what you do in some perspective. The non-thrifters may in fact be pleasantly surprised by the range of low-priced goods at the thrift and may have an epiphany of their own. They still might not truly understand why you bought a radio that doesn't work, but they might be quite pleased with the mixing bowl they got.

Thrifting with your parents is recommended for family bonding. Not only do you rack up "quality time" points, but almost *never* are your parents looking for the same things you are. Win-win. Sometimes they even go "parental" and pay for your stuff. The downside is they will sniff and tell you that glitter stretch sweater looks tacky and why would you want that when there's this nice Liz Claiborne cabbage rose sweater—look, never worn!

If you're in a competitive thrift relationship with your friends and you discover a new thrift store in your area, do you tell them or not? For some generous souls, this is a nonissue. They're on the phone in five minutes spreading the good news. For other less-caring-and-sharing types (and especially those in a fiercely competitive urban setting), they may nuzzle that little discovery close to their Mustang racing stripe jacket and not tell a soul.

I appreciate those who share, and I am respectful of people's secret thrifts. Having grown up in San Francisco, one of the most competitive thrift zones on the planet, I tended to hold secrets. The breezy "Oh, I got it someplace . . ." was my answer to any queries. I later moved to Washington, D.C., and one day, while getting from Point A to Point B via Point G, we stumbled across a new thrift in suburban Maryland. We vowed to keep it secret from our two best friends (and major-thrifters-with-similar-tastes) and we did so for three years. The weekend before we moved out of D.C. for Pittsburgh, these two friends suggested one last thrifting trip. Agreed. While en route, one coughed delicately and said casually that he'd *just* discovered a new thrift, would we like to go? Would we?! Imagine our embarrassment when we pulled into the parking lot of our "secret thrift"! Ashamed, we confessed to the crime of withholding this store. Equally ashamed, our pals admitted to shopping at this thrift for years and not telling *us*. Aren't you embarrassed for all of us?

Parking Lot Analysis

I case the parking lot before I go into a thrift. I look for the too-obvious yuppie cars—are they on some Martha Stewart–inspired slum?—and for cars with a hipster look, the Fugazi sticker or the toys hanging in the window—have they already snapped up my smiley-face glasses? What I see in the parking lot might determine where I do my primary attack inside. That said, we are talking about rash generalizations here that might prove 100 percent unfounded, but the smart thrifter is ever alert to all aspects of the environment.

Dress to Score

Wear something simple. You're gonna want easy movement for digging through that dish pile, and you don't want to get overheated. Leave your heavy coat and sweaters in the car. Same goes for raincoats and umbrellas. If you're still cold once inside the thrift, just borrow a jacket from them while shopping. Have your hands free. Wear your backpack over both shoulders and your purse strapped across you. This will keep either from sliding off you while you're bending, stretching, and grabbing. Carrying things like lunch boxes, briefcases, skateboards, coats, and boom boxes limits your mobility and shopping potential. You wanna be in there with *both* hands.

There's no hard data to support this, but it can be advantageous to dress plainly and ordinarily. While you may be shopping at the thrift to find that *ne plus ultra* item that's guaranteed to make you stand out in a crowd of a million, you don't necessarily have to advertise that while shopping. Think of this: (1) You tip off other shoppers to what you might be buying. If I see some hipster enter wearing a crazy polyester shirt, I'm gonna dash right over to that section and be there *first,* just in case. (2) You might get "followers." These are people who spot you for being some kind of expert or in-the-know and they trail behind you—looking at what you look at, staring at you—just being a nuisance. You may also be tipping your hand to a future rival. The follower thinks, "Whoa, I didn't think that muumuus were cool, but now that I see that hip-looking person wearing one, I'm gonna buy them too." (3) Should you need to deal with the staff (say, get that untagged item priced), you may merit more courtesy and attention if you look like a regular joe. As we all know, the help in thrift shops can be very mercurial. Best to keep a low profile.

Additionally, if you are shopping in a poorer area or an area where you obviously aren't a local, you don't necessarily want to call attention to yourself. It is never advisable to wear obviously expensive clothing while thrift shopping. While it may be a lark for you to score cool clothes for cheap, other shoppers are there by necessity and may resent your appearing to flaunt your high socio-economic status while slumming. Also, expensive-looking clothing can work against you should you ever engage in haggling or price-setting. A savvy clerk may eyeball your $400 leather jacket and set the price accordingly.

I know how very hard it can be sometimes to put aside your look. It might help to think of thrift shopping as some kind of guerrilla assault or covert operation that requires camouflage or special clothing. It's just for a short time, and it might help you score that completely outrageous item that you can peacock about in for the other twenty-three hours in the day. (For more advice on dressing to thrift, see Chapter 5.)

Timing Is Nearly Everything

The worst time to thrift is Saturday morning. Everybody and their mother is out. The store is packed! All the carts are taken, whole families are blocking the aisle! The other bad time is last thing Saturday afternoon (the shelves are empty). If you must shop Saturday mornings, do try to be the first one there. Thrifts that do a big business Saturday usually spend Friday afternoon stocking. This is a swell time to go. Spend a leisurely couple of hours trailing the employees while they bring out fresh merchandise. Generally, the bigger the store and the more turnover of merchandise, the more likely they are to restock continually. (I *love* pulling up outside a thrift that says "New Items HOURLY"!) If the restocking pattern isn't obvious, ask an employee.

Most thrifts have some sort of sale policy. Learn it. If it's a store on your regular circuit, tattoo it on your brain and be alert for any changes. If you're hitting a new store, check near the entrance for signs announcing sales, listen to the PA for sale info, or ask an employee.

Sales can vary. Most big thrifts have a dated-turnover policy. That is, they designate merchandise by date as it hits the floor (either with an actual date on the tag or with different colored tags—red for Week 1, blue for Week 2, yellow for Week 3, etc.). Once merchandise has sat on the floor for the prescribed amount of time (generally a couple of weeks), it becomes eligible for a discount. Make sure you understand their policy exactly. Sometimes it's only certain items (clothes, shoes, and books) that are discounted. Stores will also discount outdated seasonal merchandise (all winter coats half off, all shorts two for one, etc.).

There may be designated sale days for certain types of people. Common sale days are students' day, seniors' day, and ladies' day. These sales often occur on a weekday. If you don't fit the category, take along someone who does. Usually the discount is applied to whoever is purchasing the items. Let your grandma buy those KISS 8-tracks while you wait in the car. You can return the favor some other way.

Case the Whole Joint

Time permitting, *look everywhere* in the store! Even if you only buy dishes, you'd be surprised where dishware turns up! Remaining open to possibilities is the key to a good thrift haul. And frankly, most thrift stores are badly organized. While you may have entered the store with a jones to buy records, you may find something equally swell over in the tablecloths. You're at the mercy of where the employee decides to stick stuff—placing some 8-tracks near the Atari cartridges might make sense to them, or maybe they just got lazy and dumped stuff willy-nilly. Other customers are Public Enemy Number One, though, for picking stuff up and putting it down somewhere else. If you find one of something—like one good shoe or half a suit—do take a hard look around. The other part just might be somewhere else. Good places to look for randomly placed items are near the mirrors or dressing

Sick of looking at all those Big Ugly Lamps cluttering up the thrifts? See Chapter 17 for a solution.
PHOTO BY AUTHOR

rooms, where people discard clothes, and near the checkout, where shoppers make their final decision about what to purchase.

"No Unmarked Merchandise Will Be Sold!"

Who among us doesn't have some nightmare story about the dream item without a price tag? Most thrifts have a simple policy: "No unmarked merchandise will be sold." Instead it's returned to the back room to get reprocessed and repriced, and it makes it back out to the sales floor who-knows-when. Understandably, this is for the store's protection. Otherwise unscrupulous types would be ripping the tags off all the merchandise and trying to wrangle a lower price from the cashier. (This is a very real possibility in a big store where someone with Value Authority is pricing merchandise in the back, while the cashier is simply ringing up the price tags in happy oblivion of any value.) Bad people who rip tags off clothing aside, tags can come off innocently, torn off while trying something on or poorly stapled in the first place. And nothing is as frustrating as finding that item you dearly want without the tag.

Some thrifters give up on the spot. I don't. I at least make the trek to the checkout. I do not alert the clerk to the untagged item. I smile pleasantly until they pick up the item, turn it over, inspect it and say, "This doesn't have a tag." I feign total surprise. About 65 percent of the time, the clerk suggests a price and I accept (or decline if it's too expensive). Sometimes, despite the sign that says otherwise, there *is* a manager available for pricing and it gets repriced on the spot. (Every now and then, while I'm in my staring-at-the-ceiling smiling mode, the clerk rings up the untagged item without even mentioning it to me.) Of course, you get those by-the-book types who say "We can't sell this." I shrug and let it go. But if you're the combative type, and the aforementioned has failed to score you the untagged item, you can try arguing. I've seen it work and I've seen it fail. It's up to you how far you wanna push it.

✳**TIP**✳ **NEVER leave your cart or basket unattended. Some people are evil and will steal right out of it. Sad, but true.**

And Speaking of Unethical Behavior . . .

It's an unproven theory of mine that certain behavior may determine how well you do at the thrifts. Behave badly, thrift badly. That's thrift karma. The following are unethical thrifting activities and are pretty low-down. Imagine stealing from a place that sells things for $1 anyway?

- Swapping tags
- Tearing off tags to try to hustle a lower price
- Altering the price
- Stealing from carts (even from icky yuppies and vintage store owners)
- Stealing parts of things, like tearing off cool labels or ripping off buttons
- Stealing merchandise

You can make various arguments for creative rip-off or "settling the score" or whatever you wanna call it, but taking nickel-and-dime items from the thrifts is pretty lame behavior. Despite the increase in "collectibles" pricing mania at thrifts, they're not out to exploit shoppers. If you are some "true" anticonsumer punk, then you've probably already stolen this book, and any admonitions are falling on deaf ears.

The following actions are semi-unethical. Practice at your discretion.

- Not putting things back where you found them if you decide not to buy them. This is just sort of rude, but you could ruin the day for another thrifter who wouldn't think to look for a frying pan stuck next to the bowling balls.
- Hiding things that you can't purchase immediately but you intend to come back and get (gotta get more money or wanna wait till next week when the red tag will be half off). Aha! You think, I'll *hide* it and retrieve it later! (You're not the only one who does this, and that's another good reason to shop the whole store—you can uncover cool stuff somebody else has hidden.) Hiding sometimes works; sometimes it doesn't. Recently, I spied a fabulous ceiling light fixture, one of those flat kind with pictures painted on—in this case, images of 1950s high school teens. A blue tag and $14. Too much for me, but next week it would be $7 and I'd swing that. I stuck it down behind some really bad paintings in a hard-to-reach rack. Went back the next week and checked the hiding place. Not there. No big deal— it's a war out there; somebody else scored. While cruising the rest of the store, I saw something odd sticking out from under a giant pile of Atari cartridges. I had to remove all the cartridges and stack them up all over the floor, but underneath was the light fixture—and half off too! So, somebody else *had* found it and had rehidden it (and in a better place), but, hard cheese— I rediscovered it and won the battle.

- Stalking. Someone else in the store has the *very* thing you want. Maybe you saw it happen—they snatched it from right under your nose—or maybe you saw it in their cart as they rolled past you. Arrgh. You can follow them hoping they put it back. People almost never put the coveted item back. (It's as if they can sense you want it and they clutch it even tighter.) You're better off accepting your loss and spending time looking for other good stuff.

> "TO THE PERSON WHO CHANGE SHE/HE Their SHOES! THiS PER-SON Is going to pay 10,00 TiMES The original price of the SHoes! Mgr F.E." Sign discouraging shoe theft in a Redwood City, California, thrift.

- "Liberating" and assorted switcheroos. Liberating? This is something I'm occasionally guilty of. Take photo albums. I have a massive collection of found photos. Naturally, I check all the photo albums in thrifts. If the album is filled with photos, I buy it instantly. If there are one or two . . . or, say, fewer than six photos in the album, I may "liberate" them. It's my understanding that the photo album itself is for sale, not these two out-of-focus snapshots of the dog, right? I know of other thrifters who will rearrange paintings and frames to get the combination they want . . . I'm sure we're all paying for it somehow in the Big Thrift Karma Picture. Try to be good.

If They Want to Sell It, Why Did They Stick It There?!

The locked counter or behind-the-register display area can be problematic. Number one problem is finding an employee to assist you. If you see something you like the look of, persevere. Once you've got some assistance, try to accomplish all your "what's that?" "can I see that?" business at once. Some thrifts hang odd bits of clothing from the ceiling or high up on a wall. This is absurd. You've got to find someone to help you, then they've got to find the giant hook to get the item down—and when you don't want it after all, they glower at you as they try to rehang it. Try to be polite and maintain your good humor. It's not their fault some manager got the bright idea of putting merchandise in such a hard-to-reach place. Another quirk is items in the front windows. These are often not available for purchase until they've finished serving a purpose in the cute Valentine's Day diorama that's been set up. Some thrifts toss the items back on the floor whenever; others let you sign up to purchase something later. I've seen a variation on this where you can make a *bid* on a window item.

Other unattainable items:

- Standing floor fans or any large fan.
- The cheap plastic tub they keep the cutlery in is always marked "not for sale."
- In some thrifts, the religious art is *never* for sale.
- The great chair the clerk is sitting on.
- The clock on the wall.
- The in-store radio or TV.

The "Set-Aside" Evilness

Some thrifts have pre-existing arrangements with "special" customers or buyers (like a vintage clothing store). The desired merchandise is set aside in the back room and never makes it out to the floor. It's icky, but believe me, it goes on. I regularly scored fab old curtains at this one thrift. One day, they were gone, and for a year after, I never saw any more. I knew the outside supply (old homes packed with ancient furnishings) hadn't dried up, so what gives? All was revealed when I saw the smug owner of an over-priced vintage store swaggering out of the back room with his arms filled with curtains. I had a small victory a few weeks later when I got to a church sale before him and swooped on a huge pile of unused vintage fabric. He begged me to sell it to him, and I told him to buzz off. Still, this one tiny score doesn't take away from the awful unfairness of this set-aside policy. Thrifts like it because it's a guaranteed sale, but it detracts from the anyone-can-play pure chance fun of scoring. Thrift stores are more aware of a "collectibles market" they can tap. Capitalism beats pure democracy every time.

The Swap Party

Honestly, this is almost as fun as thrifting and costs even less.

1. Sign up six or more pals to attend a swap. Set a date, time, and place. Because of the nature of the event, it is best to hold the swap in a large place with open floor space. Stress that everybody be prompt.

2. Ask your friends to bring whatever they have at home that they don't want anymore. Tell them it can be clothing, books, records, art, knickknacks—whatever they can carry. Request that they bring the goods relatively concealed in garbage bags or boxes. There is no limit, though, to how much they can bring. Ensure them that they will not be responsible for any leftover items.

3. When swap participants arrive, have them place their unopened bags in the center of the designated floor. No one is allowed to look into the bags, but all may sit and stare at them.

4. When everybody has arrived, the swap begins. The rules are simple. Everything in the pile is up for grabs. Whoever snatches it first gets it. The call is sounded and participants may lunge forward, tearing open the bags and boxes. At this point, a frenzy of grabbing and shouting will transpire.

5. The party will then settle down while people try on their new outfits (modeling is encouraged) and former owners relate item histories to new owners. At this point, everyone can make fun of the crap that's left over.

6. When the party breaks up, one or more people volunteer to take the unwanted merchandise to the thrift store donation bin.

There are several advantages to the swap party. It's an incentive to clean out your vast pile of stuff. For diehard amassers, it's psychologically easier to get rid of stuff, if you know you'll be coming home with replacement items. You get stuff for free. You might even get that thing of your friend's that you've been coveting if they're now bored with it. The tearing open of bags and rooting through stuff is very primal and exciting. And in the end, a bunch of stuff goes back to the thrift store, upping everybody's thrift karma.

Cleaning Up Your Thrift Act

BY CANDI STRECKER

There's more to brilliant thrifting than just shopping. After you get your goodies home, they need to be cleaned. And, almost always, you'll have to undo some damage done by the thrift-store employees as they priced the goods. Just about every means of pricing leaves its mark, whether it's perversely sticky stickers, stapled-on tags, masking tape, permanent markers, or the dreaded grease pencil. But most of these marks can be eradicated if you know the right techniques and have the right cleaning products on hand. Luckily, my husband, Matt Householder, has applied the dedication of an engineer to testing and refining an array of methods for cleaning two decades' worth of thrifted transistor radios and other modern electronic collectibles. Here are some of his best tips for cleaning *almost everything*. (Since there are so many variables involved in cleaning clothing and fabrics—the fibers they're made of, their construction, age, fragility, and trimmings—you're advised to seek this information in your library, where there are whole books devoted to the subject.)

A warning before we start: many of the chemicals below are toxic, hazardous, environmentally unsound, and just plain nasty. For your own safety, please read the labels and follow the instructions there regarding handling, ventilation, and disposal. And since these are powerful, concentrated chemicals, always do a little test at the start. Dab a diluted drop of the cleaning product onto an inconspicuous part of your thrift-store find and make sure it doesn't cause fading or damage.

Over and over, Matt reaches for a few favorite clean-up tools. An old toothbrush is "the wonder tool" for all kinds of scrubbing. Toothpicks, cotton swabs, and paper towels are almost as necessary. Every year, he goes through yards of flannel (ripped into hanky-size hunks) as he polishes and cleans his finds; a cheap source of this fabric is old flannel shirts and bedsheets.

First stop in the cleanup process is the kitchen sink, where washable items get a good dunking in warm dish-washing soapsuds. Scrub away tough bits with a dab of detergent or powdered cleanser on an old toothbrush, and pry any remaining bits of gunk out of crevices and crannies with toothpicks. Items that can't be immersed in water might be wiped clean of dust (and thrift-shop cooties) with a damp cloth or by vacuuming.

Two products are vital: lighter fluid and plastic polish. If you do a lot of thrifting, both are well worth having around. Lighter fluid is the very best stuff for removing stickers, because it can be applied to almost anything, even paper items like books and record-album jackets. That's because it contains absolutely no water, and the liquid it does contain (pure naphtha) evaporates so quickly that the paper is materially unchanged. The method for stubborn stickers is to squirt a bit onto the sticker until it looks "wet," at which point you can usually lift up at least an edge of it with your fingernail. Now drip more drops onto that margin, tilting the object so the fluid runs underneath the sticker as it is loosened. After the sticker is off, any remaining adhesive can be dissolved with a bit more lighter fluid and flannel. Use flannel to polish the object dry when you're done. You know that horrible dried, mutated sticker gunk that remains years after the sticker has dropped away? Polish it off with lighter fluid on flannel. Grease pencil on books or paper? Squirt with lighter fluid, blot up with dry flannel, and repeat till it's gone.

Almost as miraculous, for *non*porous, *non*paper surfaces, is the stuff called plastic polish. Matt's favorites are the Novus and Meguiar's brands. Look for these in stores that sell plastic sheets and rods for craft and construction projects. Plastic polish is a mix of wax with mild solvents and a mild abrasive, each of which could potentially damage the thing it's applied to, so be sure and test it out first by gently rubbing it onto an inconspicuous place. Also, keep in mind that it's best for shiny or glossy surfaces; its abrasives will polish matte-finish surfaces to a glossy shine, which may not be what you want. Plastic polish is fabulous for plastic and glass, and excellent on most metals too (can be substituted for any metal polish.) This makes it useful for jewelry. Another favorite technique is to use plastic polish to brighten the painted (silk-screened) designs and logos on drinking glasses, bottles, etc. If you polish the designs with a heavy hand, you'll take the paint right off, but applied very lightly, plastic polish will take off the shadow of oxidation that so often clings to the paint, making the paint look new again. Like lighter fluid, it can be applied and allowed to soak in on supercrud. For nonporous items, it's the best product for removing marker and grease pencil; just polish the marks off with as many applications as necessary.

Another solvent that will remove crayon or grease-pencil markings from nonpaper objects is rubbing (isopropyl) alcohol, preferably in higher-concentrate form. It does have a small amount of water in it, so don't use it on things that shouldn't get wet. In a pinch, you could also use vodka.

Because it's a mild acid, vinegar is great for removing one kind of gunk you'll frequently encounter: the powdery white mineral deposits inside drinking glasses. Just pour some in and let it stand for an hour or so to dissolve the schmutz. Repeat as necessary.

You've probably seen thriftables that are perfect except for a dark, thin hairline crack. You may not be able to remove that crack, but bleach will often make it almost invisible. Bleach can be used successfully on cracked ceramic dishware and plastic radios. Again, this is a strong chemical, so apply a diluted drop with a cotton swab first, watching especially for color changes, before dunking the object into a straight bleach soak. Always rinse out the bleach with water afterwards. A great thing about this technique is that, if the crack becomes visibly dirty later, you can bleach it out again. A dollop of bleach in a sinkful of water also serves as a sterilizer. Let questionable thrift-store dishes soak in a sink full of this for an hour before you eat off of them.

Two more products should complete your cleaning arsenal. Anyone who buys thrifted things made of wood, whether salad bowls or rocking chairs, needs to know about Murphy's Oil Soap (available in most grocery stores.) Never soak and saturate wood in water; instead, make up some Murphy's suds, swish it on with a wrung-out cloth, rinse with clear water, and let the object dry thoroughly (which may take days). And if you buy many things made of leather, Lexol Leather Conditioner is the magic potion that softens faded or scruffy goods.

Scientists wouldn't be caught dead using anything as low-tech as peanut butter, but I still rely on this classic household hint to remove stickers from washable objects. Spread a little peanut butter (or vegetable oil) onto stickers or sticker gunk, let it soak in a few minutes, then wash both grease and gunk away with straight dish soap and water. You might have to repeat it a few times, but it almost always works eventually.

After he'd shown me around his workshop and demonstrated all these products, I still had one nagging question. "What about permanent marker prices on paper, Matt?" "Get another marker and cover it up!" he suggested ruefully. Along with the common cold, there are some things that even modern science can't cure.

4 Thrifts and Fashion

Clothing makes up the bulk of the merchandise in thrifts, and most thrifters appreciate the thrift stores as excellent sources of clothes, whether they're buying for the office, the rave, or all parts of their lives. It would be impossible to cover all the clothing that is available in the thrift stores, but we can examine some ubiquitous thrift garments and see what they can tell us about fashion, identity, and the clothing industry.

FASHION CYCLES—THIS SHIRT IS SO FIVE MINUTES AGO!

If it wasn't for fashion and the cycles it spurs, we might find the selection of clothing available at the thrift stores to be quite limited. While some clothing is donated to the thrift stores for reasonable physical causes (like death or the fact that it doesn't fit anymore), most usable clothing is ditched because the owner no longer considers it fashionable. Those who have good taste and money would never wear last year's clothes, right? To be seen in last year's clothes is to announce to the world that you are bereft of those enviable assets.

The hyperspeed at which clothing is now considered outdated is a relatively new phenomenon. Fashion has always changed but at a much slower rate—styles used to last for years, not for mere months as they do today. Ironically, fashion rules are no longer as rigid. Walk down any street. You'll register many "looks." Conversely, if you look at old photographs of city streets or ball games, you're struck by how nearly everyone was wearing similar clothing. Many people now wear what suits them rather than what is "in." But despite this, the clothing industry marches on. What the industry has given up in fashion dictatorship, they've retrieved with rapid-fire trends, niche marketing, and everyone's tacit understanding that clothing must be continually swapped out. You know those people who have no look—wear the same thing all the time—but still buy new clothes every two months? Well, lucky for us. All of us are itchin' for last year's clothes to hit the thrifts. We want new wardrobes like everybody else!

THE SAGA OF THE POLYESTER SHIRT

Most garment histories follow a couple of traditional patterns. Some clothing, like a wool winter coat, retains virtually the same shape, functionality, and respect for centuries. Other items such as jeans mutate slightly to reflect current social tastes, but their popularity only increases over time. Still other garments like the miniskirt are fad items, which pop up every now and again as "this year's thing."

The unique history of the polyester shirt is like a gripping summer novel, filled with near-death escapes and hairpin plot twists. You expect styles and patterns to change over the years, but it's the public's response—the love, the hate, the pity, the irony—*to the very material* that has swayed so wildly. The shirt was one of the first polyester garments introduced, has been widely worn, and exemplifies the trials and tribulations of polyester.

Test Tube Baby

The drama of the poly story revolves around the invention of a fabric seemingly out of thin air (actually air, coal, petroleum, and water—or if you prefer, teraphthalic acid and ethylene glycol) and its subsequent properties. Cotton is the way it is because it *is* cotton, but polyester has been chemically tweaked to satisfy a specific clothing market and consumer. The invention of synthetic fabrics changed the garment business for good. Or for bad. But nevertheless, it changed it forever.

DuPont bought the patent for polyester fiber in 1950 and a year later unleashed the Dacron shirt (Dacron is their polyester trade name) on the unsuspecting world. It was heralded as a miracle, a new and better type of clothing that would make life easier. Magazines were suddenly filled with new washing instructions;

housewives would have to learn new rules. But that was hardly a problem: the number one selling point of the polyester shirt was its easy care! Into the washing machine (polyester "thrived" on machine washing[1]), hang wet to dry, and voila!—in an hour, you had a beautiful clean garment that didn't need to be ironed. Continuous washing did not stretch the fabric or fade the dyes. Still not convinced? What if the fabric was "mothproof" as well? (This is like saying a concrete block is mothproof. Moths are organic creatures that live off another organic substance—wool. Why would they eat reprocessed petrochemicals even if it did look and feel like wool?!)

Gosh, was there anything wrong with polyester shirts? Oh, a few minor things. Polyester is hydrophobic; that is, it does not absorb water. This is why it dries so quickly and how it keeps its marvelous stay-press shape after washing, but it's also responsible for polyester's trademark clamminess. When you perspire in that shirt, the sweat is not absorbed by the fabric but accumulates between your skin and the garment, making you feel even clammier and hotter. And if the shirt wasn't clammy, it was electrostatic. Not only is it irritating and embarrassing to have your shirt cling to you, but static attracts dust. A polyester shirt soils more quickly than a cotton shirt just by pulling dust particles out of the air.

Many of the early problems with polyester were rectified by blending it with natural fabrics. But let's continue to follow our 100 percent polyester shirt. Soon polyester clothing was popular enough that major appliancemakers upgraded their washers and dryers to accommodate the new fabric, specifically adding the cooler settings that polyester was happier with. The ability to dye polyester improved and just in time for the explosion of colorful casual clothing in the 1960s. What could be more appreciated than an inexpensive, brightly colored shirt that never needed ironing and refused to fade? During polyester's heyday, men, women, and children hit the streets in vibrantly patterned shirts, a development made possible by heat transfer or sublistatic printing (a process whereby heat and pressure is applied to printed transfer paper to produce clear, bright, and colorfast images on the fabric[2]).

The Worm Turns . . . The Ditching Begins

Just as manufacturers were selling more polyester than ever before, a new fashion mind-set developed. Back-to-nature types eschewed the synthetics for "pure" and "natural" fabrics. Hippies didn't mind the wrinkles. Ex-hippies didn't want to give up the natural feel. Others decided the trade-off of easy care versus comfort was not worth it and went back to natural fabrics, taking their iron with them.

Said Diana Vreeland, "I went to Brooks Brothers and bought myself a Dacron shirt. We got to Boston and it was terribly hot . . . we were in a traffic jam and we couldn't move. And you know I thought I was on fire! I had to open the shirt completely, I had to get out of it and my husband said, 'In the name of God, what are you doing!' But I really and truly was in flames locked in this synthetic thing."[3] You know a garment is in social trouble when the Grande Dame of fashion is forced to disrobe on a crowded Boston freeway!

As the ascension of the natural occurred, polyester increasingly became considered cheap, ersatz, and vile (it was made from petrochemicals, and during the '70s, oil companies were demonized). The cost of polyester dropped so low that the cheapness of the fabric created a class distinction. Nice people paid extra for "real fabrics"; hoi polloi were foolishly content with the fake slimy stuff. As fashion veered away from the anything-goes outrageousness of the late 1960s and early 1970s toward a neater, more professional look, the boldly patterned polyester shirts looked silly and tacky.

What was once the height of fashion for swinging bachelors (pick up an old *Esquire* from the 1960s and see page after page of the craziest polyester shirts!) was now sneered at by Dapper Dans like Tom Wolfe. "One can't even call workingmen 'blue collar' any longer. They all have collars like Joe Namath's or Johnny Bench's or Walt Frazier's. They all have $35 superstar Qiana sport shirts with elephant collars and 1940s Airbrush Wallpaper Flowers Buncha Grapes & Seashells designs all over them."[4] Polyester was now a class issue.

Late in the '70s, the polyester shirt became a joke, an instant sight gag intended to denote the wearer's lack of taste and class. *Both* landlords on *Three's Company* (Norman Fell and Don Knotts) wore hideous polyester ensembles, as did the two Wild and Crazy Guys and Lisa Loopner's loser nerd boyfriend Todd DiLaMuca on *Saturday Night Live*. John Travolta strutted to fame dressed in a white three-piece polyester suit and a selection of poly shirts. In the ensuing disco backlash, polyester clothing became one of the problems cited by the antidisco brigade.

The gag then shifted from highlighting contemporary losers like Mr. Roper and Todd to being a signifier for "hopelessly lost in the '70s." Since the early '80s, how many bad comedies have you sat through with the loser lothario who struts on-screen in the bad polyester shirt, open to the waist, and adorned with gold chains, or the nerd in poly shirt and pocket protector? John Waters got laughs just from naming his 1981 film *Polyester*. Every ha-ha funny article about the retro '70s starts out by mentioning polyester. They make it seem like everybody in the 1970s wore really wacked-out seven-color swirly polyester shirts every day. Hardly. But it's the kooky stuff that sticks.

The Forlorn Years

Sometime in the late 1980s I got interested in the printed polyester shirt. You see an item every single day of your life, just outside your field of vision, then one day, you suddenly register the object in a different context. I came of fashion-age at the beginning of the polyester-is-bad era. I wouldn't have been caught dead in a boldly patterned polyester shirt, and I sneered at those who wore them. By the mid '80s, most people had ceased to wear them, and for me they were just an irritant you had to slog through at the thrift stores. The only thing I appreciated about polyester shirts at thrift stores was how visible they were. It certainly cut down the time spent flipping through the shirt racks—you could quickly gauge the "good" shirts from the "bad."

I wish I could remember just what it was that made me see them differently. It may have been simply that enough time had passed, that they were out of the general world sphere and were so universally reviled that it made me rethink them. I'm a sucker for that underdog drama, and they held some attraction for me as a game. Everybody agrees they're the ugliest shirts ever made, but just *how* ugly? I foresaw a fun quest where every thrift would yield dozens of polyester shirts and I could pick and choose among them, seeking out the weirdest and the ugliest. When I started a collection (and what I had in mind was some sort of wall or hanging-from-the-ceiling display—I still had no intention of wearing them), there were so many polyester shirts in the thrifts that I decided to specialize. I'd go broke buying them all. I picked two categories: the photoprint shirt (a photographic image is printed on the cloth) and the full body image (the full body image shirt has an unbroken single image that runs from the shoulder to the waist, not a series of patterns.)

And so I began. I told a few thrifting friends who also helped me search. I quickly discovered that I had chosen two categories that were less common among polyester shirts, but that was OK. I didn't

A magnificent example of a full-image poly with separate back and front scenes!
PHOTO BY ORSON

have the room to store three hundred shirts, and a little scarcity always contributes to the thrill of the hunt and the pleasure of the ultimate score.

For a couple of years, the shirts trickled in. Then in the early 1990s, the dry-up happened. All of a sudden, there seemed to be *no* polyester left in the stores. Not just the shirts, but all the polyester leisure suits, pantsuits, and house dresses disappeared as well. I was mystified. It wasn't that long ago that the world was awash in polyester. Weren't people still donating it? I could understand why old rayon Hawaiian shirts didn't turn up anymore—there hadn't been that many of them to begin with, it had been three decades since their manufacture, and they had moved on to super-retro status and were snapped up quickly. Polyester shirts seemed to defy all those criteria. Could it be simple market economics? Had the thrifts woken up and realized that nobody bought polyester clothing anymore, no matter how cheaply it was priced (most of my shirts were priced significantly lower than other similar cotton shirts) and how long it sat on the rack? I was bummed. I'd grooved on the underdogedness of the shirts, but now their total loser status had removed them from my grasp.

The Worm Turns Again . . . the "Museum Piece"

But wait! What's this? A museum show of polyester shirts!? In 1988, the Museum of Modern Mythology in San Francisco ran a show titled "100% Polyester: Shirts of Art From the Palette of Science." The "art" was compiled from museum cofounder Jeff Errick's collection of over five hundred polyester men's shirts he'd accumulated from thrift stores. Over two hundred shirts were on display from the glory days of 1968–78. "Enough great shirts together make a great collection," said Errick.[5] OK, so a small gallery space in San Francisco ain't the Museum of Modern Art, but the show was popular and was covered by national media. What is important is that a few key people decided to rescue the polyester shirt from the rock underneath which it had crawled. Their motivations weren't as pure as liking the shirts and wearing them, but they were at least recognizing the poly shirt as a cultural and even aesthetic artifact that could be re-examined in a new context.

The '90s threw a couple more bones towards the rejuvenation of polyester shirts. Poly shirts got bigtime media exposure as MTV jokesters and popular alternative acts like Smashing Pumpkins, Sponge, and Beck pranced about in them. Part of this was no doubt pure smirkiness—wear the ugliest "least cool" thing for effect. Ironically, when famous people do this, it ends up making these uncool items cool and then the fans emulate the look. (See also plastic hair barrettes, clunky boots, and saggy cords.)

The fashionable retro-decade became the 1970s. As per all retro-decades, those who did not live through it already are condemned to relive it, however vicariously. Certain items like track suits, platforms, and suede tennis shoes got rediscovered and adopted by the younger generation. Appreciation (real or ironic) for the 1970s was easily communicated by the decade's most famous piece of clothing, the wildly patterned polyester shirt.

Never one to miss a trend, clothing manufacturers actually put out "retro versions" of polyester photoprint shirts. (My trained eye could tell the difference in a second, but I'll admit to knowing more about these shirts than is really necessary.) They were just different enough to be '90s and not '70s—most noticeably the fabric was missing that characteristic sliminess or spongy feel and the images were rather sedate by '70s standards.

At last it seems the polyester shirt has been awarded the grandest fashion distinction. It has been remade as a fake vintage item, and originals are now a coveted collectibles item. Recent trips to the West and East Coasts had me agape at the prices for polyester shirts in vintage stores! When something costs more used than it did new, it's arrived, baby! Ironically, had they not been so despised once, even by the thrift stores, they wouldn't be so rare and dear today! But if they hadn't been so reviled, would they still have attracted the retro-faddists like myself? Probably not.

The Industry's Dilemma—New and Improved Polyester

"It's been a tough road ridding ourselves of the image people have of polyester."
—Ellen Sweeney of Hoeschst Celanese, the nation's second largest producer of polyester.[6]

The manufacturers may discover that it is easier to reinvent polyester fiber than it is to change the public's perception of it. Now they can make polyester by recycling plastic bottles but they still can't shake the "unnatural" image. Not to be dissuaded, DuPont and other polyester manufacturers haven't quit. The latest generation of polyester, "microfibers," is here. This new polyester thread is so thin that it can evidently mimic any number of fabrics and fool the experts. It retains the advantages of polyester such as easy care, but no longer has the clamminess and static of the hateful old stuff. Sound like another miracle? It may well be. The kicker is they have to be quiet about it. Can't even breathe the word "polyester"...

I polled some contemporary 1970s polyester shirt wearers and asked what attraction the shirts held for them. I was surprised by their answers. I expected to hear the "it's so bad it's good" ironic defense of polyester, but these young people expressed genuine appreciation for the shirts, citing such features as comfort, easy care (machine wash, no ironing), durability (colors don't fade, fabric is strong, garment keeps its shape), and their low cost. It sounds like 1952 all over again!

I AM WHAT I WEAR—CLOTHING AND IDENTITY

Clothing used to speak of class and position, now it speaks of personality. I am what I wear (or what I refuse to wear). Even the slob that says, "I don't care what I look like" is still making a statement of sorts. Since fashion splintered into a hundred looks, it's easier than ever to pigeonhole people by their clothing. Since clothes are the first thing we notice about somebody, we all strive to choose clothing that is reflective of our "real selves" or at least the image we wish people to have of us.

The fun of the thrifts is that your financial investment in clothing is so minimal that you have a lot more play with which identities you choose to project. For a hundred dollars spent on mall clothing, you can be one person. For a hundred bucks spent at the thrift store, you could be a different person each day of the week—a secretary, a skateboarder, a housewife, a sports fan, a rock groupie, a slob, a fashionable dresser, or an outright weirdo.

MY T-SHIRT HAS SOMETHING TO SAY

"If people don't want to listen to *you*, what makes you think they want to hear from your sweater?"
—Fran Liebowitz, "Clothes with Pictures and/or Writing on Them: Yes—Another Complaint."[7]

It's mindboggling that as a culture we've come to accept that you are judged by what your T-shirt says. Just because somebody bought, received, or somehow acquired a T-shirt is no proof that the shirt speaks for them. You don't have to take a test before you get the shirt that says "Co-ed Nude Volleyball Instructor" nor do you actually have to *be* a co-ed nude volleyball instructor. All you have to do is pay $10 for that shirt at Myrtle Beach. That's just a frivolous example—everybody knows co-ed nude volleyball is just a joke, right? (This shirt *does* say something about the wearer, though. It tells the world that the wearer thinks this lame-o joke is funny. That's actually a pretty valuable piece of information.)

But some T-shirts are dead serious and there's nothing to stop you, Joe Thrift Shop Consumer, from wearing them and claiming their meaning. We're a world of strangers, so we claim shortcuts by stating who we are, what we like to do, who we like to do it with, what beer we drink, and what our life philosophies are on our T-shirts. You can pick up shirts that accurately reflect your tastes, but with so many shirts to choose from in the thrifts, the fun is in subverting the meanings. Try these on for size.

My Shirt Is a Major L.A. Raiders Fan—Go Team Go, Teams That Went

Now is the time to start putting together that collection of dead sports team shirts. Experts predict that even more big cities will be swapping around professional sports teams. Lots of thrift buying in the future as disgruntled former fans dump their T-shirts. (I was thrifting near Cleveland soon after the announcement that the Cleveland Browns football team was being moved. Let me tell you, I was *wading* through Browns clothing!) I'm loathe to predict the next round of trades (watch your paper . . .) but you can begin with the Baltimore Colts, L.A. Raiders, L.A. Rams, St. Louis Cardinals, Minnesota Northstars, Quebec Nordiques, New Orleans Jazz, and Houston Oilers. Baffle the masses when you hit the sidewalks supporting teams that don't exist. (This project can be supplemented by other ghost team memorabilia: glassware, coffee mugs, hats, jackets, and football helmet lamps.)

My Shirt Is Really Fit—Be an Amateur Athlete

Strut about like a winner! You can train for months, enter a marathon, run till you puke, and they give you a free T-shirt. Or you can just thrift a marathon T-shirt. Total exertion required? Taking it off the hanger. Who's to say you didn't participate? Even if you appear to be really out of shape, you can always claim you walked it backwards or something. Another alternative is to work your way up to the marathon shirt, just like in real life. Spend three months sporting 5K race shirts. Then move on to 10K shirts. After another few weeks, get out your selection of 20Ks, and so on.

My Shirt Is a Teke—Frat Party Shirts

When they make those stupid "funny" T-shirts commemorating Friday's kegger, do they solicit the worst artist among them? Is his reward his own keg, starting the minute he picks up his pen? There's no shortage of these shirts if you live in a college town. Most are poorly drawn, but you probably shouldn't underestimate the fabled fraternal power in the big world. Might be your ticket to better seats at the ball game or a free beer at a yuppie watering hole.

My Shirt Took a Trip

Thrift T-shirts from someplace you just wish you could visit. Everybody else will assume you went—after all, you have the shirt to prove it. There's plenty of shirts from popular vacation spots (New York, San Francisco, Florida). Unfortunately, the classier the place, the less likely a souvenir T-shirt exists.

The odd thing about souvenir T-shirts is that it's the one T-shirt *not* about you that is OK to wear. If the idea of the souvenir T-shirt is for the traveler to own a memento of the trip and to broadcast to others that "I'm a Bahama Mama" (i.e., *I* went there!), why do so many tourists bring back souvenir T-shirts to give to friends and family? And why do they think you would want to wear a T-shirt from some place you haven't been? There's you—the pale fish that stayed home in Milwaukee—having to explain, "No, I haven't been to the Bahamas, my aunt brought me this shirt." Therefore, I would like to suggest some high commendation for the visionary and clear thinker who came up with the correct and proper souvenir T-shirt, "My aunt went to the Bahamas and all I got was this lousy T-shirt."

My Shirt Is Smart—Attending Colleges

Why pay the big bucks to attend college? Why study? Why go at all? Just thrift the T-shirt. By the way, there is no Institute of Higher Altitude at the University of Jackson Hole nor is Shooters University in Ft. Lauderdale an accredited institution.

My Shirt Is Covered

Does every new HMO now come with a bad T-shirt? God forbid, but if you're ever in a horrible accident, it might help to be wearing an HMO shirt.

THE WALL COLLECTIONS—SHIRTS TO ADMIRE

Some T-shirts are too fun to pass up, but you might not feel comfortable wearing them. Consider thrifting collections of T-shirts for decoration. They pin very easily to the wall. One Gulf War T-shirt is sorry jingoism, but a wall of them is a meaningful statement about our country. Well, maybe, maybe not—but think how cool it would look!

My Shirt Can Kick Your Shirt's Butt—Gulf War Shirts

Since I live in a relatively patriotic area, I see a lot of T-shirts left over from the Gulf War—or more correctly, Desert Shield and Desert Storm. Many of them are brand new. As you may recall, the conflict was over in a snap and merchants got stuck with boxes of unsold T-shirts. Some cultural anthropologist needs to be buying up these shirts now while they're abundant and cheap. They're a great window into America's most merchandised war. Selection may vary in your area, but here's some I've spotted in my local thrifts.

> **IN EVERY THRIFT**
> T-Shirt Version 1.2: The Product Release Shirt. Naturally, there's tons in the thrifts. First off, is there anything you cherish less than a shirt about your grueling underpaid job? Second, if you *are* the sort who wears software and high-tech T-shirts, your shirt is only as good as the product. When it sinks like a stone, is exposed on *Dateline*, or is obsolete in three months, of course you're gonna ditch the shirt.

"This Scud's for You," "These Colors Don't Run" (the flag), "You Can't Touch This" (usually a flag or fighter plane), "It's Miller Time" (nuclear blast over Baghdad or Saddam Hussein), "Holy War?—Holy Shit!," and "Sack Iraq" (Saddam Hussein being put in a trash truck). Maybe you'll get lucky and find the matching set of fake Hard Rock Cafe shirts: "Hard Rock Cafe Baghdad—CLOSED" and "Hard Rock Cafe Kuwait City—REOPENED."

My Shirt's a Little Buzzed—Booze Logos

Start a collection of beer-sponsored T-shirts. Try to find as many shirts as you can that somehow include the Budweiser or Miller logo. A lot of beer companies give away T-shirts or underwrite other events that give away free T-shirts.

TIP **All cheap T-shirts have good "art potential." A heavy marker will add the slogan of your choice to supplement or deride the existing slogan or image. Think of the possibilities of a closet full of Garfield shirts and a big black pen.**

LABEL LOVE

As America left the 1970s Me Decade behind and segued into the 1980s Stuff-I-Have Decade, the era of designer clothing began in earnest. By the late '70s, fashion designers represented two desirables: fame and money. Ironically, where once designer names had real cachet (the clothes were expensive and not mass-produced nor readily available), the 1970s saw an explosion of designer merchandise as designers sold their names to other manufacturers who simply plastered the designer's name on a plethora of mundane items— bedsheets, gym bags, cigarettes. By 1983 designer labels were responsible for 60 percent of the labels on the market.[8]

The idea was that the ordinary would be transformed into the extraordinary by the mere association of the designer. And generally, it *was* a mere association. Designers often had nothing to do with the revamped product other than collecting a fee for the use of their name. Easy money for them and a shortcut to sales as an eager-to-be-like-the-rich-and-famous public snapped up "designer goods."

Designers now have less influence over fashion styles than they once did. No longer do seasonal edicts come down from 7th Avenue that everyone blindly follows. The real power of the designer is now at the cash register. A lot of designer clothing is indistinguishable from the "regular" version (a Calvin Klein T-shirt vs. a Hanes T-

---

How pervasive is the "designer celebrity cult"? I bought an old metal desk at a church yard sale. Some kid had scratched into it the names "Gucci," "Esprit," "Generra," and "Polo." I hate to sound old, but in my day, we scratched in the names of our rock and roll idols, not the names of our jeans.

LET'S DO THE DESIGNER-TO-THRIFT MATH

An internationally known designer—we'll call him Bob—dreams up a shirt. It is manufactured in the Philippines at a cost of $5. The shirt is then shipped to nice stores where it hits the floor at $100. (Even accounting for various hidden costs such as shipping, ad budget, staff salaries, and standard wholesale-to-retail markup, this figure represents a colossal increase.) But the game is that consumers *expect* to pay more for a "Bob" shirt, and the high cost doesn't faze them. That's part of the sick attraction to designer clothing: "It costs a lot, ergo it *must* be good." Larry buys the "Bob" shirt for Susie. She wears it once, and as soon as they break up, she ditches it at the thrift.

This particular thrift has one of those "designer racks." The employee sees that it is a barely worn "Bob" shirt and marks it $15. To some shoppers, this would be a deal, a savings of 85 percent. But is it? The manufacturing cost of the shirt is $5. Since it's now in the thrift store and has left the circle of designer's working costs, advertising, and retail markup, the thrift consumer should not be expected to pay toward those costs. In fact, the original consumer, Larry, already paid those in full!

Pay more than $5 for this shirt and know that you too are paying extra for the designer cachet that *the thrift* has now assigned! It may be worth it; it may not. Remember, the true value of merchandise lies with you—how much you like it (for *whatever* reason) and how much you're willing to pay.

shirt), but the label has become more important than what the garment actually looks like. It's foolish to presume that all designer clothing is automatically good or of better quality. Nor should you assume there is anything *wrong* with a garment because it has a designer label. The smartest shoppers learn what makes *any* garment a good buy, regardless of the label. (See the next chapter for *practical* advice on clothes shopping.) It remains to be seen, given the overexposure of many designers, whether the names will lose their impact. We could see future thrifts just teeming with unwanted designer clothing.

DESIGNER JEANS MADNESS

"It's said that there are 40 million pigeons in the U.S.; 30 million are birds and the rest are buying designer jeans."
—Levi's executive Bud Johns. 1980.[9]

After decades of social drama, jeans in the mid-1970s were simply comfortable, casual pants that everybody—man, woman, old, young, Democrat, Republican—wore. As it became important to be perceived as well-to-do, advertisers convinced regular joes that you could work towards the desired penthouse lifestyle in incremental steps, purchasing items similar to what the rich had—one at a time. Frankly, many fell for this spiel, especially in the area of designer jeans. It was a crucial transition: from making your own personal statement with jeans (the late '60s and early '70s) to paying extra to have a designer speak for you. What did it really say about you except that you had paid $40 for a pair of jeans and you thought they were worth it?

The designer jean was a domestic retooling of a mid-'70s mini-phenomenon known as "French cut jeans." Some wily Gauls, like Yves St. Laurent, had recut standard American jeans so that they were tighter in the crotch and had long straight legs. They then shipped them to the United States where they were sold with the cachet of "being European" for two to three times the cost of U.S. jeans. By the late 1970s, domestic clothiers began to see the potential in creating a "high-class jean." If jeans were now associated with everybody, why not market a garment that let the wearer shift *up* in class, not *down*?

"Only a pig would put his name on blue jeans."
—Halston.[10]

The *exact* history of who, what, and when of U.S. designer jeans appears elusive. (See sidebar for Joe Keenan's version, which is as good as any . . .) As with any success, many claim credit. (One critical forefather was Warren Hirsch, president of the American arm of the giant Hong Kong manufacturer Murjani. He thought up the association of jeans with a status name. Evidently when couture designers turned his

"Designers had always believed that mere jeans could not be chic. On the other hand, homosexuals were wearing them, so clearly they had to be. Why else was Studio 54, the very Vatican of Fashion, thronged nightly with gay men gyrating in skin-tight denim, even as more expensively dressed straight men loitered forlornly outside, wondering if an earring would help.

"The designers got together to discuss the matter, and one of them (my source insists it was Gloria Vanderbilt) said 'Here's a thought—let's all buy ourselves a bunch of jeans, then sew our names onto the pockets and triple the price!' Everybody looked at her like she was crazy (except Calvin Klein, who was already halfway out of the room), but they went right ahead and did it, and designer jeans were born."[11]

idea down, he hit on the idea of American royalty. It's whispered that he dared to approach the Rockefellers and Jackie O for use of their names on his jeans but settled instead for Gloria Vanderbilt.) Designer jeans were suddenly everywhere, as if they materialized overnight out of some great Cosmic Big Bang on 7th Avenue.

"It uplifts her ass, fits her like a corset and takes out the flab. *For the first hour, a Sasson jean is very uncomfortable,* but then the fabric gives a bit and there's breathing room. It's not for 200 pound women."
[my emphasis]
—Paul Guez of Sasson, 1979.[12]

Designer jeans feminized the unisex/male look of previous jeans. Women's designer jeans were advertised with high heels and silk

shirts. The designers all babbled about making jeans that would "give the American woman jeans that would fit her" and that "would fit well"—all euphemisms for supertight jeans. The jeans only looked good on tall skinny models. That, of course, didn't stop everyone else from wearing them. The ideal jean look changed from loose and baggy to so tight that you had to lie down to get them on. These jeans said more than, "I'm being casual or working in my garden." These jeans said, "Look at my rich ass."

Everybody looked good in designer jeans!
PHOTO BY AUTHOR

"What Levi's does is fantastic . . . but I'm a designer. I can do things with cut, silhouette, shape that they can't."
—Calvin Klein[13]

(What he means is that he can put his name on the back pocket and charge three times the price.)

To justify their exorbitant cost, designer jeans had to be easily distinguished from less desirable pleb jeans. They were, after all, just basic five-pocket blue jeans. *You* knew they came with the designer status, but everybody else had to know, too. A standard quickly evolved. The right back pocket was ground zero. This is where the designer's name went. Distinctive stitching was added to the back pockets, and some flashier jeans used white or gold thread for an "overstitching" effect. Most had buttons or snaps embossed with the name of the designer or an associated logo. Some jeans decorated the front coin pocket as well, and the cheaper designer jeans crammed as much stitching and detailing as possible on both back pockets.

"In the jeans area, TV advertising has become so saturated, so boring and so tasteless. I don't want to become part of it."
—Calvin Klein weighs in before his Brooke ads.[14]

One of the highlights of the designer jean craze was the advertising. (Zippy slogans are in bold below.) Most ads were sexual in nature while still claiming allegiance to the upper class. What, after all, is more sexy than being rich? The best of the ads, both print and TV, created much controversy, with the topless riding-the-man-like-a-horse Jordache ads and Calvin Klein's Brooke Shields series capturing most of the network and viewer ire. In the now-infamous TV spot (titled "Feminist II"), a fifteen-year old Brooke asked us to contemplate the horror that she had no panties on. "Do you know what comes between me and my Calvins? Nothing." Ugh. By late 1980, both ABC and NBC had banned the ads, causing Calvin to drop an upcoming ad campaign that featured a bare-chested man touching himself in a suggestive manner. Calvin's response to the furor was decades ahead of its time in victimology. He claimed the ads hardly abused women but rather, "I really feel like *I've* been abused!"[15] America's response was clearer. After the ads, Calvin Klein jeans were selling at a rate of two million pairs per month!

"We've caught a moment in time. Years from now we'll think of it as an era, like the flappers of the 20s."
—Designer jeans ad man Howard Goldstein, May 1982.[16]

As with all fads, suddenly it was over. By 1983, designer jeans were being dumped at K-Mart. The proliferation of designer licenses had destroyed the cachet, and the dozens of shoddy imitators had wiped out any pretensions that designer jeans or designer-style jeans might be exclusive. In 1982, it was estimated that there were two hundred "designer" labels. Though the "designer" moniker was dropped, the production of jeans by big winners like Calvin Klein and Jordache continued.

For those readers smirking at the folly of consumers who rushed out in lemming packs to buy these overpriced jeans, look into your closet and your heart: got any $100 Docs and you're not a laborer? Do you sneer at those $19.95 Payless knockoffs? Ever pay more than $20 for sneakers because they have a certain rubber wedgey sole or they pump up with air? Figure out how much you're paying to wear company logos—yeah, that beer T-shirt and the bag that says Nike . . . We're all human. Have pity.

"Behind" Some of the Well-Known Butts
The Designers
People who had a previous reputation for creating mid-to-high-end clothing with their name on it.

Calvin Klein—the second largest seller after Gloria Vanderbilt. The jeans were manufactured by old-lady-clothing giant Puritan. They cost $7.50 to make and sold for close to $40. By 1980, there were Calvins for Men, Women, and Children. (Media-savvy Klein called his denim trousers "Calvins," never "jeans.")

Others included Adolfo (with unique square-cut front pockets), Ralph Lauren, Pierre Cardin, Donna Karan for Anne Klein, Geoffrey Beene ("Beene Jeans"), Oscar de la Renta, Yves St. Laurent, Diane von Furstenberg, and Fiorucci. (**The Fiorucci look is European. Our customers are "disco lovers."**)

Pretend Designers
They really hug your derriere. The greatest of the "pretend designers" and the biggest designer jeans seller (150 million in 1981) was Gloria Vanderbilt for Murjani. (There actually *was* a Mr. Mohan Murjani at the Hong Kong HQ.) The jeans featured an embroidered swan on the front coin pocket and Gloria's signature stitched across the back right pocket. While Ms. Vanderbilt did not design the jeans herself—merely lent her name and patrician presence in ads—she had previously dabbled in the artistic, designing greeting cards and spice jars.

I feel totally glamourous in Charlotte Ford's signature jeans. At 75 million sold, that's a lot of glamour. (Note the classy extra *u*.) Charlotte Ford's signature had "merit" not because she was a designer, but because she was a glamorous socialite herself, namely Henry Ford's great-granddaughter.

Oo la la. Sasson was founded in 1976 by Paul Guez and Maurice Sasson. The source of much consumer confusion between Sasson clothing and Vidal Sassoon, celebrity hairdresser, the issue went to court and was settled amicably.

The Jordache look. An auspicious beginning: When the Nakash brothers' Brooklyn clothing store burnt down during the 1977 New York City blackout looting, they used insurance money to start a new clothing line—Jordache. The name sounded classy, but it was a loose anagram of their names: Joseph, Ralph, and Avi Nakash. The jeans had lots of white overstitching and a white embroidered horsehead logo.

Sergio Valente (real name: Eli Kaplan) jeans had *lots* of styling—obvious overstitching and an enormous embroidered longhorned bull that covered the entire back pocket. **Jeans for the way you live and love.**

The Line Forms to the Rear (slogan for Ditto jeans)

Some existing jeans companies didn't see the craze coming and struggled valiantly to catch up, repositioning their jeans as "designer style."

Dittos—Long a favorite of bad Catholic school girls everywhere, these jeans had no pockets but had a heavy seam that curved across the backside, really emphasizing the butt crack.

Organically Grown by Arpeja—These jeans were a curious mix of high-end status and low-end hippie shit. Their ad mistakenly featured the soon-to-be-unanswered trivia question—the "star" of *Roller Boogie*, Kimberly Beck.

Others included: Chic (**World's Best Fitting Jean**), n'est-ce pas? (**A most fitting way to turn your back on the world**), Lee Tight Riders from Ms. Lee—note the Ms.!—(**They're named for the way they fit.**), Levi's Straight Legs, Lois jeans, and without question the *worst* name for women's jeans: Bend Over Jeans from Levi's Womenswear.

Celebrity "Back"-ing

In age-honored marketing fashion, celebrities and products jumped on the bandwagon "designing" their own jeans. You could strut about town in Reggies (Reggie Jackson), Gilleys (Mickey Gilley, cowboy bar owner), Willie Nelson Jeans, Kenny Rogers' Lady jeans, J.R. (Ewing) jeans, Teddy Pendergrass Celebrity Body Jeans, and Cheryl Tiegs Jeans for Sears. Make a statement in Playmate jeans (Playboy bunny on buttons and stitched on watch pocket), Candies' jeans (Candies made hooker-type sandals: **You're going places.**), Fruit of the Loom jeans, and the brazen Style Auto jeans with the Ferrari logo and two-tone (red and gold!) overstitching.

But the *ne plus ultra* endorsement-designer jeans combined both celebrity *and* product: Studio 54 jeans. A designer jeans survey in *New York* magazine pronounced them the tightest jeans available. The logo of Studio 54 was stitched across the *entire* back pocket. They had the best slogan: "**Now everyone can get into Studio 54.**" But *New York* sniffed (and probably correctly) that "these are jeans for people who have never been to Studio 54 and probably won't get in."[17] Well, excuse me. For me, they are the Holy Grail of Designer Jeans.

"Back"-lash

No fad is complete without a backlash. JCPenney (**Plain Pockets**) and Montgomery Ward both trumpeted that their jeans had *no* look. Goodwill Industries (in either a backlash or a desperate attempt to fit in, it's hard to know) sewed a "Goodies" designer label on used jeans and sold them for $4.99. A mail-order company called Mine Jeans would embroider *your name or monogram* across the back right pocket of designer jeans knockoffs. The best counter-response was Long Haul jeans. Loose-fitting, designed "for the asses of the masses," they were marketed to truckers and advertised an extra big pocket for chewing tobacco.

Buttloads of Designer Jeans in the Thrifts

For years since their moment, designer jeans have been clogging up the thrifts. They were so reviled it was hard to believe they'd ever be fashionable again. But evidently, Calvin Klein jeans are so hot again that kids in NYC are hitting retro-stores and snatching up his old designer jeans. Should you desire a pair, read on. Designer jeans should be *dark indigo blue*. This criterion will save you much time in the jeans rack. They should not be faded or scruffy, though they might show a crease or ironing mark down the middle of the leg. (This proves you cared for your jeans as much as a good suit.) While some of the designer-era brands continue to churn out jeans, those gems from the past can be distinguished by long, long (to accommodate your 4-inch mules, ladies), narrow straight legs (no tapering and not as narrow as stovepipe trousers), a high tight waist, and an extremely close-cut crotch and backside. For best fit, you'll have to try them on. A good fit will separate your buttocks, fit tight around the bottom of your butt, and take your breath away. (In jeans this tight, the pockets are useless. Make sure you thrift a disco bag.) And *you* pick the designer. I wouldn't *dream* of suggesting your taste!

> **A**fter griping about the public's emphasis on labels, let me now confess I often buy clothing at thrift stores *because of the label!* I'm speaking of those kooky weird labels. Just as with "designer" clothing, it's a shame nobody ever sees the label on your Saturdays in California Mach II or Clothes Styled for Tomorrow shirt.

Fear Not, O Fashion Victims!

There is nothing wrong with being fashionable, buying designer clothing, or dressing up to make a scene. I've been guilty myself of all three—though my sins weigh heaviest in the third category. That said, it's important to be aware of the issues that go into fashion and the clothing industry. When you see that rack of marked-up "designer clothes" at the thrifts, you realize how ingrained society's conceptions of fashion and value are. They still have impact, even at the bottom rung of the fashion ladder. The more you know, the better you can respond, whether it is the quest for this week's trend or some anticonsumer statement you've just got to make.

5 Checkin' Out Clothing

The quality of a garment may be only one factor in your decision to buy. What it costs, what effect you hope to create with it, and what you want the garment for are equally valid considerations. If you're buying a weird skirt to wear once to a costume party, you may have little regard for overall quality. You'll buy it cheap, wear it once, astound your friends, and then redonate it to the thrift.

Do get to know what distinguishes a well-made garment from a poorly made garment. Even if you don't care—and hardly anything seems to matter about a shirt that costs 69 cents—it doesn't hurt to know. You don't have to spend hours poring over each garment. But if you would like to spend your money wisely in the thrifts, read on. Thrifts are getting savvier about clothing (and marking it up!), and you should too. Is that coat *really* worth $20? And here's a bonus retail advantage. If you learn what goes into making a decent piece of clothing, you'll never shop at the mall again! So much new clothing is poorly made, you'll die when you see it! You're better off hitting the thrifts and digging up the better-made secondhand stuff anyway. That's one reason why older clothes are there in the first place. They were well made and they survived.

FIRST, READ THE LABEL . . .

Read the label. It's usually in the collar area, but sometimes you'll find the label stitched into one of the inner seams. With men's jack-

---

SANFORIZED? WHAT?!—OTHER LABEL WORDS

Sanforized: Guaranteed trademark (adopted in 1930) indicating that cotton won't shrink more than 1 percent—probably meaningless for used clothes, but now you know!

Sanfor-Set: Fabric has been pretreated in an ammonia bath to eliminate wrinkling.

Permanent Press: Synthetic and partly synthetic clothes are chemically treated and then baked in an oven. This sets them permanently and is often used with hems and pleats.

ILGWU: The ILGWU symbol means the garment was made by members of the International Ladies Garment Workers Union (organized in 1900 to combat the miserable working conditions in garment sweatshops).

---

ets and suits, the label is often stitched into the inside pocket. The Textile Fiber Products Identification Act of 1960 mandated that all garments and piece goods have a label stating the percentage of each fiber, but manufacturers are allowed to list by generics like wool, cotton, or polyester.

Don't give total credence to the label. It's like going through life taking a stranger's word for everything. Of course, the label is going to say nice things. The manufacturer wants to sell the garment, and—while it's illegal to lie on a clothing label, legitimate manufacturers do make use of qualitative terms like "tailored by American craftsmen," "made with quality," or "stitched with pride." The label can be helpful, but don't rely on it. Many thrift garments are missing labels anyhow.

One jacket I thrifted had *both* these labels. Which one can you believe? PHOTOS BY AUTHOR

FABRICS 101

I can't teach you to identify fabrics by feel, but you can *and should* train yourself. Thrifting is a contact sport—don't just look. Put your hands deep in the racks. Touch the fabric, read the label, make and remember the association. Touch things you aren't even gonna buy, just to bulk up your brain. Silk feels smooth and slippery, and so does polyester, but they are easy to tell apart with training. If you have shopping friends who are smart about fabric, ask them to help educate you. This may seem tedious now, but soon you'll have gifted fingertips and be saving plenty o' time. I just run my fingertips down a rack of dresses and stop when I feel the right things—mmmmm, linen. Touching is the solution to unlabeled garments. Older clothes didn't have to be labeled, they might be handmade, or the label might have fallen off. Ignorant pricers might not mark up a cashmere coat if it's no longer labeled, but your smart fingers can tell cashmere, labeled or not, and a cashmere overcoat or sweater is a *steal* at a couple of bucks.

Just as you can develop skilled fingertips, so can you have gifted eyeballs. Certain fabrics look different. Again, the differences can be subtle, but fieldwork will give you the skills. If I'm in a hurry, I just cast my eye along a rack; garments made from linen, silk, or old rayon just pop out at me.

Remember that "fabrics" like satin, corduroy, velvet, crepe, chenille, chiffon, flannel, gabardine, lace, seersucker, taffeta, velour, etc. are terms used to define *characteristics of a cloth* and can be constructed from a variety of sources, i.e. velvet can be made from silk, rayon, cotton, or a synthetic.

Wools

Wool is the hair cut or collected from various mammals, cleaned, spun into thread, then dyed and woven into fabric or knitted into garments. If the garment is unlabeled and you are unsure whether it is wool or a synthetic fabric, discretely moisten a small area of the item and smell it. If you don't already know the very distinctive odor of wet wool, practice identifying this smell at home. (But if it's a soft sweater with the name of a golf course stitched on it, it's probably a quality acrylic. For some reason those high club fees don't get you a wool sweater.) "Virgin wool" is no comment on animal behavior. It means this is the first time the wool has been manufactured into fabric and is not reprocessed wool or reused wool. (Navy pea coats are often made from reprocessed wool.)

Sheep: Lambswool is the first shearing from lambs, softer and finer than adult wool. Merino wool is an expensive soft wool from Australian pedigree merino sheep.

Goats: Cashmere is wool from Kashmir goats raised only in remote parts of the Middle East and Far East. One goat generates four ounces of fleece a year and must be combed by hand. One goat + three years' fleece collecting = one woman's sweater. Cashmere is often blended with other wools. The "purer" the cashmere, the spongier the garment feels. Mohair is fleece from the angora goat. Most are now raised in Texas (on mohair farms!).

Camels: Alpaca is fleece from a Peruvian relative of the camel of the same name and is often blended with other wools. If labeled "camel's hair," by law it has to be real hair from a real camel, but be wary of wool blends in camel color. Vicuña is an extremely fine fleece from vicuñas, another Peruvian member of the camel family. A very expensive wool, since vicuñas are killed when fleeced (they evidently won't hold still). Forty vicuñas = one coat.

Bunnies: Angora wool is from angora rabbits, very soft and fluffy and often blended with other wools, as pure angora is *very* hairy and sheds like a demon.

Skins

Leather is the chemically treated hide of an animal, generally with the fur removed. What says "leather" might be the skin of goats, horses, pigs, cows, deer, sheep, or reptiles and is usually not specifically identified. Good leather should be soft and supple. Patent leather has been coated with varnish for a hard glossy finish.

Fur is the top fuzzy side of animal skins. Most thrifts only stock cheap sorts of fur garments made from rabbit, dyed rabbit (have you ever seen a purple rabbit?), dyed squirrel, mouton (sheared lamb), or Persian lamb (commonly dyed black). Cheaper fur coats are also made from pieced fur (leftover bits) rather than the full pelt—common in less-expensive rabbit, mink, and fox coats. All newer furs must be accurately labeled for what fur they are and the country of origin. All spotted big cats are protected, and sale or use of their fur is illegal. You'll want that petroleum-based fake fur for your Leopard Lady Look.

Reptiles, Fish, and Water Mammals

These skins can include:

Sealskin: from the Alaskan fur seal;*

Snakeskin: from the bigger snakes: boas, pythons, and anacondas;

Lizard: various lizards;

Alligator: I saw on TV that the ban on alligator skins has been rescinded due to excess alligators near Disney World or something. Country of origin should be U.S.A., as the import of foreign alligator skins is still prohibited. Bags and shoes that predate the 1970 U.S.A. ban won't list this;

Crocodile: not commonly found; usually alligator skin is treated to look like crocodile skin;

Sharkskin leather: from sharks and not those shiny two-tone suits that Sammy Davis Jr. wore, which are made from blends of wool, cotton, rayon, and synthetics, though they are called "sharkskin" as well.

Plants Are Our Friends

Cotton is derived from the cotton plant—yes indeedy. "It's like a bush that grows cotton balls," said this amazed city child on a drive through Mississippi during cotton season. The white fluffy stuff is picked, cleaned, spun into thread, and woven into fabric. There are various grades of cotton: Egyptian cotton is considered the best, pima cotton is the finest U.S. cotton, Sea Island cotton is another good cotton from Caribbean and Gulf areas, and Indian cotton is rougher and cheaper. The more threads listed the better—300 threads is better than 200—the yarns are finer, and the fabric will be stronger and become softer over time. Mercerized cotton has had a lustrous finish added (sometimes called "polished cotton"). Fun Fact: *One-third* of the U.S. cotton crop goes toward manufacturing denim.

*These leathers/skins are from endangered animals and it's currently illegal to manufacture goods from them, but older goods made prior to contemporary regulations do show up at thrifts.

Linen is made from the flax plant through a very labor-intensive process. Linen is stronger than wool or cotton (U.S. "paper" money is made with linen). It's the oldest known textile fiber—Egyptians wrapped their mummies in it. Watch out for blends and fakes made from ramie and rayon. Ramie is a linenlike fabric made from a flax-like fiber of tropical Asian herb. Rubber is made from rubber plants by heating the juice and is the most waterproof fabric. Most "rubber" sold today is vinyl. Sniff it if you're unsure: rubber smells different from vinyl.

✳TIP✳ Don't be swayed by the phrase "imported fabric." It's meaningless. Good fabrics are imported; so are the world's cheapest fabrics.

Other fabrics originate with plants but are considered man-made textiles or semisynthetics because of the processing involved. Rayon is made from the cellulose of pine, hemlock, and spruce trees. This mixture is forced through holes to produce fine streams that harden to become the "yarn." Pre–World War II rayon is "filament rayon," which was treated with copper and ammonia and had a softer, finer texture than today's rayon, where the wood pulp is treated with alkali and carbon disulfide. Rayon is a very flexible fabric; it can mimic cotton, silk, and linen. Rayon is also called viscose. Acetate and triacetate also come from wood pulp.

Bugs and Birds

Silk comes from the cocoon of the small *Bombyx mori* silkworm (that would grow up to be a moth). Two thousand cocoons = one dress. Worms have to be fed several times a day on specially grown mulberry leaves. Pampered worms make the finest silk; less-tended worms eat other stuff, creating what is often called "raw silk." Despite its flimsy feel, silk is a very strong fabric.

Down/feather filling is from ducks and geese (down is the fluff under their feathers). Feather filling is cheaper, heavier, has sharp quills, and is less warm. Check the percentage of down and feathers—more down is better. Be alert for polyester fiberfill; it will feel solid and bulky when squeezed.

Petroleum Is Our Friend Too—Synthetic Fabrics

If a fabric sounds like it came out of a chemistry lab, it probably did. The bold names are the generic terms; trade names are also listed (in italics) here since labels may use them. These are trade-marked terms for fabric *inventions*.

Nylon was the first true synthetic fiber. In 1938, DuPont mixed together petroleum, natural gas, air, and water and used it to make hosiery. The fabric proved terrifically popular, easy to care for, and durable. *Antron, Enka, Qiana.*

Spandex was developed during World War II to take the place of rubber. *Lycra, Clospan, Numa, Spandelle, Vyrene.*

Acrylic is made from coal, air, water, petroleum, and limestone. *Acrilan, Creslan, Zefran, Orlon* (the earliest acrylic introduced in 1952 by DuPont).

Polyester is technically the generic term for fabrics manufactured from coal, petroleum, air, and water, but has also become the de facto generic for any synthetic fabric. *Dacron* was the first polyester fabric made by DuPont in 1952. *Encron, Fortrel, Kodel, Trevira.*

Modacrylic is a fake fur made from natural gas, coal, air, salt, and water. *Dynel, Elura, Verel.*

Vinyl is derived from ethylene, often used in place of leather.

Latex is rubbery elastic material in older clothes and newer sex toys; spandex is now used in place of latex in clothing.

Now you have no excuse for not knowing exactly what various fabrics are and how to spot 'em. Whether you're searching for only "natural" fabrics, avoiding animal parts, or own stock in DuPont, knowledge is power!

HOW TO JUDGE GOOD CLOTHING

Like fabric analysis, the best way to assess the overall quality of a garment and its level of workmanship is to do fieldwork. Your best training is simply to learn to pay attention. I wasn't born knowing this stuff. I learned it along my way. The more garments you examine, the more you touch them, pull at them, and scrutinize them, the better you will become at gauging quality. It's just as helpful to look at badly made clothing. Flaws are easy to see, and you can add them to your mental database of what to avoid. Once you have a little background information, most assessment will be basic common sense.

Advanced Fabric Analysis

We've already learned the origins of common fabrics. Now, assess the fabric use within the garment. Is the fabric worn in any place? Pile fabrics like velvet, velour, and corduroy are most susceptible to this. Check problem areas: elbows, butt, knees, and between the thighs. Is the fabric "pilling"? (Pills are those irritating little balls of cloth that hang onto clothing. The strands of the fabric get loose and form little balls.) A garment that is lightly pilled will have some life left in it. Pick the pills off (don't cut!) while watching TV. Be aware, though, that it will pill again. Cheaply made fabrics may have imperfections in the weave, nubs, discoloration, snags, bad dye jobs, and loose threads. Look for good things too, like woven patterns (rather than printed), richly dyed fabric (some cheapola fabric is surface dyed—check the underside), and damask patterns (fabric has a patterned weave that runs against the main weave. This can be subtle and only show up when the fabric is moved under light, like a watermark.)

Feel the fabric. With a few exceptions, most nice fabric feels good and most cheap fabric feels bad. (One exception is some of the rougher Scottish and Irish tweeds. These are good-quality woolens, and it's their nature to be scratchy.) Fabric should not feel too coarse or tacky (indicating residue from cheap dyes or treatments) nor should it be too stiff (brand new denim excepted, of course!). Age may affect the fabric of older garments. If fabric feels grainy or even seems to crumble under your fingers, walk away. We're talking "dry rot" and there's no cure. Some types of fabric have a high snagability factor. If you feel it catching your skin or the edges of your fingernails, realize that this will be most irritating when you're wearing this garment.

Pull at the fabric. If it's a giving type of fabric like wool, it should revert back to its shape. Well-worn sweaters have often lost this "bounce." Tightly woven fabrics like silk won't give much at all. If you tug at the garment and it assumes some weird shape where you pulled it and doesn't go back to its original shape, bear that in mind. Every time you bend your elbow or lift your arm, the garment may shift into odd shapes.

Other Fabric Problems

These are primarily related to the former wearer of the garment. It may have been the world's most expensive Chanel suit, but bad things can happen to it before it gets to the thrift.

Stains: Some stains can be easily fixed by a good washing. Mud on jeans is no problem. If the garment is not machine-washable, some stains may be corrected by handwashing or dry cleaning. Unfortunately, the biggest secret to stain removal is immediacy of action, and obviously, any garment at the thrift has lost this advantage. Weigh the cost of the garment, size and location of the stain, how badly you want it, and the cost and effort of cleaning. Tough stains are ink, blood, coffee, tea, dark fruit juices, grease or oil, and paint. Another bad stain is the yellowing you get from body perspiration on light garments. It's pretty permanent and pretty gross-looking. Also, if the fabric has been burnt (cigarettes and irons), there's not much that can be done.

Holes: Holes and rips in the fabric are another tough problem. Small holes can sometimes be rewoven by a clever sewer. A beautiful wool suit with a small hole that's only a few dollars might be worth taking later to a tailor for spot reweaving, especially if the hole is in an inconspicuous place. Small holes rarely stay small. The one exception is burn holes in polyester. Because the polyester fibers melt, they actually seal up the edges of the hole.

Odor: Don't be afraid to smell the garment. All clothing smells a little weird in the thrift store. (It may be a bit musty from years of storage, may have been near mothballs, or might smell of some disinfectant the thrift uses.) Learn to distinguish these temporary smells from more evil odors. Sniff the armpits for perspiration odor. If you get a good whiff, realize that that odor is buried deep in the fibers and is probably there for life. (Some garments hold the perspiration smell *until* they warm up; i.e., until you're already wearing it!) Any other foul odors should be your wake-up call to put that item back on the rack.

HOLDING IT ALL TOGETHER

Stitched Up Tight and Right

Seams: There are six things to look for when examining seams.

1. Make sure they're intact. Seams are the stress points of garments, and small holes in the seams will definitely get bigger with use. If you can sew, stitch up the ripped seam at once.

Sometimes a small sewing repair can solve minor problems. I think about sewing more than I actually undertake it, but I have included these tips for the sewers out there and maybe even to encourage those of you who haven't considered it to pick up a needle and try it yourself. It's really not very hard—and thank goodness, it's not even limited to women anymore. If you're absolutely opposed to sewing, then you should weigh "needs some sewing" into your decision of whether to purchase a garment.

2. Grab a piece of the garment on either side of seam and give a little tug. If it yawns open and you see a gaping chasm with stretched stitches across it, you're looking at a seam that was sewn too loosely.

3. If you can discern it (you may need to peek inside), more stitches per inch in a seam is generally better.

4. See what type of thread has been used in seaming. Clear plastic thread is increasingly common. I hate this stuff because it tends to get loose and scratch you. Also, I just don't like the idea of my clothing being held together with what looks like fishing line.

5. Check what the fabric of the garment looks like near the seams. Fraying is one problem, but you might have a construction problem if the fabric appears to be puckered, gapping, or not flowing smoothly into the seam. (Eyeball a very cheap men's suit at the arm/shoulder seam and you'll often see this.) Some seams are very tricky to execute, and a smooth seam area is a good indication that more care was taken in constructing this garment.

6. Look inside the garment to see that seams are "finished." This means that the edge of the fabric has been secured in some way to prevent it from fraying or unraveling.

Hems: A bad seam is like a bad house foundation: it's pretty darn hard to repair once it's in place. While bad hems will have many of the same characteristics as bad seams, they're a lot easier to fix. The hem is where the fabric is meant to stop, and since it's not meeting another piece of fabric like a seam, it's just turned over on itself and sewn in place. A well-hemmed garment should have a fairly invisible hem from the outside. Like a seam, the inside of the hem should be secured to prevent unraveling. A hem may appear slightly bunched up inside if that part of the garment is not cut in a straight line. As long as it doesn't show from the outside, that's OK.

Button, Zip, and Snap

Even if you don't try the garment on, check that all the fastening bits are present and in working condition. A nice garment will have better-quality buttons made from a good solid substance like wood, shell (including abalone), coconut, glass, Bakelite, or other early plastics, brass, heavy plastic, fabric (buttons are covered with same fabric as garment), copper, fake pearls, and rhinestones set in plastic. Cheap buttons are pretty much made from a few substances—plastic, plastic, and plastic—and mostly cheap plastic. The worst are those fake "metal" buttons made from silver-colored plastic.

Check that buttons are securely attached. A loose button is not always the sign of a poor garment. Buttons take a lot of abuse and do come loose. Resew loose buttons early before you lose them. Also, check out the buttonholes. Fraying is common in older garments. This is a high-use, high-friction area. Close the button—the fraying may be hidden. The buttonholes may be so stretched out—on a sweater or coat—that they may not hold the button very well anymore. A small stitch or two in the corner of the buttonhole will fix that. Garments made from thick fabric like a wool coat may have the button attached on a dangling bit of thread. This is to allow for the bulk of the fabric when you fasten the button.

One missing button is no problem, especially if the remaining buttons are of a standard design and color. Either replace the button or use a safety pin (if you're lazy like me). If a coat or dress has unique buttons and one is missing, first check to see if there are any spare buttons on the garment. Some manufacturers kindly hide an extra button within the garment—try inside the bottom hem area, under the lapel, or at the bottom of a shirt. (Had you been wondering what that button under the lapel was for?) If there's no extra button, see if a button already in use can be shifted. Take the decorative button off the cuff of the coat or move the top button to a more functional place. Garments missing several or all of the buttons represent a project. You may have to replace all the buttons, either from your own personal stockpile of buttons or with new buttons. (Some vintage clothes show up without any buttons, usually because somebody was more interested in the buttons than the garment and removed them.)

Zippers are another tricky piece of sewing. They should be securely sewn into the garment, with no ugly bunching or puckering around the edges. See that they blend into the garment nicely. Do the top flaps close over the zipper smoothly? When zippers go bad, they go bad in a spectacular way. Unless you want to replace them entirely, leave the garment be. If it's just the fabric edge of the zipper that's come loose from the garment, a couple of stitches or even a safety pin will right that quickly.

Other fasteners include hook-and-eye catches (those tiny metal things usually found at the top of the zipper or neckline). Any drugstore has them, you've just got to sew 'em back on. Frogs (like on Oriental dresses) and toggles (like on a fireman's coat) are harder to find and match. Snaps that sew on are also easy to replace, but snaps that have been "punched" into the fabric will require the use of a snap puncher implement. Those metal two-piece slide-the-flat-bit-into-the-slot fasteners that are often found on men's dress pants are harder to buy but can be replaced with a hook-and-eye catch.

The Garment Underneath—Linings

A lining is often the sign of a well-made and expensive garment. A coat or dress that is fully lined represents a lot of extra work on the part of the manufacturer. Occasionally, the garment may be only partially lined: the suit back and front but not the sleeves, or half the skirt (ladies, that bit goes to the front, where your knees would hit the offending fabric). There are so many blazers, jackets, and coats out there, I'd insist on one with a lining. A lining doesn't just feel nice and smooth, but it also hides all the seam work, giving your garment a nice clean look inside and out. (Pay attention next time you see a guy lean forward in an unlined jacket so that it gaps a bit. See all the seams and the inside of the pocket? Ugh.) A lining is also a blessing if the garment is made from a scratchy or irritating material like lurex, vinyl, corduroy, double knit, and some tweed. Now most linings are made from polyester or acetate, but older garments had quite yummy silk and rayon linings. I've bought coats just because of the beautiful lining!

Clean and Snappy—The Cut of Garment

The best way to judge the cut (or how the fabric is pieced together) of a garment is to try it on and look at it. How does it feel? Does it sit on your body "right"? Are the lines clean, is the hem consistent, do the back vents lie flat, does the garment move gracefully with

Sometimes it's the little things that distinguish a good garment from a bad one. Your personal taste will determine which details are important, but pay attention to:

- Pockets: Are they real? Do they button or close somehow? Are they a nice shape when you stuff your hands in? Are they in a practical place to use? A well-made patterned shirt will have a matched pocket—not just of the same fabric—but the pocket will be cut and placed in such a way that there is no break in the pattern.

- Lapels: Are they unusually cut? Do they lie flat? Is the buttonhole real, in case you want to wear a flower?

- Dresses and skirts sometimes have (or once had!) an accompanying belt. It might be a belt made from the identical fabric or a contrasting belt that the manufacturer added. (In thrifts, there's good chance it's any old belt an employee added.) If the dress is missing the belt and you don't want to wear one anyway, you can snip off those irksome little belt loops.

you? Cheaper garments have often had less attention paid to their cut—a simple block pattern for a blazer may have been used rather than lots of fine tailoring details from shoulder to waist. But sometimes even the most expensive and beautifully made garment will hang terribly on you—and it's not necessarily your fault. Your body may be a different (not wrong!) dimension, or the garment may have been altered (or hand-tailored) to fit a specific somebody.

This may seem like a lot to pay attention to, and if you've never studied a garment up close before, your first one may take a few minutes. You don't have to micro-inspect every detail mentioned on every garment. But keep the above considerations in mind. Learn to spot good and bad things about how clothing is constructed. Know ahead of time which flaws are salvageable and which garments are doomed to die. With practice, the ability to gauge a garment for quality becomes second nature, and soon you'll be whipping through the racks like a maniac.

TRYING ON CLOTHES

It's silly to buy clothing you intend to wear without trying it on first, even if it only costs a dollar. Don't count on your eyes or your mental self-image to "size" clothing for you. (Remember, your mental self-image probably doesn't look a thing like you.) Better-organized thrifts sometimes mark a size (usually a waist, inseam, or shoulder measurement) on the price tag. This is helpful, but don't rely on it. And in stores that have the clothing sorted by size, don't stop when you've looked at just your size. Check the whole aisle. Items get mixed up fast.

And never forget this: There is no reason to believe any sizing information listed on the garment! Even if the label is intact, despite what the clothing industry says, there is no such thing as "standard sizing." While ideals exist (there's a mannequin on Seventh Avenue that's a perfect size 9), they don't necessarily translate precisely to manufactured garments. Another important reason to ignore the label is the obvious fact that many clothes in the thrifts have been previously worn. With time, wear, and laundering, the garment might have traveled some distance from its original size.

Some serious shoppers travel with a tape measure—the loose sewing kind, not the metal hardware kind! A tape will give you exact measurements on waist circumference, inseam, distance from neck to waistline, collar width, sleeve length, etc. If you're familiar with your own measurements, these can be helpful. They often escape the eye, but some thrifts have tape measures and yardsticks scattered about. I've seen yardsticks bolted to the top of clothing racks. Ask at the counter. They might have a tape measure.

Try It On, Already!

The solution is to try the garment on! Then it doesn't matter who wore it previously, what the label says, what size you think you wear, what your mental image is—either it fits or it doesn't. Some thrifts have dressing rooms. If you know this in advance, then wear what you like shopping. It's always a smart idea to dress simply, though. Don't wear those stovepipe pants with giant boots.

If you know the thrift has no dressing room or you're headed into uncharted territory, then dress smart! Weather and modesty permitting, thrift in body-hugging clothing like bicycle shorts, exercise pants, and leggings, and tight T-shirt or tank. If you're wearing a second skin, you should be able to try on most anything right there in the aisle. When checking for size, do up all the zips, snaps, and buttons. It's an easy way to check that they're all present and functional, and it'll give you a true fit. I've seen shoppers just strip right down, oblivious. While this certainly gets the job done, I don't recommend it. You might take heat from weirded-out store employees, and probably nobody really does want to see you in your skivvies, thereby grossing out other patrons. But, if you're inclined . . .

If Skintight Clothing Ain't Your Scene, Try These Tips

If you're wearing a loose skirt, it is relatively easy to try on other skirts or trousers under your skirt. There's an outside chance some-

It's this simple to try on pants under a skirt!
PHOTO BY AUTHOR

body might see your underwear. If you care—and frankly I'm past that point—consider wearing opaque, dark-colored tights when you go out to thrift. The looser the skirt, the more "curtain effect" you get, reducing your chances of giving a free show. You may also want to find a quieter corner, like down behind the bedspreads, or have a friend provide a little shielding. There's an art to changing your clothes in public without giving anything away. Practice a few times at home in front of a mirror. You'll be surprised how very *un*revealing the process can be.

Gentlemen, don't be afraid. If you're serious about getting a good fit, the trying-on-under-the-skirt is a viable option for you. After identifying the pants you want to try on, head over to the women's skirts. Pick out any nice flowing skirt. You're not buying it, just

---

What to do with clothes that don't fit? Here are some suggestions that involve no tailoring.

- **Convert into gifts.**

- **Clothing too big? The hard reality is you'll probably fit into it one day, so keep it.**

- **Give to mannequin. If you're lucky enough to come across a mannequin or even a dressmaking form, you can outfit these generally svelte and perfectly sized creatures in all the gladrags you couldn't get into.**

- **Make a scarecrow.**

- **Hang cool clothes on wall.**

- **If there's a significant amount of cloth, carefully cut away all the zippers, buttons, etc., and now you have a cool piece of fabric.**

- **Hold a Swap Party (see Chapter 3).**

- **Resell at a yard sale.**

- **Give back to thrift or clothing drive—promotes good thrift karma.**

- **Give to a dog or cat to sleep on. I know a cat that sleeps on a salmon orange cashmere sweater that the owner didn't like the fit of.**

using it, so color, pattern, etc., are of no consequence. Put the skirt on over your own pants. Now, using the skirt as cover, remove your pants and try on the prospective pair. Reverse the procedure to get back into your pants. Embarrassing? Well, you'll get over it. If you can't handle the genderbending, it is possible to achieve similar results by borrowing a loose bathrobe or overcoat from the men's section. Surprise—you may find that the narrower coat or bathrobe doesn't offer as much coverage as the skirt. You can decide whether it's more embarrassing to be seen in a skirt or your underwear.

Dresses can be tricky. If it's a voluminous dress and that's the look you're going for, it can be tried on right over your clothes. Not so easy to do with a tight, fitted dress or a dress with a distinct waist. If you're particularly adventuresome, find a giant muumuu or some other large full-length loose article of clothing. Fasten this just around your neck, leaving your hands free inside the garment. This will provide a full-length cover. Remove current garments. Struggle into the prospective dress and then see how it fits and looks.

If just the waist and lower half of the garment is in question, use the skirt-cover technique. If you can't manage any of these, be sure to hold the garment up against your body, not just in midair. Position the shoulders and waist to get an idea on sizing. Be generous in your estimates of your body density. The garment you're looking at is 2-D but you're 3-D. Hold the dress waist up to your own waist. The dress waist will be halved, so make sure you can get the waist part at least halfway around your own waist. This is an inexact measure at best. It will, however, turn up dresses that are far too narrow or wide in the waist.

Other Fitting Tips

- When buying a suit or other two-piece outfits, try on both top and bottom! Older suits especially were custom-made, and although the top might fit, the bottom might not.
- Shoes that slip off and on easily will enable you to try on those go-go boots right there at the rack in seconds. Try to wear socks or stockings that approximate your usual wear. Bare feet will not always give the best indication of shoe fit. A stocking will help your foot slide in nicely to test the fit.
- Jackets and coats you can try right on over whatever you're wearing. If you live in a cold place, think about sufficient room for layering if purchasing a winter coat. Sure, it fits great over your T-shirt now in

September, but in January you'll be wearing a heavy shirt and big sweater under it as well. Get a good gauge of how much free space there is around the neck, shoulders, and armpits.

- Always try belts on. Some belts are self-adjusting. On others, make sure the holes are punched where you want them to be. You can use an awl or other sharp pointy object to punch a new hole, but see how far away that hole would be from existing holes.

- Try hats on. A hat either fits or it doesn't and most aren't adjustable (unless it's a baseball cap). Also, find a mirror. It may look fab and oh-so-snappy lying on the shelf, but be realistic about how you look in it!

And Finally . . .

Don't be embarrassed about trying on clothing in the store. First off, who cares? It's not like you're strippin'. Second, so what if somebody stares at you—like you know them and are ever gonna see them again or even care what they think? They should be thinking, "Hey, there's a smart shopper. Trying the garment on." Even if you cannot fight your own embarrassment, weigh it in the larger context. Which is worse? To be embarrassed for a minute? Or to get home and find the really swell dress doesn't fit at all! Not just a loss of money, but a disappointment. Better you should be embarrassed.

Use your common sense. You needn't spend your whole thrifting time laboriously changing under muumuus. Some garments have a better success rate (pants with draw strings or something that's obviously deliciously huge), or maybe it's only 49 cents and you wanna take the chance. Should you try some item on—be it spike heels, fedora, or cowboy shirt—and it does *not* fit, but it's the dreamiest thing you've ever seen, go ahead and buy it anyway! Shoes can be displayed on a shelf, hats can hang on a hook, clothes can go on the wall, they can be given away as gifts, or you can just delight in the acquisition.

6 A Partial History of Thrift Shoppers

"I long to turn myself into a Bohemian, but lack the proper clothes."
—author Joyce Johnson describing herself at age 13 in 1949.[1]

Why do people who in theory can afford to shop new choose to shop secondhand? Often, the goal is not just to save money but to purposefully make a larger social statement. The rise in recreational thrifting corresponds neatly with two important developments in post–World War II America: the development of youth subcultures, and the mass media's fascination with them.

Clothing has been the main thrift-store purchase of youth subculture members throughout the post–World War II decades. It's the easy participatory element: you can be an office drone Monday through Friday but, by changing your clothes, be somebody quite different on weekends. Joining a group by donning used clothing is a *cheap* way to belong. When the subculture is co-opted into the mainstream, the clothing is the easiest thing to imitate and market. Media attention also makes that once-outrageous look "standard," giving rise to newer subcultures that return to the thrifts to distinguish themselves from previous groups now considered part of the majority.

Most subcultures do not rely *exclusively* on secondhand clothing. Some groups will make or design their own clothing (e.g., the classic hippie tie-dye). Others will incorporate key garments that must be purchased new (e.g., the 25-zippers punk bondage trousers). The sartorial gift is in supplementing meaningful new garments with supposedly meaningless discarded clothing to achieve the perfect integration.

Because clothing and appearance (and the personal distinction it can bring) are so important to youth cultures, this is where many don't-need-to-thrift people begin their thrift shopping. The thrift stores start as easy repositories of kooky outfits, but shoppers are soon educated to other advantages of thrift shopping. They discover that they can purchase needed kitchenwares, decorate their home in a unique and inexpensive manner, or buy a handful of good books they've always meant to read. When the youthful moments of participating in the subculture have passed, they may continue to shop at thrift stores, having long ago learned that there are bargains to be had that support any age or lifestyle.

By examining these subcultures and their use of secondhand clothing, we can trace the development of today's accepted Thrift Fashion Concepts: antifashion, antimaterialism, fashion-as-personal-statement, emulation of entertainers, political statement, and campy, fun dress-up. Each generation of thrifters brought a new spin to thrifting. Let's take a look at our thrifting ancestors. Grab your bongos and follow me to the 1950s.

BEATS AND BEATNIKS (1945–1965)

The Beats must initially be distinguished from the beatniks that came later and grabbed all the good media. "The Beats" was a term loosely applied to a small group of writers and artists (Jack Kerouac, Allen Ginsberg, and William S. Burroughs were the most well known) who achieved some small fame in the late 1940s and early 1950s, first for their works and second for their appearance and lifestyle. The Beats weren't young enough to be youth culture nor did they have a specific look. Still, Ginsberg stated that one of their purposes was to be against the "iron regime of fashion." They adopted a nonchalance in their dress—any old pair of khakis would do. They railed mightily when most of the mainstream reviews of the Beats' works began with a physical description

From Joyce Johnson's autobiographical account of living among the Beats: "Socialites too would appear at the Cedar (Bar), fairy godmothers in extraordinary furs—potential collectors of artists as well as art. Some painters' old ladies retaliated by picking up the wilder stuff in the thrift shops—Spanish combs and beaded dresses from the twenties that ripped under the arms if danced in too energetically."[2]

ANTICONSUMERISM

In his unintentionally hilarious I-was-there 1959 study of Venice Beach beatniks, *The Holy Barbarians*, Lawrence Lipton explains the fascination with secondhand living in a chapter entitled "Down with the Rat Race: The New Poverty":

> Disaffiliation is a voluntary self-alienation from the family cult, from Moneytheism and all its works and ways. . . . Why, then, disaffiliation in an era when Time-Life-Fortune pages are documenting an American Way of Life that is filled with color-matched stainless steel kitchens, bigger and faster cars, electronic wonders, and future of unlimited luxuries like television-telephones and rocket trips to the moon? Because it is all corrupted by the cult of Moneytheism. . . . The New Poverty is the disaffiliate's answer to the New Prosperity. . . . It is an independent, voluntary poverty.[3]

Later in his book, Lipton posits that thrift shopping is not just the only shopping alternative left once you've adopted "voluntary poverty," but that it is a revolutionary act in itself!

> The pressure is toward conformity, with regular working hours and consumer spending in ways and in quantities that will make the American Way of Life look good in the Labor Department reports and Department of Commerce statistics. Buying a second-hand suit for five or ten dollars at a Windward Avenue uncalled-for clothing store or a three dollar second-hand dress at an East Side rummage shop does nothing for the statisticians or the Chamber of Commerce.[4]

Here is the development of an important sideline to thrift shopping. The deliberate refusal to participate in the retail marketplace is not just to save money or to get a unique look, but to be a purposeful economic affront to that very market. Later subcultures like hippies, punks, and riot grrls will also claim the same subversive act.

of the artist ("shabbily dressed," "dressed sloppy," "unwashed minstrels," "shaggy"). Whatever their dismay at this attention to the superficial at the expense of their art, it nonetheless laid the groundwork for the beatniks of the late 1950s.

Welcome to 1959. This is the watershed year when we have the first complete mass-media takeover of a youth subculture. Nobody cares about the Beats anymore; they're old. There's a hot new group of young people who wear way-out clothes, cohabit unconventionally (shack up), play bongos, recite poetry, and drink cheap plonk. Now *these* people are photogenic and media-friendly! They're beatniks. The well-publicized beatnik image the media created was a caricature of the erstwhile Beats—just a bunch of layabouts who played at being artists till the money from home ran out.

Unlike the Beats, the beatniks strove to emphasize their distinctive look. The beatniks created a "costume of cool" that is still imitated today. For the cats: a general sloppy look, black sunglasses, black turtleneck, striped boater T-shirt, shabby over-coat, beret, jeans, sweat clothes, shorts, sandals, and bare feet. Fashion is always more complex for girls and there were two fashion camps for beatnik chicks: the good-natured spaghetti sauce stirrer and the disdainful glacial beauty. Choose from black stockings, copper jewelry (preferably in some abstract shape), thrift-store dresses, sandals, bare feet, house-dresses, slacks, sunglasses, beret, toreador pants, flat ballet slippers, long black dresses, and black leotards.

Co-opting the scene. A "beatnik-style" totebag.
PHOTO BY VANESSA DOMICO

Not all of this attire—that abstract copper jewelry, for instance—could be purchased at a thrift store. The properly gifted beatnik would mix the new earrings with the old black thrifted dress and bare feet. Voila! In the event that the shabby old clothes didn't deliver the intended look (you wouldn't want to be mistaken for someone who was just poorly dressed!), a key garment like copper jewelry or a black beret would.

Not to go overboard on the poor beatniks, but they were the first fully exploited-for-their-look youth subculture. The media attention accomplished several things (that we will see occur again and again). The "look" was cemented, especially through photojournalism—and young people in weird clothing are always delightfully photogenic. If you were young and you didn't live in Venice Beach or Greenwich Village, it didn't matter because now you knew how to look like a beatnik even while living in Squaresville, Indiana. Advertisers and retail manufacturers couldn't resist the attraction of marketing the allure of the "exotic youth culture." The easiest thing to co-opt and deliver was the clothing. To "escape the Rat Race" all you had to do was dress up—a simple *surface* transformation—add black clothing and stir.

HIPPIES AND POST-HIPPIES: ANYTHING GOES (1965–1975)

The next significant subculture group that made a deliberate trip to the thrift stores was the hippies. Whereas the beatniks had had a

> **R**ock music critic Joel Selvin makes a case in his book *Summer of Love* that the crazy old-world look that some hippies fancied was created by one rather obscure rock band in 1965. A San Francisco band called the Charlatans played and pranced about town dressed in elaborate Victorian costumes. "Their women dressed like Victorian queens in lace-trimmed velvet. They had perfected their old-timey look through countless hours of rummaging through San Francisco's well-stocked thrift stores."[5] They were a major influence on other blossoming psychedelic bands and the San Francisco Summer of Love scene in spite of never having released an album! (The long-awaited album came out in 1969 after founding members of the band had left and the hippie look and lifestyle was already passé.)

tenuous relationship with an art movement (the Beats), the hippie look was irrefutably linked with the rock music scene of the mid- and late 1960s. Bands had ditched the buttoned-up suit look and were mixing and matching outrageous fabrics (brocade, velvet, leather) and odd garments with wild abandon. Unlike the beatniks, who had been categorized by a rather narrow look (the minimal dark and dull antilook clothing), these bands blew the fashion door right open by juxtaposing one kooky garment with another.

Hippies kept the anticonsumerism and antifashion sensibilities of the beatniks but also added two new important thrift fashion concepts: personal expression and political statement.

When the hippie youth culture began to jell in 1965, an important fashion aesthetic developed. Like the beatniks, what you chose to wear would signal your allegiance to a group, but rather than adopt a uniform, your clothes were now supposed to reflect *your unique personality* as well. Clothing was a form of expression. The more singular your clothing, the more personal your statement. Everybody's favorite venue for one-of-a-kind-items? The thrift store!

There was plenty of exposure to everyone's stylish experimentations. The hippie and rock scenes were covered extensively in mainstream and alternative media. There was inspiration from movies like *Monterey Pop* (1969), *Gimme Shelter* (1970), and *Woodstock* (1970), which showed what hundreds of thousands of oddly dressed *real-life* people were wearing. Just walking down the right city streets let you see what crazy costume somebody else had put together. Modesty and imagination were the only limits, and you could really tax these! The more "regular" people adopted elements of the hippie look, the weirder and wilder *your* look had to get.

The Beats and beatniks had made a half-hearted social stand

Dig the cobbled-together thrift look of Frank Zappa's girl group, the GTOs: "They [the GTOs] travel in a pack looking much like that section of the Goodwill store where clothing is sold by weight; worn cowboy boots, rotting thirty-year-old blouses and acres-large skirts and dresses, limp boas, pink tights, 75-cent army belts . . . "6

through their secondhand attire. The conceit was "I'm sloppily dressed so I'm not buying into Madison Avenue." When the hippie scene spilled over into the counterculture movement, the wearing of certain garments or combinations of garments easily served as political and social protest. It was critical to be perceived as antimaterialistic. It was an honor and a responsibility to reuse old clothing and take a stand against any kind of bourgeois fashion imperative. Excess military clothing from the thrifts and army-navy surplus stores was especially useful for making statements against the ongoing war. A flak jacket removed from its military context and worn over a patchwork skirt is more than just a fashion style or a cheap aesthetic, it's a public confrontation.

Much of the hippie dress aesthetic lingered throughout the early 1970s, although with a lack of an organized social or cultural movement, there was less media attention. Ironically, all the fringe experimentation of the hippies helped to loosen up fashion rules for *everybody*. With the increased acceptance of colorful and casual, you could sport nearly any look. Being weirdly dressed was losing its shock effect.

THE VINTAGE YEARS (1975–NOW)

"The latest trend in shopping, apparently, is the shift to thrift," said *Time* magazine in 1975. The article cited the recession as a possible cause of the trend but concluded that "some of the bargain hunters could well afford to shop in regular stores, but they have discovered that secondhand can be chic."7

In 1975, an important book was published, *Cheap Chic*, that transformed thrifting and the wearing of secondhand clothing from a funky, kooky, raggy hippie pastime to a unique fashion statement. *Cheap Chic* defined the vintage clothing fad and DIY dressing while still paying dues to a traditional sense of style. This book was not written for any fringe youth culture, but for women of any age and station in life (a handful of men were featured). Primarily, *Cheap Chic* encouraged *all* to seek an *individual* look. We take it for granted but this was a relatively new idea. The book's opening line said it best: "Personal style is what this book is all about. Fashion as a dictatorship of the elite is dead. Nobody knows better than you what you should wear or how you should look."[8]

Lack of money was not an impediment to style. The book implied that the less money you had to work with, the more creatively you were apt to shop and the more interesting your final look would be. In a groundbreaking approach to shopping, the authors emphasized the delight in the hunt and the scavenging. Suggested clothing venues ranged from thrift shops, vintage stores, army-navy surplus outlets, the family closet, and yardage stores. The individuality and the quality of older garments was praised over new mass-market clothes. Secondhand stores were also lauded as a source of historical retrieval. A shopper could help preserve the past and relive the associated romance and nostalgia of bygone times. Vintage clothing was the ticket back.

The Vintage Scene Established

Vintage stores selling a "sophisticated" look soon sprang up across the country. (Some of the older, funkier hippie secondhand stores went upmarket vintage.) Those who couldn't afford the vintage shops, or preferred the hunt themselves, raided the thrift stores to stock up on desired vintage clothing. Hawaiian shirts, pre–World War II fashions, leather bomber jackets, handpainted ties, evening wear, and costume jewelry were all popular scores. At the same time two other subcultures, those of Latinos and gay men, hit the secondhand stores in search of vintage clothing. Among Latino youth groups on the East and West Coasts, there was a revival of the early 1940s look: zoot suits, '40s platforms, above-the-knee vibrantly patterned rayon dresses, hats, and resort wear. Some got deeply into the look. The girls would sport towering pompadours and cruise with guys in shiny '40s automobiles.

Out of the Closet and into the Thrifts

A new subculture of recently liberated gay men was also snapping up vintage clothing. (*Cheap Chic* recommended having a gay male friend help you navigate used clothing shops and flea markets on the West Coast![9]) Besides recapturing the allure of past glamour, it was a fun way to dress up the "neat look" favored in gay ghettos at that time. How campy to pin a '30s brooch on your jacket or to wear a '40s handpainted tie to the office! You could set yourself apart from the mainstream (boring straights), from your own group (the no-style clones), or from anybody who lacked a sense of humor or fun.

Cross-Gender Dressing for the Masses

Any drag queen worth her high heels knew where all the good thrift stores were, but 1977 was the year *everybody* knew about cross-dressing for women. Two words: *Annie Hall*. Ruth Morley, a long-time film costumer, designed the "Annie Hall Look" for the very popular Woody Allen movie. A classy update on the recycled, eclectic look that had developed since the late 1960s, the costume showcased the character—urbane, kooky, youthful, neat, but with a unique style. Annie Hall didn't look like a hippie; she looked stylish. Many women quickly adopted the look. Morley concurred, "[This is] not a designer-dictated style, anyone can gather up pieces from her closet or the neighborhood thrift stores. . . "[10] Though "cuter" and less extreme than a lot of the other thrift looks in our history, the "Annie Hall Look" helped establish the general acceptance of women wearing men's clothes.

PUNK AND ITS DESCENDANTS (1976–NOW)

Scholars and sixteen-year-olds are still arguing over the meanings of "punk" and "punk style." It has been a subculture with incredible longevity. Though much of the look has remained consistent, the motivations of the participants have varied widely in twenty years. The style has been adopted by so many and in so many forms and with such varied intentions (from class overthrow to bugging the parents to band appreciation) that it is hard to determine its true meaning. The moment of birth, though, *can* be isolated. We do have to cross the Atlantic here for a moment. This is one youth culture that didn't pop up first in America.

While they were no doubt influenced by outrageously dressed kids hanging about the West End of London, the "official" punk look that sparked all the attendant media and mimicking sprang from the minds of two professional scene-makers: clothing designer Vivienne Westwood and impresario Malcolm McLaren. They had both previously dabbled in marketing other subculture styles including Teddy Boy (nostalgic 1950s) and sex fetish looks. They had the brilliant business sense to link their new "look" with a ready-for-total-media-exploitation band, the Sex Pistols. McLaren later admitted that one of the reasons he had started the band was to "sell more trousers."[11]

Though the punk look seemed unique, it contained a purposeful mishmash of previous subcultures: black leather and the vintage clothing from the Teddy Boys, narrow pants and blazers from the '60s mods, boots and suspenders from the skinheads, pork pie hats and fatigues from the ska and rasta camps, and shiny plastic, colored hair, and extreme makeup from early '70s glam rock. Much of its uniqueness was in the juxtaposition of these disparate garments. When punk arrived stateside, it lost much of the socioeconomic import it once had in Britain and was most often associated with a musical subculture. In contrast to highly stylized UK punks with bondage gear, rubber clothes, and full face makeup, the U.S. punks adopted a sloppier look. (Most American subcultures favor scruffiness.)

Similar to some beatniks and hippies, punks attempted to recreate themselves with an air of poverty and dishevelment, but the extreme nature of some of the clothing was an ironic statement, the deliberate playing up of the artifice rather than the reality of poverty. If you purposely rip your clothes and then hold them together with safety pins, this is about pushing the look of poverty to an absurd extreme. It is a parody. Even the very term Westwood used to describe her clothing—"confrontation dressing"—acknowledges the wearer's self-awareness. The use of inappropriate clothing was encouraged but it had to be obvious. Secondhand markets were ideal for finding trashy fashion. The ironic or agit-prop use of established garments, easily found in the thrifts, used out of context or in sharp contrast to another garment was common: the misuse of religious or political imagery, the glamorous made ugly (wedding gowns with boots), the dowdy made cool (grandma's rhinestone jewelry, old guy sweaters), and anything trashy or slutty looking (leopard skin, too short, too tight, too shiny).

Though perceived as a rebellious antifashion, the punk look is problematic. It was conceived by a designer as an antifashion that *was* a fashion. For a subculture reputedly based on anarchy, the look was quickly frozen into a uniform. In certain circles, slight deviation or the inappropriate article signaled not personal expression but phoniness, poseur crimes, or a lack of commitment. To *really* be against everything, you had to have just the right outfit. Nonetheless, plenty of punks got their look from the thrift. And why not? All the "real" clothing was often quite expensive. Participants either didn't care about the "authenticity" of their look or they decided there was a larger message from punk—and that message said, "Of course, you can thrift your own outfits. It's about *not* following rules!"

NOBODY LIKED ME IN HIGH SCHOOL BECAUSE I WORE WEIRD CLOTHES. . . OR HOW I WENT OUT OF MY WAY TO BUY WEIRD CLOTHES AT THE THRIFT STORES SO THAT NOBODY IN MY HIGH SCHOOL *WOULD* LIKE ME

You don't want to hear my silly nobody-liked-me tales about high school? Well you must, because it's all about thrifting. It was thrifting that provided me with the benign outlet, the shortcut to "class weirdo." And I choose to relate this story because the search for adolescent identity through unique clothing found at thrift stores is a common tale and how many of us thrifters began. Sure, the names, dates, places, and desired objects may be different, but many readers may recognize themselves.

No matter what they tell you about the importance of appearance in the corporate world and how micro-subtle difference like the width of the paisley in your tie can make or break your career, *nothing* compares to the rigid detail of fashion dos and don'ts in high school. I went to a Catholic all-girls high school—a thousand girls all dressed in bad plaid skirts and Peter Pan–collared blouses. You'd think the uniform would be the great equalizer, but the presence of the uniform only increased the importance of tiny things like shoes, socks, and what is worn on the rare free-dress days.

I attended high school in the late 1970s, a transitional time for youth fashion. The sloppy anything-goes-fashion of the early '70s was mutating towards the-label-and-cost-is-the-most-important-thing '80s. The funky cork wedge high heel gave way to the dressy disco high-heel sandal. Those earth-mother dresses were gone; velour dresses with a slit up the side were in. Denim maxicoats were out; down jackets from North Face were in (especially with the ski ticket!).

Why didn't I wear this stuff? Mostly because I didn't like the majority of these girls and consequently did not want to look like them. I mean, *I really didn't*. Other nonplayers adopted a beige look and disappeared into the wall. Not me. I said, I'm going to shove it in your face that I have chosen to not be like you and you will know it every time you look at me and see what I'm wearing. This all seems like silly posturing now, but you gotta remember how important silly posturing is to adolescents. I was blessed to be having my I-hate-girlie-girls crisis at a time when popular culture handed me the blueprints for full-out visual assault. Hello, punk rock, new wave, new music—whatever they called it. I was an immediate fan of the music and there was an easy marriage between dressing for fandom and dressing for shock effect. I got to be "part of the scene" *and* piss off Suzy Creamcheese. Win-win.

Like any besotted teenager, I studied intently. Every album cover, fan magazine, imported punk film from England, odd late-night video, concert, and even a walk down the city street let me see another article of clothing presented in a new manner. Thus educated, I'd hit the thrift stores, pawing through rack after rack of clothing, acquiring one necessary piece at a time for a couple of bucks each. I did covet new "punk" items that could be found in record stores or certain retro stores—two-tone shoes, tight black trousers, boots—but all beyond my wallet. I noted what the look was and used the thrifts to approximate this cheaply. Sometimes I would mimic faithfully (the day I found the black-and-white super pointy flat patent leather shoes!); other times I would venture out on my own fashion limb.

The passage of time has made my must-have list a giant alternative-dressing cliché (who *hasn't* worn this stuff in the past twenty years!), but at the time...Thermal underwear bottoms (to simulate the look of skintight stovepipe trousers), sweaters from the '50s and '60s (men's striped golfers and women's beaded cardigans), muted plaid shirts, dresses from the '40s, '50s, and '60s (any dress or skirt could be made "punk" by wearing it with black tights and inappropriate shoes), plaid skirts, anything leopard skin, gigantic men's shirts, men's blazers and overcoats, odd little hats, old sunglasses, rhinestone jewelry, gloves, flat shoes, old scarves with crazy prints, and—the de rigeur item—the black leather motorcycle jacket.

Dressed to alarm at Disneyland, 1981. The "thrift look" wasn't in yet. Disney didn't think my look was appropriate for their park, but I bought a hat at the parking lot gift shop anyway.
PHOTO FROM AUTHOR

The black leather motorcycle jacket was a watershed event. I dearly wanted one. It seemed to mean the difference between the pretenders and the credible. The Salvation Army on Valencia had recently opened a "boutique" of better clothing, and one afternoon I found the black leather jacket. It was far more than I had ever paid for anything (and frankly, it was priced far higher than it was worth), but it was the Holy Grail. I returned home triumphant and clad in black leather, already secure in how much "different" it would make me look. My mother was not pleased, not with the "look" or that I had spent money I was supposed to be saving for something. "Nice" sixteen-year-olds didn't wear black motorcycle jackets— but hello, that was the point! I "debuted" the jacket at a bootleg screening of the Sex Pistols flick, *The Great Rock and Roll Swindle* (could you even ask for a more perfect event?!), where my like-minded friends, green with envy, completely validated my purchase.

Important, I paid for my look myself. This raises another lesson learned early about thrift shopping. Buying your own clothing is about control, your total control over what you want. If you take outside money, it nearly always comes with strings attached. Is this velour sweater really "you" or does your mother think it's "you"? Especially for teenagers, what prevents this control over clothing purchase is the prohibitively high cost of new clothing. Ten bucks' baby-sitting or lawn-mowing money goes a l-o-n-g way at a thrift store.

KARMA CHAMELEONS AND OTHER ASSORTED LOOKS (1981–NOW)

Probably the biggest boon to thrift-shop dressing was the creation of a TV channel that broadcast nonstop music videos. There's always been an easy link between the costuming of a band and their subcultures of fans. Previously it may have been difficult for a kid out in the boonies to see what bands wore or see how it affected street dress in larger cities. Now, you didn't have to be old enough to go to Los Angeles or to see a show. Switch on MTV and there it was. The ascension of music video as the preferred medium for pop music exposure meant that the *style* of a band could be more important than the actual music. During the early to mid-1980s, there was no shortage of musical acts heralded for their look, and so many of the fashions could be pulled right from the thrift. It's no coincidence. These bands came up after the big vintage and punk dress fads of the 1970s, and many band members wore an updated (or watered-down) version of these looks. Besides dressing up for the videos, they were also available to discuss important topics like clothing during hours of promotional interviews.

What MTV acts looked like they shopped at the thrifts? Cyndi Lauper, Madonna (in her earlier incarnations), the Stray Cats, the Bangles, the Go-Gos, Bananarama, the B-52s, Julie Brown, 'Til Tuesday, Madness, the Clash, and nearly any band that turned up on the "alternative" show, *Post Modern MTV*. Other popular acts like Duran Duran, Eurythmics, Culture Club, and Prince seemed to at least give the impression that you could dress as outlandishly as you wished—and why not thrift it? You wouldn't find anything like Boy George's caftan at the mall, but given a little imagination, the thrift might yield a similar garment.

An Akron, Ohio, thrift makes an attempt to cash in on the alterna-youth market.
PHOTO BY AUTHOR

The 1980s disgorged so many looks as youth culture continued to splinter. In 1980, you might have run into a few punks scanning the clothing racks in the thrift stores, but by the mid-1990s, you'd almost need a score card to keep all the hip kids straight! Look who is digging through the bins for their look—California-style punks and thrashers (there really are enough flannel shirts and giant T-shirts to go around), old-fashioned 1970s style punks (same old, same old), goths (all black, all the time—a timeless look), retro hippies, Deadheads and Phishfollowers (it's colorful, it's ethnic, it's floppy!), rave kids (1970s clothes, anything kooky), grunge (still more flannel, lots of pretorn, shabby "no look" clothing), kinderwhores (raiding the kid section for tiny T's and the lingerie aisle for slips), riot grrls (old lady dresses, car coats, baggy sweaters), and the all-purpose alterna-kids (dressing down, sloppy, an amalgam of any of the above styles.)

1980s Retro Party

If you're old enough to be reading this book, you probably remember the 1980s. In practice, an '80s retro party is dead easy. The thrifts are currently overflowing with '80s discards. I'd recommend narrowing your focus: pick a representative '80s theme. You can't possibly recapture a whole decade in one evening, so relive your favorite part or mock something you despised. Persons under ten should be cautioned against holding a 1980s retro party without assistance from older family members. I undid my memory block on the '80s and came up with a few party ideas. There's so much raw material available in the thrifts you can put together another dozen '80s theme parties in a snap.

- **Big Players Power Party:** How about a group play of the thrift perennial Trump: The Game? Some good prizes for the winner: a selection of yellow power ties, meaningful 1980s books—*The Art of the Deal* (Donald Trump) and *Iacocca*—or an outdated cellular phone. Dress should be appropriate for corporate takeover, although women may wear sneakers with their suits.
- **Fantasy Big Player Power Party:** Throw a *Dynasty* Party. Perfect if you have a lot of drag queen friends. Everybody can be Alexis for one evening! You'd think big-shouldered poufy party dresses would be hard to find, but you'll find quite the selection of never-worn-again bridesmaid dresses perfect for that Nolan Miller trash-class look.
- **Thrift AID:** Throw a Swap Party (see Chapter 3), but request that only '80s goods be donated.
- **Primetime Wrestling Party:** Remember when Hulkamania was running wild? Stock up on spandex, exercise wear, gym T-shirts, Zubaz, neon sunglasses, and bandannas, and come as your favorite wrestler. If you're not cut out to be an athlete, show up as an overdressed manager or hanger-on girl-

Classy Freddie Blassie, professional wrestling's King of Men, says, "Come to my party!"
PHOTO BY VANESSA DOMICO

friend. Thrift two dozen or so of those wrestling action figures and then pass them out to friends as party invitations. Tell them to come as the wrestler they received.

- **New Wave Party:** That awful mall version of new wave in the 1980s may be too "personal" still for some readers, but those who dare can throw a New Wave Do. Lots of vinyl out there from pop acts that were once considered "cutting edge": Duran Duran, OMD, Romantics, Spandau Ballet, Adam Ant, Culture Club, Human League, Thompson Twins, etc. You're gonna need skinny ties (leather is the most!), wraparound shades, zebra-striped T-shirts, tight stovepipe black jeans, checkerboard miniskirts, little suede boots (no big clunky boots—look for boots with a stiletto heel), high-top Converse (red or black), and lots of bangles. Rent some mid-1980s peek-into-teen-new-wave films like *Pretty in Pink* or *Valley Girl* and you'll get a lot of great ideas for really bad outfits.

- **"It's Going Down"—the *Miami Vice* Party:** Another fun dress-up party. The men should wear loose pastel blazers and pants with casual shoes like Italian-style loafers or canvas slip-ons. Absolutely no socks! Sunglasses optional. Women dress up as slutty drug lord girlfriends, prostitutes, or women-cops-undercover-as-prostitutes. Let the men figure out which one you really are! The soundtrack to the TV show is mandatory for the turntable, but extra points are scored if anyone can thrift Don Johnson's or Philip Michael Thomas's solo albums. A perfect summer party, since warm humid air is a must.

- **Preppy Party:** Thrift enough copies of *The Official Preppy Handbook* to pass out as party invitations and instructional guides. It might take a year or so, but I think it could be done. Plenty of available clothing in the thrifts: madras shorts, skirts and blazers, golf jackets, golf skirts with mushrooms and frogs appliquéd on them, penny loafers, docksiders, polo shirts (Lacoste only please, Ralph Lauren is an interloper), green belts with whales, monogrammed crewneck sweaters (ladies, wear these over turtlenecks with a pattern of little ducks), and dark blue double-breasted blazers with nautical-motif brass buttons. Award a prize to the landlubber who arrives in the best go-to-hell pants (middle-aged guy slacks made from patched madras, half a dozen colored corduroys, bright green fabric with golf clubs printed on, or some other sartorial atrocity). I think preppies just drink and mingle at parties, so once you've got everybody dressed, the rest of the party is a snap. Should be super!

ANTIFASHION BECOMES FASHION

What do we have finally but a *loss of impact* as antifashion officially becomes fashion. Each successive thrifting subculture look has been absorbed by mainstream fashion and has lessened the impact any of these looks ever had. Now the generic "thrift look" is in. Look at all the contemporary groups listed above that support the "thrift look"! If you were a new clothing manufacturer, wouldn't you have noticed you could clothe a lot of young people by selling knock-off versions of goods previously scavenged from thrifts . . . You bet! So now we have the bizarre phenomenon of retro-fashion.

A Cycle of Fashion chart from 1945 by James Laver listed clothing as dowdy at one year after its release, hideous at ten years, amusing at thirty, and romantic at one hundred.[12] What would Mr. Laver think of today's microspan retro cycles? While, generally speaking, all nostalgia timelines have shortened considerably, Mr. Laver still could not have foreseen antifashion and irony and their bastard child, retro fashion.

When today's trendy kids wear a 1970s-style T-shirt with the iron-on logo of *Star Wars* or *Schoolhouse Rock*, it's not about wanting to be the dweeb who would have worn that in the real '70s. Retro-dressing of this sort requires a certain level of sophistication. It's nostalgia but with ironic distance. It's kin to another

Sure, Adidas can slavishly copy their best retro shoes, but none will have the original 1970s cachet of a Billie Jean King endorsement! PHOTO BY VANESSA DOMICO

semihighbrow activity, the deliberate cultivation of bad taste. "I like wearing the leisure suit jacket *because* it looks weird and outdated. *I know that.*"

Fashion has always drawn upon the past for inspiration, but now rather than reach back for suggestions, clothing manufacturers just smash-and-grab from the past. It's not about homage but slavish reproductions. As antifashion has been adopted by the mainstream, we now have a curious situation where retro clothing is made new. "New retro clothing" is an oxymoron, but it's out there! You don't have to rummage through the thrifts looking for '70s suede tennis shoes, photoprint polyester, or gas station jackets. Head for a nearby department store or youth outlet like Urban Outfitters, where retro clothes are not so subtly sold *as antifashion* when it is in fact mainstream fashion.

These stores praise the thrift shop *look* while they are selling you expensively priced new garments that only *seem* to have come from a thrift store. There's not even the tacit acknowledgment that this stuff can actually be *had* at the thrifts! It's perfectly OK to want to wear a '70s T-shirt, but where's the fun in going to the mall to drop $25 on a fake new one? What about the excitement of the hunt? The satisfaction of knowing that your thrifted garment is historically authentic and unique? What about the thrill of snapping it up for $2? And never mind the guaranteed adolescent fun of wearing odd things to annoy people. Fashion sold as "thrift antifashion" is a scam and robs all the fun and meaning out of secondhand clothing that our thrifting ancestors waged such mighty battles for.

7 The Living Room

"Mira let herself down into an overstuffed chair of maroon velvet... and the arm of the chair fell off.... Iso darted over and replaced it. 'Sorry,' she said between closed lips, 'My furniture all comes from the Goodwill.'"
—The Women's Room[1]

If there's one phrase I see again and again, it's "thrift-store couch." The phrase is usually shorthand for the same thing—a grubby little student/artist/bohemian/lowlife apartment, distinguished by a sad, obviously used couch. But this phrase is something of a misnomer. Sure, there's a lot of bad (ugly, cheaply made) furniture out there, and you have to persevere to score the good pieces. (I hit a Salvation Army in Illinois once, counted more than four hundred pieces of perfectly functional furniture in decent shape, but there wasn't one piece I would have paid a dollar for.) But there is smart-looking, sturdy furniture in nice shape out in thriftland. Some sofas and chairs live outright luxurious lives—maybe they've been in a parlor or guest room where only a dozen people have ever sat on them. Maybe the previous owner covered the couch with those awful plastic slipcovers. A decorating abomination to be sure, but that's a nice clean, unfrayed couch going to the thrift.

First find a thrift with a good selection of furniture. Smaller thrifts may not carry furniture because it takes up so much floor space, requires hefty people to move it in and out, and it's generally a pain to deal with. That said, don't overlook the smaller thrifts. They might only have three armchairs in stock, but one might be the one you want and they might be more inclined to make you a deal to get it off the floor. Thrift chains like Goodwill and Salvation Army often desig- nate one or two stores in a

PHOTO BY MICHELLE GIENOW

region as their furniture showrooms. They might be in a warehouse-y part of town or out in the 'burbs. If your nearby thrift has little or no furniture, ask at the counter if there's another more furniture-friendly location.

It's the age-old thrift law-of-desires rule: If you're specifically looking for an armchair, you won't see any. The other truism is that the day you are traveling by bus or Honda Civic is the day you see the perfect sixteen-foot long *Dick Van Dyke Show* couch for $8. If you don't own a large vehicle, at least cultivate a friendship with someone who does. Some thrifts will deliver—ask. If an enormous item is an absolute *must*-have and it's priced low, consider renting a U-Haul for an afternoon. Even adding the cost of the rental to the cost of the furniture, it still might be a better deal than buying something new.

If you have to leave the thrift to get your friend with the van or rent a trailer, *pay* for the furniture first. No matter how unwieldy and permanent it looks, somebody else could snag it in your absence. Also, if you spot a large item of furniture early, but need more time to shop or to telephone your roommate to come pick it up, take the sale tag off the item and hold on to it. This prevents somebody else from buying it while you're still browsing since most thrifts will only ring up the tag. Don't be selfish or greedy. Pull the tag only if you're 75 percent sure you'll buy it and don't take tags off of half-a-dozen chairs because you can't make up your mind. The purpose is to "reserve your inevitable purchase," not to deprive other shoppers of what is still for sale. And if you don't purchase the item, please put the tag back. With a smaller item like an end table or footstool, I throw it right in my cart while pondering its purchase. Nifty pieces of furniture get snapped up quickly in thrifts.

"YOU'LL BE SLEEPING IN THE CLOWN ROOM TONIGHT"
—CREATING THEME ROOMS

Deciding to do a theme room is a great excuse for years of thrifting. Make sure you tell your friends, too—you'll want to solicit donations. The other plus is in discovering how a little organization really brings out related objects. A cowboy figurine on your mantel looks OK, but the same figurine in a room full of western objects is part of a more pleasurable wall-to-wall experience.

You don't need to have a multiroomed mansion to do theme rooms, although that is surely the dream scenario. You can designate a functional room like a bedroom or bathroom. A guest room is also a handy place to experiment with a theme. If you're short on space, find a free hallway or nook somewhere.

Besides the bounty of stuff ready for purchase at the thrifts, your best asset is your imagination. A lamp base covered in shells will work well in a tiki room or a nautical room. It is also not unreasonable to start with one fantastic object and then devise a theme to build on it. Remain open to all possibilities and be patient. A good theme room doesn't happen overnight, but the acquisition and development will bring delight for years.

Free ideas for theme rooms:

- Pick an era. All-'50s is pretty tricky these days (but not impossible). All-'80s is dead easy (but people won't recognize your genius for several decades).

- Pick a color. Imagine a room done only in orange! If you're not so bold, pick two colors. The trick to this room is to be very very consistent. Not mostly orange, *only* orange.

- Pick a popular motif like cowboy/western, colonial, tropical/tiki, flowers, or clowns.

- Some people *love* Christmas. Why not have a year-round Xmas room? Use fake trees, as real trees can quickly become fire hazards.

- A nautical or undersea-themed bathroom is easily assembled. Cover the walls with those plaster fish and thrift anything with a shell motif.

LOUNGING NECESSITIES—SOFAS AND CHAIRS

When purchasing a secondhand couch or armchair, examine it carefully. Look on all sides, the back, underneath; lift and examine all sides of the cushions. An expensive couch should be close to flawless, but a $10 couch, whatever its faults, might be fun to have around for six months. And always always always: *Sit on it!* Flop, sit, squirm, slouch, do everything you can. You'll get a good feel for the piece plus turn up defects like that loose spring you didn't notice till you slid waaaay down. Also, if getting it home is an issue, check to see if it can come apart for easy transport. Some armchair legs unscrew easily. We had a monstrously heavy 1950s sofa bed that took six guys to carry, till the day we realized that unscrewing four screws meant you could remove the bed part and carry the sofa, the mattress, and the metal bed frame separately.

> **Impress your friends. Know the right terms for couch shapes:**
>
> **Camelback:** Back of couch is humped. If there is only one hump, it is still a camelback, not a dromedaryback!
>
> **Chesterfield:** Arms are the same height as the back.
>
> **Club:** Back is straight and the arms are lower than the back.

Most problems with used furniture are not structural. If a piece of furniture feels flimsy or is missing a significant portion of itself, don't even bother. Occasionally I see armchairs and sofas that might be missing a small three- to six-inch leg. Some can be easily replaced at a hardware store, or if you're lazy, a couple of Norman Mailer novels will do. Furniture flaws tend to involve the outer covering.

Surface Flaws

Most of the chairs and sofas you find in thrifts are upholstered with fabric. The fabric will rarely be identified. It will have to meet your eye and fingertip test. Always *smell* the fabric and smell in a couple of places. If it smells icky like cat pee or some other unidentified funk, ditch it. Barring some industrial cleaning process, it's gonna smell. Naturally, color and pattern of fabric is up to you.

> **Pet hair or fuzz:** If it's odor-free and you can pick the fuzz off easily, it's probably redeemable. Remove fuzz or hair with vacuum or the sticky side of packing tape.

> **Stains:** Stains are probably there for life. The secret to stain removal is immediate action, and who knows when Aunt Gertie tipped over that cup of coffee. Some might be minimized with furniture shampoo products. If one side of the seat cushion is stained, see if the other side can be used instead. Also, check if the seat cushion has a slip cover that can be removed and washed.

Grime: Grime areas are the headrest, near the floor, the edge of the seat cushion, and especially the ends of the arm rest where sweaty palms have lain. Crud around the headrest and arms can be disguised by placing odd bits of fabric there. Some pieces of furniture already have these–and this is precisely what they're designed for. An anti-macassar is a piece of fabric made to protect the back and armrest or cover up previous damage. (Macassar was a brand of hair oil, hence the term "*anti*-Macassar"!) A little dirt builds up on the arm slipcover and you just wash that, not the whole chair. Look in the linens section of your thrift for crocheted arm coverings. For the back of a chair or sofa, use fringed satin pillowcases that say "U.S. Navy—I Love You, Mother" or some other such sentiment. Or toss a folded throwrug, bedspread, or quilt along the top.

Torn fabric: A small hole on the armrest or seat cushion will just get worse over time. It's better if the hole is around the back or side, because you might be able to put that part against a wall. Torn fabric on the underside isn't much of a problem (unless you have those kind of parties where furniture gets tipped over!). And while small tears might be disguised, split seams are gonna give way fairly quickly. It's the seams that bear the stress of people sitting in the chair.

Missing cushions: If a chair or sofa is missing the big seat cushion, let it go. While you might locate the right-shaped stray pillow one day, it won't be the same fabric. Your couch will end up looking like those cars that are all blue except for the brown door that says "79 Chevy Caprice." If it's the smaller throw pillows that are missing, you can buy any old pillow and cover it with a complementary or contrasting fabric.

Movement: If it's meant to move, test it for mobility and see if any defects turn up when shifted. Rock in the rocking chair, spin in the spinning chair, BarcaLounge in the BarcaLounger. In rare cases of vibrating furniture (some recliners have "massagers"), find a nearby plug and check for action.

Vinyl

Two major problems to look for with vinyl-covered furniture: dirt and cracks. Simple dirt will clean up easily. Use some hot soapy water or a basic household cleaner like 409. You can also buy products specifically for cleaning vinyl (most easily found in auto supply stores). Cracked or split vinyl is trickier. I've never had much luck fixing torn vinyl, though in fairness, I've never tried that miracle product they advertise on late-night TV. A couple of vinyl repair products I've tried are essentially goopy glues that cement the crack, and the repair doesn't hold up very well. Don't use cellophane tape. It looks gross, it yellows, and in the long run it looks worse than the original crack.

Leather

Leather furniture is pretty yummy, but look out for dirt and tears. Some dirt can be cleaned up using a leather-cleaning product. Like fabric, leather will absorb stains and body oils. You may find the armrests to be permanently discolored from years of hand gripping. Some products claim to fix tears and cracks, but you'll have the same problems as with fixing vinyl. Another concern is the suppleness of the leather. Over time, leather dries out, leaving it vulnerable to splitting and cracking. There are products available like mink oil that will "remoisten" leather, but it involves a lot of elbow grease and is a big project for a chair or sofa. Also, these products are best used when there is still some life left in the leather to preserve. They can't bring really old leather back from the dead. That said, one of the best chairs I ever had was a beat-up scalloped-back maroon leather club chair from the 1930s. The seat cushion was cracked beyond repair (I put a smaller cushion over it), the scalloped back had cracks, and the ends of the armrest were black with decades of grime. Still, it was a great-looking chair and one of the comfiest I've ever owned. I paid very little for it and enjoyed it for years despite its uncorrectable flaws. Even when I finally got rid of it, it still had enough charm that a friend snapped it up instantly and is still using it today.

All Solid Material—Wood, Plastic and Metal

Furniture made from all solid material is pretty easy to gauge for flaws. Look for big defects like missing pieces, large gouges, and check to see that all connections like screws are intact. Plastic furniture should be inspected for cracks and metal furniture for rust or other deterioration. Some metal and wooden furniture can be easily repainted to suit your tastes, match your other furniture, or cover up any stains or minor surface flaws. Conversely, painted furniture can be stripped to show the original wood or metal. Slightly uncomfortable hard furniture can be made more inviting by adding pillows of any shape and fabric.

Rehab: What to Do with Crappy-Looking Sofas and Chairs Until You Find the Ultimate Piece

Reupholstering—consult your financial adviser. This is not cheap. The other expensive professional fix is slipcovering. A slipcover can be a single piece of covering—like a big condom for your couch—or can comprise smaller pieces that cover the frame and seat cushions separately. A standard size couch will take about 18 to 20 yards of fabric. (By comparison, a queen size sheet is just 6 yards.) If you're a clever sewer, you may be able to do it yourself. The local library will have a book on slipcovering. It's a big project, but I've seen it done and it may be just the thing to occupy you during some long winter months. Obviously a plain fabric is more forgiving to work with than a patterned fabric. Stripes are for the very, very clever. Be aware of what original fabric you are covering. A pal slipcovered a very cool-shaped vinyl-covered couch. It looked swell, but in the summer months, even with the heavy canvas slipcover, you still got that "wet-seat" effect from the vinyl underneath.

The thrifts are a handy source of quick-and-dirty rehab. The easiest and cheapest thing to do is simply to cover the offending piece of furniture with a gigantic piece of fabric—bedspreads, blankets, sheets, and curtains all lend themselves nicely. Even a bedspread for a twin bed will cover a standard-size sofa if the back of the sofa is against the wall and not visible. (Pushing the sofa up against the wall will also anchor the bedspread in place.) Simply drape over gross chair and you're done. When it gets dirty, you just throw it in the washing machine. When covering a couch, remember that a couch runs long from left to right whereas most bed coverings and curtains run long top to bottom. Keep this in mind when you purchase any *patterned* covering. You don't want to have a couch covered in some sideways-looking image. Covering furniture this way doesn't give you the classiest-looking living room on the planet, but it'll probably look better than the bad plaid couch underneath. (I know someone who covered all their living room furniture with heavy white sheets, and the totalness of it made it look intentionally decorative.) Plus it's hardly permanent. Easy to do, easy to change.

SWINGER'S LIVING ROOM FURNITURE SUITE

by Tisha Parti

The best thing I ever left behind, I did for the larger thrift-karma good. This one little thrift had a wonderful display of someone's living room in its window. This living room ensemble included one gold velour couch with matching swag lamp and pillows; one glass-top coffee table with a life-sized gold (as in *Goldfinger*) statue of a naked woman on all fours (as support), with really large breasts and a look of ecstasy on her face; and a gold end table with a two-and-a-half-foot high statue of Michelangelo's David with one minor . . . uh . . . major change—the penis was enormous, hanging well past the statue's knees.

As I gazed at this whole tableau, I was convinced a guy should have first crack at all this really keen stuff. I really loved it, but it was so "Swingin' Bachelor Pad Guy" that I decided to leave it for some cool guy to snag and impress girls with his ribald and robust taste. I took one last gaze at David (breaking up the set was unthinkable, although David temptingly called. . .) and left behind one of the coolest sights I've ever seen. And I'll always wonder who got it . . .

Park Your Feet—Footstools

Occasionally, a chair or couch hits the thrift with a matching footstool, but most often not. It takes luck and imagination to thrift footstools that coordinate well with your existing furniture. I take the lamp–lampshade approach to buying footstools. I buy what I like when I see it, regardless of whether it matches anything I already have. It's just as easy to buy a chair later to match the footstool as it is to buy a footstool to match an existing chair.

My two favorite footrests are a pair of black and white vinyl dice, and they illustrate the serendipitous nature of acquisition. I bought the first one—a black die cube with white dots—at a small flea market in Maryland. While strolling about the flea market, a woman approached me and *begged* to buy the cube. She related a sad tale about how her family had the set—a black cube with white dots and a white cube with black dots—and that the black one had been lost or destroyed and she had been searching for years to replace it. I was moved by her story and grateful to learn of the "matched set" but clung to my purchase. That was ten years ago, and I still haven't seen the matching white-with-black-dots cube, *but*, not long after I bought the first cube, my husband was driving home through a grimy part of Washington, D.C., and there in the roadway lay a completely flat, mud-covered, black-with-white-dots cube. He

MOVIES THAT THRIFT

No one has yet made a movie about thrifting. It's odd that none of the recent rash of Gen-X-oriented films have covered or even alluded to thrifting. In some of those films there seems to be an implied understanding that the weird, floppy clothes or quirky home decor came from a thrift store, but evidently filmmakers do not consider this an important enough cultural activity to be given precious screen time. (The accidental giving away of some valued object to a rummage sale or thrift store does seem to be a popular sitcom plot device. Unfortunately, TV is pretty ephemeral.) I did unearth a few films that feature scenes of thrift shopping or other secondhand venues like flea markets or yard sales. If cinema is our cultural mirror, let's see what significance we can draw from it about thrifting and secondhand shopping.

Tales of Manhattan (1942) Secondhand Connection: This film is a series of five vignettes that follow the life of a tuxedo coat in its new-to-used downward spiral. (1) The coat is custom-made for a society wedding. (2) A wedding guest, who has borrowed the coat, is shot while wearing it. The ruined coat is discarded. (3) The wife of a poor composer buys the coat from a pawn shop for her husband's debut night. She mends the bullet hole. (4) A street mission gives the coat to down-and-outer Edward G. Robinson. He wears it to his class reunion and pretends to be a successful businessman. (5) After being used in the commission of a robbery, the coat falls from an airplane into a poor sharecropping community. The now pretty-ragged coat is given to a scarecrow. Significance: To my knowledge, the *only* cinematic work that provides such detail of the life cycle of used clothing. A classic.

Blown Away (1994) Secondhand Connection: Mad bomber Tommy Lee Jones visits a neighborhood street sale and purchases a Rube Goldberg–type toy and cassette tape of U2's *Joshua Tree*. The toy inspires the bomb in the climactic scene, and Jones puts the finishing touches on it while rocking out to "With or Without You." Significance: If you're gonna blow something up, why not be thrifty?

Thelma and Louise (1991) Secondhand Connection: Next door to the honky-tonk where Thelma and Louise get in the fight, there is a big giant thrift store! Significance: Hello?! What if they had gone, like any of us would have, *into the thrift store* instead of the honky-tonk?! Why not female-bond over thrifting instead of being on-the-lam-from-the-law?

Serial Mom (1994) Secondhand Connection: Serial Mom Kathleen Turner and daughter Ricki Lake both sell items at a flea market during an extended sequence. Prior to this scene, much discussion occurs about selling at the flea market, and Ricki Lake is seen constantly pricing items for sale. Significance: You gotta love John Waters because his script has so many in-jokes about collecting and flea markets for those of us in the know. The Pee-Wee Herman doll ("Still in the box!") sells for $158 to a gentleman who offers "New York money." Two Gen-Xers are thrilled with their purchase of an amateur painting that resembles Don Knotts. And we all can grimace in unison when we learn that the flea market has a Franklin Mint booth. And bad karma happens to the guy who shops *that* booth instead of Ricki Lake's cool tchotchke booth . . .

Something Wild (1986) Secondhand Connection: Melanie Griffith and Jeff Daniels stop by a small-town thrift to reoutfit themselves for "meeting Mom": a sundress for her, and a sharkskin blue suit and handpainted tie for him. Significance: This illustrates the worthy concept of "thrifting as temporary costume." Why spend good money on a nice outfit you only have to wear once when you can score one cheap at the thrifts?

Psych-Out (1968) Secondhand Connection: Susan Strasberg is taken to an everything-is-free thrift store in San Francisco's Haight-Ashbury. Here she sheds her suburban nice girl costume for something more appropriate to the Summer of Love scene. The sequence also features a montage of her trying on various "kooky" outfits. Significance: Fanciful clothing from the thrift store was a key source of the craziest hippie looks. Thrifts have continued to remain a good stockpile of odd clothing for later subculture looks: punks, riot grrls, grunge, etc.

Dad (1989) Secondhand Connection: Back-from-the-dead old guy Jack Lemmon drags his family to an L.A. flea market to purchase clothes for his "new" wild-and-crazy lifestyle. Shopping is not seen, but the next scene in the film shows Lemmon, his son, and his grandson modeling the crazy outfits they bought there. Very pleased with his purchases,

retrieved it. As it was made from a quality heavy-duty vinyl, it cleaned up beautifully. He restuffed it with a cardboard box and an old blanket, and now we have two matching black cubes. Sure, it would have been a better story if the cube in the gutter had been the white one, but it's still a mighty strange occurrence.

FOR MAGAZINES AND MARTINIS—END TABLES AND COFFEE TABLES
The most important consideration for an end table or coffee table is strength and stability. These pieces will most likely be in high-use areas and be expected to bear up under day-to-day living, entertaining, and the piling up of all your stuff on them. Give 'em a good shove or shake in the thrift—see if the piece feels sturdy. Check the legs and the supports (if it's a bilevel piece). If it's a coffee table you plan to entertain around, the surface material should be easy to

Lemmon wears these new outfits throughout the rest of the film. Significance: Using unusual secondhand clothing to reinvent yourself is not uncommon, though it's a practice found primarily among the young. Despite his complete lack of fashion sense, Lemmon is delighted and empowered by his purchases, so what more could you ask for?

Alice Doesn't Live Here Anymore (1974) Secondhand Connection: Newly widowed Ellen Burstyn sells off her stuff at a yard sale before embarking for a new life in the West. Burstyn scores karma points by giving leftover merchandise to an old lady. Significance: Before picking up and moving, it sure is smart to move a lot of your junk into the secondhand sphere and make some traveling cash to boot.

A Home of Our Own (1993) Secondhand Connection: Hard-pressed single-mom-of-six Kathy Bates takes her brood to a church thrift store to outfit them for school and winter. Initially, they all seemed pleased with the selection of goods. But the priest offends Kathy Bates by offering her the clothing for free. Rather than accept his charity, she dumps the clothes and thrifts some sewing patterns and fabric instead. Significance: Ah dear, pride. Kathy Bates kept hers, but she made the wrong choice. One, her kids looked extra silly in the outfits she made. More important, when you factor in her labor time of sewing for six (!) kids, it would have been far *cheaper* to thrift the ready-to-wear clothes. Since she wasn't above thrifting the patterns and fabric, she should have just *paid* the priest for the clothes she wanted. If necessary, leave your pride at the door when you thrift.

clean (glass, Formica, ceramic tile, or a high-gloss veneer). I know many thrifters who use mirrors as coffee-table tops. Either lay the mirror directly on a coffee table of corresponding size or support a heavy mirror from underneath using bricks (glass bricks are nice!) or two smaller end tables. This setup is not 100 percent stable, so make sure it suits your lifestyle. A large, heavy, glass-framed piece of art can also double as a tabletop.

Don't sweat the small surface gouges and stains that often come with used coffee and end tables. As long as the piece is integrally sound, these small marks can be disguised by placing plants, ashtrays, books, lamps, or bits of cool fabric to strategically cover the flaw. A little luck can rescue even the most colossal flaw. I bought a bilevel comma-shaped coffee table. In the lower small end of the comma, somebody had sawed a huge hole, about 9 inches in diameter. I can only guess that they might have had a plant growing through the table? Whatever. The table was so cheap I bought it and, once home, found that I had a big dish-shaped ashtray that fit perfectly into the hole.

The easternmost piece of '50s populuxe in North America
PHOTO BY AUTHOR

Everyone's dream coffee table is the 1950s boomerang. I'd been hard-core thrifting furniture coast-to-coast for fifteen years and never even seen a boomerang table in a thrift—not even one marked up too high to buy. Desired objects are out there somewhere; you just have to wait till fate throws you and that item together. In the end I found my boomerang coffee table—3,274 road miles and a fourteen-hour boat ride away from my homebase—at a Salvation Army in the *easternmost town* in North America, St. John's, Newfoundland. A bargain at $15 Canadian.

FABRIC FOR YOUR FLOOR—RUGS

Nothing like a rug to make a home feel homey. The bad news is, very few cool rugs come through the thrifts. There's essentially two kinds of rugs: big floor rugs (at least 5 by 7 feet), and small occasional rugs. A lot of thrifts won't even accept a donation of a large rug. They may lack the floor space to display it (even rolled up), and they may feel the item is too dirty to resell. When a decent big rug does come in, there're still problems. (1) They're usually priced pretty steep. New rugs, especially wool rugs, are not cheap, and thrifts mark up rugs accordingly. (2) They may be rolled up and tied, leaving you with a giant logistical problem trying to get the thing unrolled to look at. Would anybody buy a rolled-up rug without looking at it? Now you've got to find some employee to help with the untying and unrolling—and heaven help you if you *don't* want the rug after all! (3) They might be dirty. Rugs soak up dirt, dust, pet hair, spilled drink and food, baby pee, whatever. Unless you're prepared to spend the time and money to get the rug deep-cleaned, it may not be worth it. (4) They're old, torn, frayed, or faded. If they're priced reasonably, a little "distress" might be workable. If you're angling for that shabby genteel look or just anything to put down on the kitchen floor, this could be your bargain. Some rugs styles take distress better than others—a threadbare shag rug looks cheap and horrible, but a frayed Persian (or more likely Persian-style!) rug can be passed off as a family heirloom.

You'll have better luck in the occasional rug department. Actually, there usually isn't an "occasional rug department" in thrifts. I find most of my small rugs hanging up in the linen section somewhere. There's more variety among occasional rugs—hook rugs, Southwestern stripes, fun fur and novelty rugs, chenille bath rugs, tiny narrow hallway rugs, rag rugs, and assorted other fuzziness. Utilize occasional rugs by purchasing what you like, and then don't limit their placement in your home. A pastel chenille rug with raised flowers may be rubber-backed so that it can go in the bathroom, but you can lay it anywhere! I have bathroom rugs all over my house—either nobody notices or if they do, I hardly care. Also, if you're already living in a mismatched house, you may never thrift a full-size rug that coordinates with everything, but by thrifting a lot of smaller rugs, you can divvy them up and match them with single chairs or appropriate areas. Small rugs also have the advantage of being cheap. Buy them as you see them and replace them when they get too grungy.

Typical state of rugs in thrift stores. PHOTO BY AUTHOR

Persevere—there are good rugs out there. My favorite, pictured here, cost less than a dollar. PHOTO BY VANESSA DOMICO

THE MANLY DEN—THE LOST ROOM

"Every man needs a corner of his own."
—Better Homes and Gardens (May 1949)[2]

Prior to the domestic liberation of women and men, the understanding was that the woman undertook the frou-frou decorating of every nook and cranny in the house. The house may have been a man's castle, but the king was only allowed to decorate one little corner. He was typically restricted to the library, the study (now "the home office"), the TV room, the rumpus room, the work room, the bar, the basement, or, in the saddest cases, literally just a corner somewhere. But in his own space, a man could forgo the pink Formica and frilly curtains for more masculine trappings.

Home-decor manufacturers kindly provided suitable building blocks. A man might choose curtains and furniture with patterned fabrics that featured hunting or fishing scenes. (There were 1950s and 1960s fabrics that depicted team sports like baseball or football, but these were traditionally used in the boy's bedroom. Cowboy scenes were also common for the lad's room, but some object-based Western patterns with guns, horses, spurs, saddles, etc., can be used in the Manly Den.) Chairs designed differently for men and women are now a lost substratum of furniture merchandising. Furniture sold with the man of the house in mind was heavier looking (often with exposed wood) and featured appropriate fabric. No mercerized chintz, but bold plaids and stripes, fishing tackle pattern, or woodsy scenes. It would be difficult today to shop retail and put together a traditional Manly Den. The concept of the man's corner has been lost now that both sexes are expected to contribute to domesticity. No matter, for the thrifts are filled with discarded odds and ends to help men construct their own little lair.

Start with a chair. It should be large, comfortable, and sturdy enough to support the biggest and weariest man flopping into it after work. If you can't unearth one already covered in manly fabric, at least look for masculine colors like forest green, brown, deep rust, tan, and bronze, and go for dark or knotty woods. Think autumn. Get a footstool to park your barking dogs on. A plain chair can be jazzed up by adding patterned pillows. Sometimes they turn up premade at the thrifts or you can thrift some manly fabric and cover a few pillows yourself. (Ideally, the little lady could help here . . .) A plaid lap blanket is the perfect accessory for lounging.

Make sure you have a nearby end table. You don't want to reach far for that Manhattan, ashtray, or magazine. (Some chairs have a

---

CEDAR PLAQUES

The Manly Den may be a lost room, but a key piece of its decor, the All-American Cedar Souvenir Plaque, is still very much with us. The cedar plaque is a simple, flat piece of wood, usually with a bad epigram stenciled on it. Fancier ones have a shellacked picture. The cheesiest have some generic image (deer or tree) and the name of a local attraction ("Enchanted Forest") poorly stamped on it . You can still buy these jokey things new at many tourist traps, but plenty come to the thrifts. (Another proverbial souvenir gift bought for someone who doesn't appreciate it . . . Why wouldn't somebody want a cheap piece of wood that says: "If Men Were As True to Their Country—As They Were to Their Wives—Goodbye Country.") An entire wall or corner covered with cedar plaques would look quite stunning! When shopping for your manly den, don't overlook the other delights of souvenir cedar: flat wall clocks, cigarette boxes, toothpick holders, key pegs, coin banks, drink coasters, and hat racks.

built-in magazine slot on the side.) You'll also need a lamp that says "manly"—decorative lamp bases with crossed rifles, pine cones, pheasants, or leaping fish are good. This is a good place to use that sentimental-object lamp like the one made from a military shell or bowling pin. In a pinch, just keep the lamp simple. A metal base and an understated shade will complement any manly room.

This wood and metal ship/clock would be right at home in a Manly Den.
PHOTO BY AUTHOR

Decorate the walls with taxidermy. (Whole heads are hard to come by, but deer antlers and feet are fairly common. An upturned deer hoof is ideal to hang your smoking jacket from.) There's a fine selection of art available at thrifts that's suitable for the Manly Den—mix and match from hunting scenes, fishing scenes, and landscapes of woods, mountains, and deserts (maybe with a discrete cowboy or Indian). Check for paint-by-numbers. Their popularity coincided with the era of Manly Dens, and many were designed with manly decor in mind.

Look for arts-and-craftsy things men have made: wood whittling and carving, the painted saw, the shellacked plaque (often a photograph rescued from a calendar or magazine shellacked onto a piece of wood), leather craft, and handmade gun and fishing pole racks. Other manly knickknacks include sports trophies, fishing tackle, a bag of golf clubs, sports mementos from your supposed youth (well-worn baseball mitts or the football you won the Homecoming Game with), pipes and pipe racks, automobilia, figurines of horses, fish, and dogs (faithful retrievers, not sad-eyed Chihuahuas), as well as appropriately themed ashtrays, lighters, and glassware. Depending on how secluded your Manly Den is and how understanding your cohabitors are, you may want to include ribald knickknacks: dirty joke ashtrays and shot glasses, a deck of girlie cards, and pinups. Keep a pile of pulp novels with lurid covers handy.

Slip into Something More Manly . . .

If you don't completely change into something more comfortable, you should at least remove or undo half of your work outfit: remove blazer, loosen tie and belt, undo collar buttons, and roll sleeves up. You'll be more relaxed after donning a lounging garment—a bathrobe, smoking jacket, or that favorite moth-eaten sweater you refuse to give up. Take your shoes off and slip your feet into a cozy pair of slippers. Ahhhhh. . . . Now, doesn't it feel good to have your own little corner?

ON BEYOND THRIFTING PROFILE NO. 2

Who: Paul Wilson, Phoenix artist born after the 1950s.
Thrifting Origins: First thrift experience was purchasing a wig and bag at the Goodwill for a high-school banquet with a comic-strip character theme. Paul went as Mary Worth.

• • •

In the mid-1980s, Paul became obsessed with recreating the 1950s after wistfully paging through his mom's old *Better Homes and Gardens* magazines. He initially hit the thrifts in search of small '50s items like dishes, lamps, and tchotchkes. Soon, *anything* from the 1950s was being reclaimed by Paul. In 1991, he set up residence in a 1957 ranch house, which, after dragging all his stuff out of storage, he decorated—pure '50s—in one day! It was here, in 1994, that his ultimate '50s recreation was born: the Kimbles.

The house seemed perfect for a set, Paul recalls thinking. "Wouldn't it be fun to take a photograph of myself, a self-portrait, and make it look like I'm really in the 1950s?" He garbed himself from his extensive collection of thrifted 1950s clothes and began posing around the house. Inspired, he began posing as the quintessential 1950s family, the Kimbles (dad, mom, and three kids), in ever more elaborate settings—Tupperware parties, bowling night, Christmas morning. Soon, he was also dressing up as family friends as well.

The Kimbles live through the miracle of photo-collage. Paul poses as all the characters, takes the individual photos and develops them at Walgreens (ever thrifty!). Using the tiny scissors from a Swiss Army knife, he carefully cuts out each person and pastes them all onto a background photo. The collage is then color-photocopied, retouched with colored pencils, and reshot to create the "original" snapshot. Paul assembles the photographs in an album, meticulously recording the small personal moments of the Kimbles' life. He tries to represent typical photos that would be found in any 1950s family album.

Paul's scenes look so disturbingly real. "I'm so familiar with the '50s now, it's second nature to be accurate," he says. "I'll change the lampshade if I wanted to make it look like 1959 as opposed to 1955 because I put all these pictures in a family album and they have to be chronological." Paul does most of his research from original 1950s sources. He scrutinizes movies, books, and magazines. His first love is still *Better Homes and Gardens*. "It has everything—car ads, kitchens, living rooms, clothing, the whole bit.

The Kimbles give a cocktail party, 1958. From left to right, Dick Kimble, Lurene Kovatch, waiter, Charlie and Gay, Dottie Kimble, and "Hutch." Paul really is each person! PHOTO BY PAUL WILSON

"The men's clothes don't change a whole lot. I wear the same baggy pants. I just switch ties, jackets, hats, and glasses. The ladies, though, their clothing looks so much more dated, so I have to buy more for them. I've been collecting size 14 dresses for two years now. My bedroom has become just a big walk-in closet—dresses, wigs, bags, and shoes.

"I thrift everything for my photos—furniture, lampshades, fabric, housewares, appliances, dishes, Melmac, clothing, big women's shoes and dresses, menswear—absolutely everything. It's all I spend my money on—old clothes and thrift store stuff. All the stuff I buy, I try to validate the purchase. 'My *pictures.* . . Might do a *photo.* . . It's for *research.*' And I *never* get rid of anything!

"I even buy small things, really boring stuff most people would have or should have thrown away. That's what makes the photos realistic. People look at my pictures and they'll say, 'Good God, where did you find a still-shrinkwrapped package of vintage pipe cleaners?' and I'll say, 'Well that's what thrifting does, you find these things!' It's kind of a bitch storing all this stuff, but it's vitally important to integrity of the pictures, because if you look in old photographs, you see that stuff. You see pots and pans and obvious things, but there's little things like matchbooks and envelopes in a box with a logo on it. I love it when I find stuff like that in the thrifts. For me, the whole thrifting thing is such a joy because even then I pretend that I am back in the 1950s and that the thrift store is a great big five-and-dime. I try not to go in with a goal, but then when I do find that one tiny thing, even if it's just a bag on the wall with some old cocktail napkins in it, I think, 'Oh cool, I went to the five-and-dime and bought some napkins.'"

Paul is hardly worried about his mad quest to relive the '50s. "The Kimbles project has been very cathartic for me because it's like I'm living that wonderful time period that we'll never see again, even though it's all fantasy." But what's going to happen when the '50s stuff dries up in thrifts? "I don't know," he muses. "Friends have asked me whether I'll ever move into 1965 . . . but I'm very happy here in the '50s."

• • •

8 The Office

All serious thrifters share a love of objects, and I'd bet that a lot of thrifters are affected by another common object-lust sickness—the obsession with office supplies! While thrifts won't offer you that same excitement you get when you're standing tiny and helpless before a 25-foot-high stack of pens and binder clips, you *can* score lots of great office supplies at thrifts, getting a double dose of shopping pleasure. Not only are thrifted office supplies cheaper, but the older pieces are sturdier and more attractively designed. Fill up your home office, or take bags of this cool stuff to the workplace. You'll work better surrounded by objects you like, feel like Joe Friday, and you might even get brownie points for saving the company a few bucks on office supplies.

THE FULL-METAL OFFICE

Today most office supplies are made from cheap plastic, but the standard materials used to be wood and metal. Finding a wooden desk is not that hard, but wooden office chairs and file cabinets are not as common. Putting the all-metal office together is much easier. Start with a big solid metal desk. You'll have plenty of choices in green- and gray-painted steel. Look for the chair you like—some have wheels, some have arms, still others can be adjusted for height. While you can certainly find chairs made entirely of metal, you might want to relax your requirements slightly to include a bit of seat padding. If the chair hasn't got a cushion, thrift a small flat

CONTACTS ARE ALL!

The ultimate way to organize your many important contacts is to Rolodex. The granddaddy office organizational tool was introduced in 1950. During its glory years, no secretary, boss, or player was without a Rolodex—never more than a second away from alphabetically spinning contacts. Rolodex made several hundred models and at one point controlled 90 percent of the market! The computer chip killed the Rolodex, and today go-getters are more likely to own a tiny handheld address organizer. But how can you tell now how important that man is? Not by eyeballing the personal organizer in his hand! The days of discerning Mr. Connected by his three-wheel Torque-A-Matic (holds six thousand cards!) are gone.

cushion. You'll only need one more big piece of furniture, and that's a file cabinet—as little as two drawers or as many as eight! Some have odd-shaped drawers for storing index cards (good for loose photos) or flat paper. Check that the drawers open and close properly. If the cabinet is missing those metal racks to hang folders from, you can pick those up later at an office supply store.

Additional all-metal office items include wastepaper basket, file storage boxes, index card filers (perfect for keeping small supplies like Post-it Notes and rubber bands in), and a desk lamp. Now clutter up the surface of your desk with the following metal items: tape dispenser, pencil holder, ruler, vertical file holders, in/out trays, metal binders, stapler, binder clips, paper clip holder, hole punchers, ashtray (for butts or small things like stamps and thumb tacks), Rolodex or a small flat metal address book that flips open, clock, pencil sharpener, and message holder (the giant paper clip is cute, but the big spike you spear phone messages on is better). Imagine the great clanging noises you'll make as you work work work. You'll have security knowing that your office is rock-hard and indestructible (no plastic bits snapping off) and have loads of fun sticking magnets to every bit of your work space!

What's an Office Without Paper?

Plenty of paper at the thrifts. Pick up envelopes, notepads, memo pads, phone message pads, or boxes of leftover typing paper or business stationery. Stock up on good greeting cards and blank postcards as you see them. I throw all the greeting cards and envelopes I buy into a big box and then no matter what the occasion—birthday, holidays, graduation, etc.—I always have a card ready. I recommend always keeping a nice selection of no-message-inside greeting cards with some generic picture like flowers or sail-boats. Perfect for thank-you notes, last-minute birthday greetings, or really, any occasion. Also popular in thrifts are those precious little sets of matching notepaper and envelopes. (Isn't there somebody out there who'd appreciate a word or two from you on Ziggy stationery?) Thrifts often keep stray stationery in those hanging plastic bags. Don't sweat mismatched envelopes and cards-missing-envelopes. Get enough stationery and you can

Bulletin board, pencil sharpener, and trash can—all ready to make your office a *happy* place!
PHOTO BY VANESSA DOMICO

mix and match it later. Also keep your eyes peeled among those bags for stickers—kids' stickers, freezer stickers, promotional stickers—they're all prefect for decorating your mail.

Pick up an el cheapo bulletin board to help make sense of your paper clutter. Bulletin boards are usually stored with the paintings, but sometimes I find them in the toy section. Bulletin boards with kiddie pictures on them are common, but don't worry about the clown train image—you'll be covering it up with paper anyhow. Paperweights are nice office *objets* you don't see around "real" offices anymore. Air-conditioned offices and modern construction mean the windows (if you were ever lucky enough to have an office with a window) don't get opened, and there aren't fans running all summer blowing stacks of paper over.

Thrift Some Knowledge

Make sure you've got reference materials! Pick up a couple of dictionaries, thesauruses, and other word-helpers. Sure, the older dictionary is missing important new words like "telecommute," but all the old words still work.

A globe is classier than a map. What with recent world upheaval, it's almost guaranteed that the country boundaries will be out of date on any thrifted globe, but remember that the big sections of land in relation to bodies of water have remained unchanged. (Thrifts have begun marking up old globes. Doesn't it seem like they should charge *less,* not more, for an old globe that's hopelessly out of date?) Keep an old globe (the one with black oceans look pretty cool) in your office and see every single coworker comment about how on your globe Germany is two countries or that the

Rubber stamps are currently popular (but not so cheap!), and I'm secretly hoping the fad will die and bags of swell stamps will go to the thrifts. Still, sharp eyes will uncover rubber stamps at the thrifts. Be open to possibilities—you can have a lot of rubber-stamping fun with date and price stampers. Those blessed plastic bags will sometimes yield "basic" stamps like "Air Mail" or "PAID" or "Return to Sender." Don't forget to check the toy section—I've found quite a few rubber stamps there.

I have a *really* big date . . . PHOTO BY VANESSA DOMICO

Soviet Union still exists. It's a good office trick to pull on coworkers you can't stand to express complete surprise that Germany is now one country. Watch them waste time explaining it to you while you shake your head in amazement.

And Speaking of Yuks. . .
No office (especially a real one) is complete without a few work gag items—a small plaque ("You Want It When?" or "You Don't Have to Be Crazy to Work Here But It Helps"), a figurine of the harassed worker, a coffee mug ("Don't Ask Me—I Just Work Here") or the all-time classic, a framed photo of the kitten dangling in midair that says "Hang in There Baby." By all means "hang in there," but hang in there in style!

The All-Metal Typewriter

BY JOHN MARR

The showpiece of any all-metal office is a good, sturdy manual typewriter. They may seem quaint next to a Pentium-class computer running the latest Word, but you can clack out a letter while a word-processing wizard is still putzing around with the printer drivers. And where would the long-suffering protagonist of Stephen King's *Misery* have been without his manual typewriter? Bench-pressing an IBM-compatible keyboard never rehabilitated anyone.

Thanks to the rest of the world embracing the digital age, the thrifts and flea markets are *filled* with manual typewriters. Because they're both functional and virtually indestructible, people have hung on to 'em for years. It's not at all hard to find good specimens predating the plastic scourge. Unfortunately, some thrifts equate age with value and price accordingly. Don't be taken! You'll probably see the same machine next week for a quarter of the price. Even the casual thrifter can score the right machine at the right price with a little patience.

Most common are big, hulking office machines. As any working gal who spent her career in front of one can attest, typing on one of these behemoths gives you a solid feeling of accomplishment that no computer ever will. Fringe benefit: no carpal tunnel syndrome! Late-night typists working on their *noir* novels in thin-walled apartments should look for a *noiseless* model. Your roommate

Not nearly as cute as manual typewriters, the thrifts are filling up with the office dreck of the 1980s.
PHOTO BY AUTHOR

may not find them any quieter, but their "thunk, thunk" is less penetrating than those crisp clicks. Portables are somewhat flimsier and often lack basic features like tab stops. But they're so gosh-darned cute. What they lack in majesty they make up in niftiness—some aren't much larger than laptops. While three or four typewriters can clutter up any room, it's easy to stack a dozen portables in their cases (always insist on the original cases!) in an out-of-the-way corner. If you ever have the urge to play foreign correspondent, you'll have something to peck out your dispatches on.

If you're going to be doing any typing at all, the test run is vital. You don't even have to hunt for an electrical outlet! *The quick brown fox jumps over the lazy dog.* Check the tabs, the space bar, the backspace key, and the carriage return. Don't worry about ribbons; most machines take the standard half-inch size. At worst, you'll have to thread it on the spools yourself. Most minor problems can be cleared up with a little cleaning and lubrication at home. Use mineral spirits, diluted dishwashing detergent, and 3-in-1 oil—sparingly!. Unless you're the tinkering kind, machines that don't work mean hunting for a manual typewriter mechanic. Only a *really* cool, really cheap typewriter is worth it.

And once you have your baby up and running, put it to work! You might want keep the trilogy on the computer, but you can't beat a typewriter for quick notes. And, thanks to the sterile perfection of laser printing, typing has a warm, individual look perfectly appropriate for the personal letters of folks with poor penmanship. Just remember—no death threats, ransom demands, or manifestos!

9 The Kitchen

GET READY TO COOK—COOKBOOKS

Some thrifts treat cookbooks as a precious commodity, storing them behind the counter (like there aren't fifty million copies of *The Joy of Cooking* out there?), and plenty of thrifts significantly mark up their cookbooks. There's no harm in acquiring cookbooks—as long as the price is right. Thrifting a load of cheap cookbooks and lining them up on your kitchen shelves creates the superficial impression that you are quite the cook! Old cookbooks can be loads of useful fun. You can find great recipes for "lost foods" like "Broiled Grapefruit" and "Emergency Soup." Some older cookbooks contain other handy-around-the-house advice too, like how to bargain with the butcher, stain removal, cooking dinner for your husband's new boss, homeopathic health care, and how to stretch-dry your curtains.

Exercise some caution when dealing with thrifted cookbooks.

1. Beware of measurements! A lot of older books give recipe amounts in weights, not the standard cup measures we use today. (Also, make sure it's a measuring system you understand. Some more recent foreign cookbooks use metric measures.)

2. Skim one or two good-sounding recipes to see how much *time* might be involved in preparing this food. In the past, people (well, women mostly) spent a lot more time preparing food than we do today.

An Odd Old Cookbook: *Men Cooking* by Outstanding Men Cooks (Sunset Books, 1963). You couldn't market this book today—how very sexist to distinguish recipes by men from recipes by women. The point of the book was to encourage men to cook by proving that other men did too. The book's foreword emphasizes the "manliness" of the cooking—barbecue coals made from prunings and freshly caught fish cooked in a gunnysack. Compiled from the popular men's cookery section of *Sunset Magazine*, the editor swears the recipes have been vetted, both for taste and to discard those recipes sent in by "wily women, attempting to crash the select fraternity."[1] To think this once mattered . . .

3. Check to see what portions of food are made. Some older books erred on the side of large gatherings, and "serves 16" might not be practical for your lifestyle or budget.

4. If you're on any kind of reduced bad-food substance diet (either by choice or by doctor's orders), be forewarned. Older recipes can be chock-a-block with butter, eggs, raw eggs, meat wrapped in fat, booze, cream, sugar, lard, etc. Still, there's a certain vicarious pleasure in just *reading* about extravagantly prepared forbidden dishes (food porn), so it might be worth the dollar investment even if you never make "Maitre d'Hotel Butter" or a chicken drenched in heavy cream and champagne.

Cooking with Famous People—Celebrity Cookbooks

Am I the only one that believes that celebrities don't cook? I figure they're too busy, too glamorous, or at the very least too rich—don't they just pay somebody to cook? Now that we're encouraged to view celebrities' "human sides," there's no shortage of "celebrities who cook." At the very least, they're photographed in *People* magazine stirring something in their kitchen, but the really committed P.R. agents . . . uh, I mean, celebrities . . . publish cookbooks. Below are some of my favorite kooky celebrity cookbooks—you may not find these, but you'll find others—and even more marvelously, celebrities keep churning them out! Look for copies of *Cooking with "Friends"* and *Stand By Your Pan: Country Music Cookbook* in thrifts soon! Now, let's go sauté something with the stars.

Jolie Gabor's Family Cookbook (1962): Jolie was "mama" to the Gabor sisters, Magda, Eva, and Zsa Zsa. Can't you just see a rhinestone-encrusted Zsa Zsa whipping up a batch of "Transylvanian Potato Salad"? (A bonus joy of a secondhand cookbook—on this recipe, the previous owner scratched out the ingredient "2 tablespoons of white wine" and huffily wrote above it, "one is enough.")

The Mondale Family Cookbook by Joan Mondale (1984, Mondale for President Committee): Thrifted in Washington, D.C., this book still had an enclosed handwritten note, "Fritz and I thank you for all your help! Joan"! The book opens, "Next to fishing, Fritz's favorite hobby is cooking," but we only get a couple recipes from the former Veep. The bulk of the recipes come from Mondale family and friends. The standout is Betty Friedan's "Garlic Soup," which she says "cures a broken heart" but I'd suspect it *causes* heartbreak.[2]

The catch-all . . . *The Celebrity Cookbook—Favorite Recipes from the Famous* (1978): This book has the look of those celebrity recipes that the *National Enquirer* features. Each recipe has a little bio of the "cook" and the celeb's autograph. A lot of the "celebrities" are long-forgotten congressmen, but Governor George C. Wallace's "Smothered Alabama Doves" sounds intriguing. It's also gratifying to see how many of the rich and famous cook with canned and frozen produce.

And speaking of food porn—no need to eat! You can just read and drool over some of the carnally detailed recipes from *Liberace Cooks*! And how! "Liberace may have traveled all over, but he remains as American as hamburger. He has a way with ground beef. . . . He begins with sirloin, defatted and twice ground. . . . The raw beef is piled up about half an inch thick on halves of hamburger buns . . . [T]he prepared half sandwiches go under the oven broiler. Not a drop of the luscious juice escapes; it is all caught by the bun underneath."[3]

Cooking with Famous Food—Some Bad Ideas

Food companies often publish recipe books or booklets that feature a zillion different yummy things to do with their product. These books are often free for the asking, available by redeeming product seals or sold at low cost. Some foods—say, butter—truly lend themselves to being used in a variety of dishes, but food companies can really push the envelope with a limited product. I'm particularly fond of the product cookbooks that start with an already unappetizing food item and then take said product to horrifying new culinary depths. A few to whet your appetite . . .

Flavor Sparkling Recipes with Tang (General Foods Corporation, 1965). Scariest Application: Tang-Sauced Beets.

The Touch of Taste from None Such Mince Meat (Borden, 1977). The very first line of this book will get your taste buds going: "None Such Mince Meat comes in two forms: Ready-to-Use and Condensed." Scariest Application: Mince Sauce Flambé.

63 Wheat Germ Recipes (Kretchmer Wheat Germ Corporation, late 1950s). Wheat germ wouldn't come into its own till the big natural food craze of the 1970s. Scariest Application: Pineapple Cheese Ball Salad (cream cheese and pineapple juice balls rolled in wheat germ and served with salad dressing).

Put Some Kraut in Your Life (The National Kraut Packers Association, early 1970s). Scariest Application: Kraut Conquers All . . . Chocolate Cake. "This rich fudge cake has a coconut-like texture and the kraut keeps it wonderfully moist and fresh for several days."[4] No fools, the Kraut Packers Association—they recommend that you not inform your guests that the cake contained sauerkraut until after they have eaten it.

RELIABLE COOKWARE—THINGS THAT STILL WORK

Once armed with recipes, the thrifts are a swell source of things to cook in. The beauty of cookware is that it is designed to withstand very intense conditions and therefore is fabulously durable. (Some of the best developments in cookware have come from the defense and aerospace industries!) While it may not have the same cachet as a '50s cocktail set and can be rather ugly, good cookware is one of your best buys in a thrift store. A few dollars will net you a fully functional piece of cookware that may even outlive you. Best to avoid cookware with the so-called miracle coatings (they are prone to deteriorating). It's hard to go wrong with the basics: glass, cast iron, and ceramic. Some shoppers aren't interested in these items because they can be bulky and heavy, but that's why they last and all those new lightweight miracle products come and go.

Watch the Food Cook

In 1915, Corning Glass rolled out its first piece of Pyrex ovenproof glass in the shape of a pie plate. By 1936, they'd invented Pyrex Flameware that could go stovetop. If it doesn't say "Pyrex" (which is a Corning Glass brand name), make sure it says "ovenproof." (Fireking and Glasbake are two other common lines of oven glass.) Never put anything that doesn't say "ovenproof" in the oven! Not all glass is ovenproof. Older oven glass may be slightly yellowed. This is a factor of age and has no effect on the durability of the glass or on your cooking.

✳TIP✳ A cool ashtray makes a good spoon rest.

Heavy Metal

Enameled cast-iron is a favorite of good cooks and wannabe kitchen snobs everywhere. Cooks like it because iron is a good conductor of heat—an iron pot will heat evenly and will use less energy to maintain a high temperature. The snobs love it because the bright, colorful pots look like they belong in a well-decorated French country kitchen. (In fact, most enameled ironware does come from Europe.) This is expensive cookware to purchase new (another reason why kitchen snobs love it)—a stewpot can cost over $200 in a department store. While enameled cast iron doesn't turn up as frequently in thrift stores, when it does it's usually priced like all the other cookware at a couple of bucks. It's easy to distinguish from other cheaper enamelware (covered steel or aluminum) by being very, very heavy.

Sometimes you'll find that the pot is stained or scuffed. Pay no mind. A light enameled interior takes on various food stains over time (one round of black bean soup causes permanent discoloration). Any stain that doesn't come off with scrubbing is purely cosmetic and will have no effect on your cooking or the taste of your food. You may also find pots where the enamel has chipped off. The enamel has been fired on and it takes a pretty dramatic event like dropping one piece of cast iron onto another to cause chips. Don't sweat small chips in the enamel. The metal underneath is not harmful nor will the chipped area affect cooking. Avoid pots with large areas of enamel missing since there can be a temperature discrepancy between enameled area and exposed iron that could cause "hot spots" and food burning.

Make sure the pot or pan is enameled inside and out! It looks nicer, and you'll find that it's a dream to clean up the inside of an enameled pot, no matter what culinary disaster occurred in there! Soak in warm water and watch burnt caramel corn just sponge off! (Do not put in the dishwasher!) It's hard to find something much sturdier than iron. These pots are built for life. One downside is the major hazard they pose to other things in your kitchen. I've broken plenty of glasses and plates by accidentally dropping a piece of ironware on 'em.

Non-enameled cast iron pans, skillets, and griddles get seasoned with age, so used ironware can be a plus. Scrape out any rust or grime, wash, dry *thoroughly* with a cloth, and massage them with some vegetable oil. (Non-enameled iron should never go in the dishwasher or soak in water.) The totally iron pieces can go on the stovetop or in the oven. Very versatile piece of cookware.

Be prepared for any dessert. Stock up on cake tins of all sizes, pie plates, cartoony cake molds, and Jell-O molds. The nice thing about muffin tins—even the grimy cheapola aluminum ones—is that they're all salvageable if you use paper or foil baking cups. I hate standing by the oven making several batches of cupcakes with one measly six-cup muffin tray. I thrifted an armful of muffin tins, and now I can make three dozen cupcakes at one go. Saves energy too.

From Orbit to Oven

You'll find Corning also leading the pack in ovenproof ceramics. Some oven ceramics are earthenware, but most are ceramic glass. Ceramic glass is that opaque (usually white) glass you see plates, bowls, and mugs made from. This material was originally developed for use in the nose cones of space missiles, so rest assured it's pretty impervious to heat and trauma. Check that it says "ovenproof," and hold out for the casserole dish with the matching lid.

Fresh Squeezed!—Juicers

That innocuous cardboard can of frozen pulp killed the old juicers. Sure, food and health snobs today buy those high-tech juicers, but in the old days, every household had a juice maker. If you enjoy fresh-squeezed juice, why not rescue a sad old juicer from the thrifts? (At the low price, they're still a bargain even if you only make one glass of juice a year!) Dedicated mixologists will want to have a juicer on hand for the most delectable fresh-squeezed tropical drinks. The basic juicer is a solid reamer you twist your orange around. Insist on a glass one—no plastic! The Juice-O-Mat (cousin of the chrome-domed Ice-O-Mat ice crusher) is a common simple-physics juicer: you pull a lever

The dependable Juice-O-Mat
PHOTO BY VANESSA DOMICO

to exert the force of a gigantic chrome lid down on your orange. Occasionally, you'll see an old electric juicer (like the 1950s Juicerator). These reduce any fruit or veg to juice, but they can be very loud and hard to deal with first thing in the morning.

Oh, how those kitchen appliances pile up!
PHOTO BY AUTHOR

ELECTRICAL KITCHEN APPLIANCES— THE GOOD, THE BAD, AND THE UGLY

As with any electrical appliance, plug it in and see if it works! You don't actually have to make toast, but look to see if the heating elements come to life. If you notice an electrical burning smell, leave it be! In my travels, I have found these two basic electrical housewares to be good buys—that is, they tend to be available, working, and cheap. If it doesn't work or showers sparks later, you can ditch it without much remorse.

- **Toasters:** While ancient toasters look really cool, make sure the one you buy has a thermostat attached to the pop-up mechanism (usually disguised as the how-brown-do-you-want-it? setting.) Plenty of shiny chrome-domed toasters out there—don't settle for that ugly rectangle shape.
- **Waffle irons:** The waffle iron dates back centuries. Decorated flat breads were made for religious ceremonies using metal plates with

---

ELECTRICAL KITCHEN GADGETS YOU SEE IN EVERY THRIFT IN MASSIVE QUANTITIES

- **Popcorn poppers (both dome and upright shapes):** Evidently the Pilgrims popped corn for the first Thanksgiving. *They* didn't need some plug-in contraption the size of their best pumpkin to do it in!

- **Electric warming trays (don't get up!):** The "Hotray" was first marketed by Salton in 1950 and they've been piling up in the thrifts ever since. Either they don't work or *nobody* wants them.

- **Coffee percolators:** Coffee snobs say no! no! but there is something cool about listening to the coffee perk and watching it bubble up under that little glass bit.

- **Electric can openers:** In one thrift alone, I counted *ten*, priced randomly from $4.95 to $7.95.

impressions like today's waffle iron. Personal experience has taught me several important things about modern waffle irons to insist on: an indicator light that tells you when your waffle is done, removable iron, plates for easy clean up, and plastic or wooden handles. I thrifted an all-metal waffle iron, and a very poor design concept it was indeed. With no temperature settings, it just got hotter and hotter while I figured out how to open it without getting third-degree burns. Good waffles, though . . .

> **Y**ou can get a lot of practical use out of a toaster, but a lot of silly kitchen items *suffer* from being electric. Consumers quickly realize this and dump the contraption at the thrifts. Do you really need a special electric thing for heating hot dogs—a Hot Doggery? An electric wok? Could you buy something called M'sieur Crêpe with a straight face?

TIP **The iron was one of the first electrical household appliances. The old ones don't make very good functional irons—no temperature settings and no steam—but they do make quite nice doorstops. Cut the cord off first before you trip over it.**

ASSORTED KITCHENWARE

Storageware

Tupperware was another miracle use of post–World War II plastics. Mr. Tupperware (Earl S. Tupper) proudly produced the first of many pieces—a polyethylene tumbler—in 1945. Then came the lidded bowls, the pie-slice keepers, the boiled-egg holders, and a thousand other specific-use storage containers. (Naturally, the Tupperware imitators followed, too.) By the early 1950s, Tupper discontinued selling his products at retail stores in favor of home parties, where enterprising housewives sold one another ever-more-fantastic burping food containers. I've seen several warning signs that older Tupperware is about to become "collectible." While I can't quite wrap my head around this possibility, don't fall for it. No need to bother with expensively priced "original" Tupperware—just thrift the stuff that works and is in good shape. Some plastic storageware gets warped from too many spins through the hot dishwasher.

Keep your flour, sugar, coffee, and tea in canisters marked as such and you'll always know where they are. Coffee and tea stay fresh longer in airtight containers, and sugar-seeking ants and flour-hungry meal worms have a hard time negotiating through a can of aluminum. Ideally, you'll want to thrift all four basic canisters as a package deal, but some are so common (like the aluminum and plastic-that-looks-like-metal ones), you can probably assemble a set singly. I'm partial to the roundish brushed aluminum canisters, because they made lots of smaller labeled canisters besides the Big Four. Over time, I've added "cookies," "salt," "pepper," and another dozen spices, as well as the essential "grease" canister.

Kitchen Linens

Any small terry-cloth towel is great in the kitchen for wiping your hands or cleaning up spills. More absorbent than paper towels and more ecologicaly sound, too. A souvenir item I find regularly in thrifts is the linen tea towel from the British Isles, usually unused. I give everybody one for Christmas—they're the *best* for drying dishes. Never pay a lot for outdated calendar tea cloths. They're close to worthless—that year will *never* come again!

Perfect for your calypso parties! PHOTO BY VANESSA DOMICO

It's sad that nobody seems to buy aprons anymore. They're cute, protect your clothes from icky food spills, are a handy place to wipe your hands, and they're so cheap in the thrifts. So many appear never worn! True, there aren't many *manly* aprons available, but anybody can wear a ladies' apron in the privacy of one's own home. Remember how fetching Jim Backus looked in *Rebel Without A Cause*?

Aprons have four basic designs:

1. Waisted full apron: A retro favorite, this apron hangs from the neck and is fastened tightly with a big bow at the back of the waist.

2. Loose full apron: Like a deli apron, it starts at the neck but is only loosely secured mid-body and has no distinct waist.

3. Basic thigh protector: This begins at the waist and hangs to just above the knee.

4. Hostess apron: An absurd delight they don't make anymore, this teeny treat starts at the waist and barely covers the abdomen. Completely useless for protecting clothing and made from practical kitchen linens like taffeta, satin, appliquéed felt, velvet, and netting.

THEME ROOM: LITERALS

A popular 1970s housewares trend was to label the obvious. There was the bowl that said "bowl" on it and the book bag that said "book bag." Seventies historian Candi Strecker has dubbed these objects "literals," and that seems to be a perfect name for them. Literally. Nearly all the literals used the same typeface to spell themselves out and usually in lowercase letters. Another common motif was to have the literal name turned on its side so it ran bottom to top vertically, instead of the standard left to right. It seems stupid now, but at the time literals were considered a hip little joke. Sort of postmodern. We were all so *over* coffee mugs that had every other image and motif on them. Why not just reduce to the obvious? I used to assume that a mug labeled "mug" was for the benefit of the very dumb, but now I realize literals were in-jokes for those who *thought* they were quite clever.

Most of the literals were kitchen items, probably because there was already an established labeling pattern in kitchens with basic storageware like "sugar" and "flour." Also, a popular '70s kitchen decor idea was to be bright and fun. But other household items were literalized. While most people only had one or two literals in

their home, I really like the idea of a room stocked *only* with them. It'd be maddening—everything you looked at would shout back the obvious at you until the whole space was reduced to meaninglessness. And it would be the perfect accommodations for a visiting foreign exchange student or Mr. Short Term Memory: "What is this again? Oh, right. A mug."

Hey! It's my bag!
PHOTO BY VANESSA DOMICO

Below is a list of common literals to look out for. This fad has not died out entirely. The original '70s literals will be distinguished by that unique typeface. You can guess what the object might be from the "literal." For instance "ice tea" would be written on a container intended to serve ice tea from.

KITCHEN

mug

glass

bowl (also: popcorn, soup, chowder, leftovers, salad)

mixer

oil

vinegar

names of common spices

wine

juice or orange juice

ice tea or sun tea

beans

rice

salt

pepper

nuts

nut mill

crackers

cheese

crackers and cheese

snacks

OTHER

book bag or homework

lunch or lunchbag

trash

yarn & needles (bag for knitting)

clock or time

T-shirt

socks

umbrella

money (bank)

FOREIGN LITERALS

Le Bag

La Machine

NOT QUITE LITERALS BUT EVEN CLEVERER

bed sheets that said "sleep sleep sleep"

towels that said "dry dry dry"

aprons that said "eat eat eat" and "diet diet diet"

1970s LITERAL STORES WHERE YOU COULD BUY THIS STUFF

The Door Store

Crate and Barrel

DRIVE THERE IN A . . .

Le Car

LOSE WEIGHT WHILE YOU THRIFT!—DIET BOOKS

There are scads of diet books in the thrifts. Obviously, people buy the book, follow the sensible plan presented, lose the weight, and then no longer need the book. Right? Real World Scenario: People buy the book, hope they'll lose weight, flip through the book, hope they'll lose weight, maybe try a new recipe or exercise, hope they'll lose weight, and finally, put the book on a shelf. Later they discard the book and buy this year's "better, easier, quicker" diet book and the cycle begins anew. Most of these diet book fads follow a wave pattern: the book comes out (low); it is hailed by media as the amazing new diet (middle); everyone buys it and tries it (high); somebody irritating like *Consumer Reports* issues a public statement saying the diet is no good or dangerous (middle); there is mass media hype (same sources as "it's a great diet") about the worthlessness/danger of the diet (low); some people reputedly die while on the diet (plummet). New book comes out.

If you wanna go on a diet or truly try out new low-cal recipes or new exercises, there are plenty of choices in the thrifts. For the cost of one new diet book, you can take home a dozen books from the thrift. Mix and match—eat like Richard Simmons but do Cher's arm stretches. And if you blow off the whole regime (and the chances are good . . .), you've wasted almost no money. If you lose the fat and keep the muscle, then good for you. You just paid a quarter for the same results other people waste tens, hundreds, even thousands of dollars to achieve.

Diet books are fascinating in themselves. Picking one up and reading it is a free peek into the curious psyche of America. Leaf through them and wonder about our country's overriding obsession with weight and fitness. Diets very much mirror contemporary times and it's interesting to see how this obsession changes. Some earlier diet books from the 1950s and the 1960s flat-out claimed to be "starvation diets," but that was a perfectly acceptable method to achieve fashionable slimness. There really wasn't much concern whether the diet promoted health (or even robbed your health)—it's about how you look!

The concepts of health and nutrition begin to appear in 1970s diet books. Some diets are pitched as "miracle health cures," like diets meant to prevent cancer. Others up the ante by claiming to improve your health *and* help you lose weight. By the 1980s, fitness is king and now you must eat healthy, exercise, *and* lose weight! Most contemporary books aren't even pitched as strict weight-loss

Hooray for Loose Bowels! or A Diet Worth Reading. *The Beverly Hills Diet* by Judy Mazel is a laugh-out-loud diet you can actually read! One of the diet "classics," the book spent eight months on the *New York Times* bestseller list in 1981. (So hot it inspired a parody book, *The Burbank Diet*. I thrifted both books in one shop.) Filled with chirpy talk about your "skinny voice," the "science" of this diet is that "conscious combining" of foods will result in weight loss—that is, Food A should be eaten with Food B—ta da! weight loss. If Food A is eaten with Food C—uh oh, instant weight gain. The miracle food was enormous quantities of tropical fruit—pineapple, watermelon, papaya, and mango. "If you have loose bowel movements, hooray! Keep in mind that pounds leave your body in two main ways—bowel movements and urination. The more time you spend on the toilet, the better."[5]

diets, but are sold as guides for you to reorganize your entire lifestyle around health and fitness. It seemed easier in the old days when you just had to stop eating!

The increase in general science and health knowledge has also affected the diet books. Americans have assimilated a lot of information about good and bad food, and most people can discuss at length blood cholesterol, binge dieting, or bran flakes. (What they know and what they practice often remain incompatible, but that discrepancy keeps the diet industry flush!) You couldn't sell the very popular 1972 diet book *Dr. Atkins' Diet Revolution* today. Dr. Atkins recommended an unlimited consumption of saturated fats and cholesterol-rich foods. As long as you didn't take in any carbohydrates, you could eat *as much fat* as you wanted and *still* lose weight! It *does* sound yummy, but most people know better now. At the time of its release, the diet was widely denounced by doctors, but it still became one of the bestselling diet books in history. Today, virtually every thrift has a copy.

FONDUE: FUN-TO-DO FUN-DO!

The ancient (or so they claim) Art of Fondue had a big resurgence in the late 1960s. As a fad, it must continue to bubble under any contemporary trends, since in my lifetime there has *never* been a shortage of fondue pots and accessories at the thrift stores.

DEAD ·FAD·

Fondue is the perfect excuse to throw a small party and requires very little in the way of materials. It's a casual affair and great for these informal times. Plus, there's the added carnal pleasure of bonding over food. In the 1960s, highbrows likened it to a "latter day version of huddling round the fire," but it was apt to be more like a titillating adult version of some child's party game. Never mind "Pin the Tail on the Donkey," how about "Stick Your Fork in My Bubbling Cheese"?

Fondue was such an amusing excuse for social interaction that a set of cute rules intended to speed up the fun soon developed. To wit:

- You don't just dunk your bread in, you make a figure-eight swirl.
- If you drop your bread, you must kiss your neighbor or buy the next round of drinks.
- The cheese crust left in the bottom of the pot is considered a delicacy and is reserved for he who has not dropped his bread during the dinner. A variation of this rule allows the crust to be presented to the honored guest, if there is one.

Fondue sounds foreign and sophisticated, but it's all about poor eating habits and bad food. Imagine *dunking* your food in a communal bowl! How gauche. And suggested foods to dip, besides the traditional crusty bread, can be positively low-rent: hamburgers, hot dogs, and pizzas, sauerkraut balls, cheese fingers, marshmallows, and donuts. (A good fondue host should provide a selection of raw vegetables just to cover his culinary butt.) During fondue's heyday, you could shortcut the cooking process by buying cheese fondue ready-to-go in a can. You can still take fondue to its nadir by thrifting a recipe book that calls for cheddar cheese soup or pasteurized processed cheese spread. Yummy. It doesn't get any less foreign than this.

Fondue Starter Kit

Book: Thrift one or two of the *many* available fondue cookbooks. Decide which sort of fondue you'd like to attempt. There are four basic types: two dipping fondues—cheese or chocolate—and two dip-and-cook fondues—hot oil (fondue bourguignonne) and hot broth. You'll note below that different equipment is needed for specific types of fondue. (Chocolate fondue is a dessert entrée and should not be substituted for an entire meal, no matter how delicious that sounds.)

Pot: Most fondue pots I see in the thrifts appear never used.

Probably another never-appreciated wedding or housewarming gift that has likely sat around homes for 20 years till somebody finally said, "You know, we're *never* gonna have a fondue party."

No more than six dunkers to a pot, so if you're having a largish fondue feast, thrift enough pots to go round. Fondue pots come in ceramic, enameled aluminum, and steel, copper, and cast iron. Your energy sources are limited to electricity, denatured alcohol burners, and Sterno cans. Electric fondue pots are easier to use, but some traditionalists insist on the warm flicker of real flame. The big plus of the electric fondue pots is that you can control the temperature to keep your cheese or chocolate at just the right consistency. A good electric fondue pot will have a detachable base so you can clean the pot separately without risking electrocution.

After learning of some no-doubt spectacular domestic disasters, *Consumer Reports* had the good sense to recommend diners avoid the fondue bourguignonne: "Deep hot oil right on the dining table?"[6] The cooking oil can get as hot as 450 degrees Fahrenheit, and is just the kind of spilled liquid that can ruin any party. Look for a narrow-mouthed pot for hot oil fondues (it will help contain splattering), and do exercise caution.

Plates and Forks: While fondue forks do show up singly in the flatware bins, it's best to hold out for the package of six. You need six forks with different colored handles (so that each guest can keep track of his own fork). If you thrift the bins, you may end up with four red forks and risk a public health crisis. Serious fondue-ists take note: the proper cheese fork has three tines. The meat fork has two barbed points, and the considerate host provides *two* meat forks—one for cooking and the other for removing the hot meat from the first fork. Some meat forks have hooks that allow the diners to hang them from the edge of the pot during cooking. This leaves hands free for getting to know your fondue pot neighbor.

There's a specific plate for meat fondues—a sectioned plate that looks something like an airline food plate. The large section holds the meat, and the smaller areas are for savory dipping sauces. Any plate can be used for cheese fondue. Guests are apt not to need a plate—they'll just spear the bread from the communal pile and eat it right off the fork. Small plates are recommended, though, for catching cheese drips. Fondue soon—it's cheese-easy!

10 The Dining Room

THE SAD WORLD OF UNWANTED DISHWARE

So many housewares items are ditched at the thrifts. Here's the dining room thrift caveat in a nutshell: Everything you can buy for your dining room has lost *none* of its function! Take one perennial item: dishes. Can you conceive of a more basic and utilitarian object around the house? No matter what its shape, weight, color, pattern, translucency, age, etc.—unless *shattered*—it *never* loses its function! You put food on it, you take food off it. It never fails. Dishes are discarded for many reasons. China can suddenly look "out of style." Dishes are tricky things to move. Better kinds of dishware are developed. People scale back big sets and dump unwanted dishware gifts. So many dishes in the thrifts—each similar yet each different—like grains of sand on the beach. A bonanza for us thrifters!

Most dishes are ceramicware, a general term that refers to items made from clay and fired in a kiln. It's understating it slightly, but a china plate is simply soft rock pressed hard into a shape and solidified with heat. Once shaped, the dishware is dipped in glazing and baked. Most ceramicware is patterned before the glazing and baking process. Such "underglazed" colors and patterns remain impervious to wear. Printed dishware, most commonly seen as souvenir plates, have paint or decals added after the glazing process, since more colors can be used with an "overglazing" process. Such patterns are subject to chipping and fading if used as an eating utensil, which, in fairness, they were not designed to be.

To Mix or Match?

NO, I don't want to match: Start shopping now. My first apartment was stocked on one thrift trip. I bought the first eight plates I liked. Each different. Used them for years.

YES, I do want to match: The easiest way to get a matched set is to stumble across a donated matched set. Usually the thrifts are smart enough to put these in a bag or box and sell them as a matched set. Other times you may notice that there seems to be an unusual number of the same pattern on the shelves. Pricing varies. Sometimes it's a better bargain to buy the set—40 pieces for $8 rather than individual plates at 50 cents each. Sometimes "matched set" means "thrift markup." Abide by your own limits.

The matched set may not be complete—you might have eight plates but only three bowls. I like this setup. I get a lot of matching dishware and an excuse to keep thrifting. The fun of a matched set comes not just from serving food in a "real" way, but from the treasure-hunt aspect of searching out new pieces of "your pattern." Make sure your thrifting friends see and memorize your pattern. You'll want their help in acquiring stray pieces.

You can begin acquiring a matched set with just one piece. Buy a plate you like, then on return trips look for more. At any given point, I usually have three or four pattern searches going with varying degrees of success. Years ago I thrifted this one pink and green saucer with a cool shark on it. Haven't seen it again, but someone I know has four cups and four saucers of this pattern, so I know it's out there somewhere. Be reasonable in your search criteria. Older dishware is quite collectible, therefore the odds of finding sets of certain styles and patterns are poor. Visit the dishware section and take note of what's there fairly regularly.

Mixing AND Matching

Between the polar extremities—the perfectly matched eight-piece setting for twelve and the postnuclear survivalist look of twelve completely different plates—lies the common ground most of us tread. Given the slimmer chances of a matched set, you may wish to consider the attractive compromise—semi-matching. Some suggestions for mixing *and* matching:

Similar Pattern: Some large dishware manufacturers keep a similar look with all dishware. Though you may be buying from several different patterns, the overall effect is one of sameness. You could build a stock of "diner china" (heavy thick institutional china made for restaurants.) Most of it is white with simple decorations around the edge of the plate.

Color: Once you've picked a color, you can be as selective as you like picking up coordinated pieces.

Motif: This requires a little more work than color, in both searching out and determining suitability, but the effect could be fab! Blue flowers on white, pictures of wheat, Pennsylvania Dutch look, etc.

Ugly Plates: Maybe you're over dishware or think searching it out is a waste of time. You could play the Ugly Plate game. Buy the ten ugliest plates you see. Revel in their hideousness. Swap them out as you discover worse ones. At 50 cents a plate, it's a fun pursuit and great passive-aggressive way to keep your friends and family on edge.

BYOP—The Bring-Your-Own-Plate Party: Replace your old dishware in one fell swoop! Throw a party and tell everybody to bring a piece of dishware that meets your specifications ("pink," "stripes," "plastic"). It could be quite a success depending on how many party attendees you have and how good their thrifting skills are. Keep it simple and even nonthrifters can play. Anybody can make it to at least one secondhand venue and find a pink plate.

Searching out dishware is no spectator sport! This is one of those hands-on areas that brings out the dedicated thrifter. Because of their accumulated weight, the dishes in thrifts are often stacked on the floor. You gotta grub around down there while you laboriously inspect each plate. Unlike clothing, where a sleeve can reveal much about the rest of the hidden garment, the edge of the plate often says nothing at all. And not just the front of the plate either—serious dish-thrifters gotta check the back to see the manufacturer's mark!

When stocking your pattern, keep an eye out for those odd pieces of china—the sugar and creamer sets (sometimes with lids), the gravy boat, the covered butter dish, the salt and pepper shakers, the serving bowls and platters, the coffeepot, and other specialized dishware. Occasionally, some pieces in the set may not have the pattern—the saucers, for example, may be a solid color. This makes stocking trickier. If you're seriously committed to one pattern, you'll need to research the pattern (if it's "interesting" enough to have made some collectible book) or use your imagination and good judgment to "fit" unmarked pieces into your set.

Don't get discouraged. Getting just the right set can be a gradual process. Swap out bad plates for good plates as you go. And remember, most of the fun is in the hunt. Once you get your whole set, you may not experience elation with your completed set but rather profound disappointment that the game is over. You are free to start up again.

THE MIRACLE OF MELMAC—PLASTIC DISHWARE

The plastic melamine was developed in 1834 in Germany and then ignored. A hundred years later, the American Cyanamid Company "rediscovered" it and brand-named it "Melmac." In the late 1930s, the U.S. Navy went in search of a sturdy dinnerware better suited to rough handling by seamen and ocean journeys. Melamine, being a hard, break-resistant plastic, satisfied the durability criteria. The fact that it could be easily and quickly molded into the thousands of plates and bowls needed sealed the deal. Following World War II, the companies that had supplied the war effort were free to make and market civilian Melmac dinnerware. Initially they only shifted their focus slightly and pitched Melmac dinnerware to other large institutions like hospitals, schools and cafeteria chains—all no doubt delighted to find a close-to-unbreakable, easy-to-clean dishware.

An assortment of Melmac sugar bowls
PHOTO BY VANESSA DOMICO

Improvement began at once on civilian Melmac. The plastics industry had to overcome a public distaste about plastic—that as a material it was "ersatz," or a pale imitation of some finer substance; in this case, ceramic china—and to present Melmac dishware as something other than institutional. To shed its mental hospital look and its cheap "plastic" association, American Cyanamid asked the designer Russel Wright (who had already designed a successful line of ceramic dishware) to create new molds for Melmac dishware. With an artful design, consumers might be persuaded to purchase Melmac dishware for their home. New colors were added, the scratch- and stain-resistant qualities were beefed up, and more specialized dishware (like the butter dish) was added to the list of available pieces. Melmac was heavily promoted, and as the volume of production increased, the costs dropped, making Melmac even more attractive. Not that it was hard to sell. Imagine being a young housewife with a passel of kiddies and discovering there was a virtually unbreakable dishware!

Melmac came into its own when manufacturers and consumers realized the vivid colors (much easier than glazing pottery) and the

---

CARE AND FEEDING OF YOUR MELMAC DISHWARE

- Melmac *will* scratch. Don't scrub with sharp or rough things. Best to wash with a sponge.

- Technically dishwasher-safe, but repeated exposure to all that very hot water will "age" Melmac sooner.

- Do not put in microwave.

- Not ovenproof. Do not even warm plates in low oven.

- Don't leave coffee, blueberry pie, or other stain-making foods in it. Wash quickly.

---

fabulous shapes it could be poured into. It seemed that once designers discovered Melmac's inherent plastic nature, they couldn't resist molding it into the most absurd and delightful shapes—shapes that would have been physically impossible or prohibitively expensive to achieve with ceramic!

Despite the explosion of plastic dinnerware in the 1950s (by 1960, one in four families had a set), all was not perfect in Melmac World. Although it had big-name designers and the pretty new patterns, plasticware never achieved the high-class status of ceramic china. Most homes had a set of each—Melmac for outdoor or everyday use and china for nice occasions. Some problems didn't materialize until after use. Light-colored plasticware stained easily. And be careful scrubbing! Despite its rock-hardness, Melmac took a beating from cutlery, and the plates became scratched and dull. For others, the idea of plastic dishware was a novelty. Once the fun was over, they reverted back to their china.

No matter. Plastic dinnerware was here to stay, but having established the market, the industry began to loosen quality standards. When manufacturers discovered how to inlay colored patterns into plasticware, they did a curious thing. They began to design dishes to look like ceramic dishware—white plate with colonial designs or a ring of blue flowers. While Melmac had once reveled in its otherness, spilling onto the table in glorious weird outer-space shapes, it now began to look like a very bad imitation of ceramic dinnerware. In addition, the heft and width of melamine dishware was reduced, making plastic dishware feel even cheaper—too light and too thin. Melamine eventually gave way to polystyrene as the material of choice for plastic dishware. Not only was polystyrene lighter, but it tended to

PLASTIC VERSUS POTTERY

Irecently (after moving to a house with no dishwasher and an enameled metal sink) have stepped up my search for Melmac. I'm sure you'll be delighted like me to find you can drop the dishware anywhere, hurl them into the sink, and slam 'em around during washing. I'm not a big plastic person, but I have been won over by their durability and the astounding shapes they come in.

In an unscientific study here at Thrift SCORE HQ, I subjected a ceramic-ware bowl (C) and a Melmac bowl (M) to a series of rigorous durability tests. The results are summarized below:

1. *Boiled for 5 minutes in water*
   C: No change
   M: No change, but smelled weird afterward

Let the games begin!
PHOTO BY AUTHOR

2. *Froze first, then boiled for 5 minutes*
   C: No change
   M: No change

3. *24-hour coffee bath*
   C: Appeared stained, but cleaned up completely.
   M: Appeared stained. Cleaned up, but left faint, faint stain.

4. *24-hour grape juice bath*
   C: Appeared stained. After cleaning, left faint stain.
   M: Appeared stained. Cleaned up, but stain remained in edges of bowl that couldn't be scrubbed.

5. *Attacked with sharp knife*
   C: No change
   M: Left barely discernible scratches

6. *Left cigar burning in*
   C: No change
   M: Barely perceptible burn mark

7. *Ran over with 2-ton Ford truck*
   C: No change
   M: Remained intact but sustained bad scratches from contact with pavement

8. *Left on curb overnight*
   C: No change
   M: No change
   (no one stole either)

We have a winner!
PHOTO BY AUTHOR

9. *Threw from 3rd floor onto cement path*
   C: Shattered
   M: Bounced on impact and landed upright. A quarter-inch deep chip came off of the bowl's base.

have sloppy visible seams and wasn't as indestructable as melamine.

Plastic dishware didn't go away, but it lost its luster. (One wag in the housewares industry declared that much plastic dinnerware had been converted to "petware.") The ceramic dishware industry responded by introducing lines of china designed to approximate the good things about plastic dishware (dishwasher-safe, less breakable, lighter in weight) while keeping the cachet of ceramic dinnerware. By the early 1970s, Corning had introduced its extremely popular Corelle line—lightweight, inexpensive patterned china with a *guarantee* against breakage!

Wither plastic dinnerware today? It's still out there. Supermarkets and discount stores still sell plastic dishware generally intended for outdoor picnic use. The days of "formal" plastic dishware are over. There are, though, huge reserves of Melmac still in use. Recently I was dragged to a community function that involved a dinner. The highlight of the evening? Finding the hall set with hundreds of pieces of pale yellow Melmac!

Thrifting Melmac
Melamine or Melmac is easy to distinguish from inferior plasticware. It is hard, very smooth, and has a good heft much like ceramic china. It is not a flexible plastic at all, but rigid. Melmac is virtually seamless. You can't distinguish where the mold was broken and there are no stray knobs or lines of plastic. (Look at a cheap plastic cup and you will see these nasty characteristics.) Later Melmac from the '60s will not have the same density as earlier pieces. Of course sometimes it just says "Melmac" right on the bottom of the piece.

Like ceramic dishware, sometimes you get lucky and find that someone has dumped a whole set and you can quickly acquire forty matching pieces. However, I don't think plastic dishware moves that well at thrifts, and I often see large bags—albeit very cheap—that contain a jumble of plastic dishware, some great pieces, some crappy pieces, all colors and shapes. (The plus side of this is that thrifts, unlike some tony stores and fleas, have not designated older plasticware "collectible." To them, all plastic dishware is the same crap.)

Should you desire a set, you must make the same commitments we discussed in acquiring china. Obviously, the narrower your search ("just the 1953 Boontonware in pink, please"), the slower your progress. It's quite easy to pick a common color, like pink or yellow, and build a fun set of dishes that have varying shapes and styles.

Oddly, unlike ceramicware, I find Melmac plates much harder to come by than cups or peripheral pieces like the creamer or sugar bowl.

Other Dishware

Despite the prominence of ceramic dishware in thrifts, you'll occasionally see other types of plates. Older colored and patterned glass plates that predate World War II are very collectible and pretty much out of thrift circulation. Sometimes they turn up in the boutique area or behind the counter. Every so often I do see a solitary piece of Depression glass make its way out to the "regular stack" and go for 49 cents. You'll never collect a set this way, but it is pretty glassware and even one piece makes a nice dessert serving plate. More common are the plain clear glass plates and ceramic glass. Some may be ovenproof, some may not, so be careful. Clear glass dishes get horribly scratched (which is probably why most people dump them at the thrifts!)

Dishware made from metal does exist. Obviously, metal is not necessarily the smartest material to hold hot food, but it's been done. I have seen plates, bowls, and drinking glasses made from aluminum (scratches horribly, dents easily). Enameled tin makes a very attractive rustic place setting, but it's impossible to serve hot food or drink in, and spots where the enamel coating has come off are susceptible to rust. You could return to the ways of our forefathers. I like the idea of setting your table with those commemorative Bicentennial pewter plates! There were some misguided attempts at wood dishware in the 1960s and 1970s. Yuck. Obviously, it gets gouged with knives and forks, soaks up food and water, splinters . . . ugh.

HOT AND COLD DRINKWARE

Coffee Mugs

Some people despise coffee mugs because they are apt to be cluttered with pictures of Garfield, so-called witticisms ("In case of emergency, administer chocolate."), or the name of your bank. Others adore mugs for this very reason! Count me in the latter group—I'm a sucker for cheesy slogan/image mugs. There's my CB and trucking company

> **THRIFT ITEM OF THE FUTURE**
> Sure espresso's hot now, but when everybody gets tired of taking fifteen minutes to make a teeny cup of coffee, the thrifts will fill up with precious demitasse and espresso cups. Pick up an espresso machine while you're there too.

MUGS THAT MATCH

Like plates, the only thing standing between you and a set of matching mugs is your imagination. Ten mugs that look identical are boring and no fun to find. Ten mugs that have a similar look, motif, or theme are cool, clever, and a great excuse to go thrifting. Here's a starter list of suggestions:

- Stemmed mugs
- White glass mugs with stupid slogans
- Pick a color
- Sports teams
- Banks
- Radio stations
- Hospitals
- Tourist traps
- Motivational company mugs ("XYZ is #1 in 1987!")
- Self-referential (mugs about coffee)

---

mug collection, the religious mug collection ("Here I am Lord, use me"), the bad '70s cartoon collection—I tell you, the mug section gets me going in the thrifts!

Wacky mugs make swell gag gifts. (Your pal in the death-metal band would bust in half if you gave him that mug that says "I'm part of the Bible translation team".) I keep plenty of mugs in the Gift Box for any occasion that pops up. Though they might not get the joke or like the pattern, everybody can use a coffee mug.

Mugs advertising pharmaceuticals are great fun. They often have medical "in-jokes" that will send you scrambling to your *Physician's Desk Reference* to decode. The smiley face and the exhortation to "Have a Happy Day" on this mug are courtesy of Sandoz's drug Mellaril, an antipsychotic. Thanks! I think I *will* have a happy day!
PHOTO BY VANESSA DOMICO

Drinking Glasses

The variations in drinking glasses must number in the millions!— height, width, thickness of glass, color, pattern, etching, frosting, beveling, shape, etc. And for something that is so mortal, so break- able (even so recyclable), it's astonishing how many discarded glasses are available. Many homes had several sets of glassware. Cartoon glasses for the children, a complementary design to match the good china, kooky motif glasses for the BBQ, glasses for card games, glasses for the ladies' luncheon, glasses for summer, glasses for winter—the "needs" were unlimited.

But fashions come and go, and glasses come and go (many go tragically), and the odds and ends of glassware end up at the thrift— yours to acquire for pennies. Glassware should be approached simi- larly to dishware: Do you want a matching set? How closely must they match? Because of the fragile nature of drinking glasses, it's uncommon to see large sets (more than three or four) of matching glassware. If you're committed to it, you can invest the patience to acquire sets gradually. If you're really good, you'll also find the matching pitcher!

Like dishes, a more practical approach to matching is to use crite- ria that are looser than "identical." The variation in patterns, col- ors, and motifs is so delightfully wide in glassware, it's almost a shame to limit yourself to one rigid pattern. Consider these match- ing glassware ideas:

- Geography: souvenir or promotional glasses from all states, one state, tourist traps, places that begin with the letter *D*
- Color or motif: polka dots, leaves, flowers, automobiles

THINGS YOU SEE IN EVERY THRIFT

The proliferation of cheap plastic giveaway cups and Big Gulp refills in today's thrifts is alarming. Buy what you like, but I make no recom- mendation for this stuff. It's low-grade plastic, prone to cracking. The images are cheaply painted and flake off easily. For me, they hold no aes- thetic or cultural value. (Will I be shaking my head twenty years from now when McDonald's Batman cups are "collectible," wishing I'd snapped them up when they were 25 cents each? I hope not—not just for my sake, but for the sake of our collective culture that we never inflate the value of this shoddy promotional merchandise. We'll see.) Currently, this crap takes up valuable shelf space in the thrift, and I swear I have never seen anybody buy one of these cups!

- Souvenir glasses from proms
- Theme: local industry, sports-related, Bicentennial

If you find colored or patterned glassware to be too unbearably tacky, relax. It is even easier to match plain glasses. And they're easier to look after. Painted-on patterns and decals on older glassware can be wiped out in *one* visit to the dishwasher. Wash any glass you treasure by hand and with a soft sponge—don't scrub.

WASHBASINS FILLED WITH FORKS—THRIFTING CUTLERY

Buying real silver silverware is a discussion for another type of book. If you find it, great, but don't call me to come over and help you clean it. Nearly everything you'll find in the thrift silverware bins is made from stainless steel. You may find pieces of silver plate (stainless steel electro-coated with the thinnest possible covering of silver)—usually distinguished by the fact that the plate is visibly wearing off.

I always wondered why stainless steel was called "stainless." The answer is so obvious as to astound you! Previously, flatware had been made from carbon steel. While it was durable, it stained easily and necessitated an endless drudgery of cleaning. Stainless steel flatware was first marketed in the 1920s. Like melamine, it was sold to hotels and restaurant chains that were delighted to find they didn't have to scrub black stains off hundreds of pieces of cutlery every night. Well, who would?! Stainless steel quickly became the de facto standard for everyday flatware. I doubt very much that any dining or kitchen implement is made these days from steel that stains, but the distinguishing term "stainless" has never been dropped.

TIP If the handle is made from anything other than stainless steel (celluloid, catalin, bakelite and other early plastics, bone, wood, bamboo, horn, etc.), don't put it in the dishwasher.

It's pretty tough to find perfectly matched flatware. The thrifts usually have grab-bag bins of cutlery—sometimes separated into knives, forks, and spoons, sometimes not! However if you're in a matching mood, you'll find that there are really only a few "motifs"—curlicued edges, Art Deco stripes, plain handle, flowers, little stars, etc.—so it's not really that difficult to put together a set that looks similar.

SALT AND PEPPER SHAKERS

There is no shortage of salt and pepper shakers at the thrifts. They come in any imaginable shape and material. Maybe you stumble across a matched set you adore—lucky you! Don't be afraid to work a "theme" or "motif" as previously discussed.

TIP If you want a pepper mill, pay close attention. There are many, many things in the thrifts that *look* like pepper mills but are in fact just decorative objects shaped like pepper mills. Turn the object around and examine it closely. Look for the hole the pepper-corns go in and the hole ground pepper comes out. You may think I sound downright ignorant, but I looked for more than six months for a *functioning* pepper mill. And yes, I did accidentally buy one of the nonfunctioning kind.

SIT DOWN AND EAT, ALREADY—DINING ROOM FURNITURE

Unless you're the type who prefers to eat out of the LeMenu tray while standing near the sink, you're gonna need some dining room furniture. At least the essentials: a table and some chairs.

Matched dining room sets and dinette sets—a "dinette set" being defined as something that looks better in a fabulous kitchen than a stately dining room, usually a small Formica-and-chrome table with matching vinyl-and-chrome chairs—do turn up in the thrifts. Whereas the bag of matched dishes can be a bargain, a table and four matching chairs is often grounds for Thrift Markup. It's easier to find odd pieces—and if you're out of luck looking for the matched set and you still want to be coordinated, have no fear. As you do with your dishes, make it a hunt. Get a fast-and-dirty table and four random chairs cheap, then gradually swap out your temporary chairs as you acquire the ones you want.

- Don't sweat any missing plastic leg tips on dinette chairs and tables. You can buy these in any hardware or discount store.
- Got a small car? You'd be surprised how many tables have legs that unscrew easily. You have a screwdriver in your car, right? Other table legs are secured with cotter pins, even simpler to remove.
- Can only find hideous tables? This is the *other* reason people use tablecloths!
- Old wooden folding chairs turn up a lot. You can buy them singly,

and once you've got a group, an hour spent with a can of paint will make them all match. They also fold up (duh) and store away neatly.

Don't be limited by preconceived ideas of what a dining room chair (shiny wood with red velvet upholstery) or dinette chair (marbleized vinyl with sparkling chrome legs) should look like. *Any* chair of a standard height will do (though most people find it easier to eat from chairs that have no arms.) How about half a dozen of those old dark-green vinyl-and-brushed-aluminum office chairs? They'd look swell around a table.

Fortunately, a table and chairs is about all you need for the dining room. If you have the room to put it and the luck to find it, you could add a sideboard. Just the place to display your fab dishes. The hostess-with-the-mostest might also investigate a serving trolley or tea cart—

> ## JUST WHAT IS FORMICA ANYWAY?
>
> **F**ormica was the trademarked name of "laminated thermosetting plastic" made by the Formica Company of Cincinnati, Ohio. The tremendous popularity of the product in the 1950s bestowed upon Formica the highest marketing honor: generic status. Formica is a thin, squished-together sandwich of plastic and paper—$\frac{1}{16}$ of an inch thick—eight sheets of resin-soaked paper, one sheet of metal foil (to conduct heat away from the surface), and a clear armor coating on top. These layers are squeezed flat together and permanently fused with heat. Formica was a huge hit. It was attractive, inexpensive, easy to clean, and impervious to boiling water, staining, cracking, and even cigarette burns.

a two- or three-shelved unit on wheels. Imagine your guests' delight when you wheel in the cake and after-dinner coffee from the kitchen! (For full effect, be sure to wear a tiny taffeta hostess apron.)

DINING BY CANDLELIGHT

Even if you're not a mushy sentimental fool, every home should have candles. They are so useful when the power goes out, for dripping on people at orgies (I saw this in a movie once), for home shrines, for. . . gosh, loads of stuff! And they make any humble meal of macaroni and cheese a romantic occasion.

The thrifts have a fine selection of candleholders in a variety of shapes, widths, heights, colors, and materials. Most are designed to hold a single candle, but wouldn't a tabletop candelabra look stun-

The Un-candle: What could be less traditional than the Un-candle? Technically, a "wet candle"—you lit a floating wick in a cocktail of water and vegetable oil. A popular product manufactured by Corning Glass, the Un-candle came in a variety of sizes and shapes, some suitable "for even the most elegant tables," and was available during the Un-Decade (the 1970s). The thrift store is now the only place to score some Un-candles.
PHOTO BY VANESSA DOMICO

ning! Sometimes they're paired, sometimes they're not. Consider how interesting your table might look set with a variety of different candleholders of varying heights and widths. You could pick a material—say, wood—and thrift an attractive batch of unique wooden candleholders. Or go the nontraditional route and display your candles on attractive saucers, soap dishes, small bowls, or even upturned aluminum Jell-O molds. And don't forget candles! These are a perennial thrift item, most often found in those prepackaged plastic bags. You'll never want for wax again.

DINING ROOM LINEN

The linens sections is often overlooked in the thrifts, and yet it holds so many delights for your dining area. A tablecloth is by far the easiest way to disguise an ugly table. Most tablecloths are made of cotton. Some cheap ones are made of polyester, expensive ones are made of linen, and older ones may be made from rayon or rayon/cotton blends. The fabric will most likely not be identified by any tag, but remember nearly all tablecloths are designed to go right into the washer! (Do be careful if something looks really old and fragile or has lots of delicate embroidery—the washer may be too violent for it. Rinse it in the sink by hand.)

I find so many tablecloths in great shape. I bet many are given as gifts and never used. Nice tablecloths like a linen one with hand-

TIP "I'm having an outdoor dinner party and I'd like to use a tablecloth to cover up my rancid old picnic table, but we're having Chesapeake crabs, watermelon, and a blueberry-pie-eating contest and it's gonna be a mess . . ." Of course, there are vinyl-covered tablecloths (nearly all in a red-checkered Italian restaurant pattern), but perhaps this is the time to dig out that cool black and white op-art shower curtain you thrifted and never got around to using? Cut to fit just under the picnic table—thumbtack in place, eat, and hose down later.

stitched edging work may have been kept for special occasions and hence rarely used. However fantastic it is to find a pristine tablecloth with rich colors, I never overlook those with more wear. I'm not bothered by small stains (#1 culprit: coffee). After all, it *is* a tablecloth! It's designed to be stained. If the price is right and I like the pattern, I'll buy 'em. It's very probable that when you use them, a plate or bowl will be covering the small stain anyway. Less than perfect tablecloths that still have a great look are perfect for everyday use. You'll end up spilling on them yourself anyway. Like the generations before us, you can save the "good" tablecloth for company.

> **HINTS FOR HOMEMAKERS**
>
> **R**emember to wash your matching napkins each time you wash your tablecloth, or else your tablecloth ends up fading earlier.

It's rare to find the matching napkins with a tablecloth. Not impossible, but uncommon. Mix and match your napkins—use solid colors with patterned tablecloths, patterned napkins with solid tablecloths, choose a single color like pink and hunt down six different but equally lovely pink napkins—or give up and use those extra paper napkins you picked up at Taco Bell.

What to do with those linens that aren't in perfect shape? Maybe you got that swell tablecloth home and unfolded it completely only to find a sizable hole or stain. Or you up-ended the espresso cup on that creamy linen. Maybe you don't even have a table, but you like the look of a tablecloth? Stop thinking "tablecloth" and start thinking *fabric*. Most tablecloths are a good-sized piece of yardage and a very cheap way of acquiring fabric. (You might get six yards of tablecloth linen for a couple bucks—cheap linen in a yardage store starts at about $15 a yard! Even cheap cotton is $4 a yard.)

If you can sew (or can talk somebody who can sew into it . . .), a good-sized tablecloth can yield a small dress, skirt, or shirt (depending on your size). Even allowing for cutting around stained or torn areas, you can salvage enough material to make an article of clothing. You will need to be careful working with patterns (even damask patterns) to keep images aligned. Maybe you're no sewing whiz, but you had Home Ec once and can sew a straight line? A tablecloth can be turned into pillow shams, a drawstring

Former tablecloth masquerading as pillow slips
PHOTO BY VANESSA DOMICO

PLACE MAT PARTY PLANNER
Collect a dozen of those souvenir photograph place mats, each from a different tourist trap. An instant icebreaker at any dinner party when guests comment on which scene (Niagara Falls, Great Smoky Mountains, San Francisco cable cars) they got. Really inventive dinner-givers might use them as place cards. Tell your guests to sit at the place that best defines them, the place they want to go, the place they've already been to, etc. You've got a lively party already and nobody's even sat down yet!

PHOTO BY AUTHOR

laundry bag, small curtains (perfect for the kitchen or bathroom), kitchen towels, or napkins. Still too troublesome for you? If the tablecloth's too ruined to give back to the thrift, you can always put it in the doghouse or cut it up for rags. It's nice soft cotton and ideal for dusting all those fragile tchotchkes.

Place Mats

Some diners prefer place mats to tablecloths. The thrifts have plenty to choose from once you discover where they've stuck them. Some thrifts hang them up near the aprons or tablecloths; others stack 'em near the dishes or even in the bric-a-brac section. You'll find more diversity in material here than with tablecloths—cloth, quilted cloth, cork, raffia, vinyl-coated fabric, and plastic. Again, you may or may not find a matched set, but use your imagination.

ON BEYOND THRIFTING PROFILE NO. 3

Who: Nick Fetterick, Furnishings Manager for Dallas-based restaurant chain Uncle Julio's/Rio Grande Cafe
Thrifting Origins: Nick started thrifting in high school when he was involved in student theater and had to provide his own costumes.

• • •

Hey, hardcore thrifters! Imagine being paid to thrift! Spending hours rooting through thrift stores unearthing cool stuff, amassing it in a gigantic warehouse, and then using all the wacky stuff you bought to decorate! Sounds like a job that exists only in your fantasies? Take heart—this job *does* exist, and Nick's got it! He works for a Tex-Mex border-style restaurant chain and rounds up its decor from thrifts and secondhand markets all over Texas.

Because the restaurant theme is a Tex-Mex home, all sorts of merchandise is eligible for purchase and placement. "I work with the interior designer. We'll go over the plans together to recreate a Tex-Mex border home. We'll go through each room . . . one room is the kitchen, another the living room, a library. The designer might say, 'We need some kitchen items here, we'll need some flat things for the walls there.' I'll throw out ideas about what things I think might work. Pretty much anything vintage from the 1920s through 1950s can be used. Folk art pieces. *Lots* of thrift art. We just come up with a general idea and then I start buying the stuff wherever I can find it." It takes *thousands* of items to decorate one restaurant. "The stuff goes on walls, shelves, everywhere! The restaurants just suck up material!"

After sketching out the rough plan, Nick hits the road, traveling mostly in a big circle around Dallas. "I can drive as many as two to three hundred miles a day." He hits some flea markets, junk stores, estate sales, and garage sales but says thrift shops are probably the best place to get the things. "I have a budget and the corporation likes me to get as much as I can for the least amount of money, so thrift stores fit the bill. I'll always find something at a thrift shop that we can use." Nick does look everywhere. "You never know what you're going to find where. That's the fun part of the job." Or sometimes not! Nick was once bitten by a poisonous spider while poking around a barn full of junk and spent four days sick in bed. The upside? "There was some stuff from that old barn that I bought and we used in various restaurant remodels."

The job has given Nick a perfect outlet for the Number One problem many thrifters face: buying way more stuff than they can ever feasibly use. "Before I'd go into a thrift store and buy some cool funky things and they'd sit in my closet. Now when I buy those things, they'll be used in a restaurant. The stuff definitely gets a second life and it's still being used for what it was designed for, as decor." It's a great form of recycling, says Nick. "Even when we remove stuff from restaurants, it's usually rotated to another restaurant or stored for an upcoming one."

And it's not just buying loads of cool stuff—he gets to do the decorating, too! "I love pulling the stuff from the warehouse and then throwing it on the walls, and sometimes we literally just put it anywhere on the walls. It has to look sort of kitschy, and that in itself is a talent, but I have sort of weird taste."

Nick knows that Dallas is a pretty competitive thrift market, especially for the sorts of items he's buying. "There are supply stores where you can buy decorations that are new and they're made to look old but it's expensive and it just doesn't have that authentic feel to it. If I buy something from a thrift store, at some point it *was* in someone's home. You bring that karma from the home and transfer to the restaurant." And unlike less-scrupulous picker-types, Nick does not prearrange set-asides with the thrift stores. "I figure if I miss something in the thrift store, well, there's another thrift store where I can buy something just as cool. That's part of the fun. It would turn into a drudgery if I went around and said, 'Hold all this stuff for me' and then had to make regular rounds to pick everything up. The coincidence and synchronicity of finding the perfect decoration is half the fun, and really, there is plenty of stuff to go around."

Nick couldn't be happier that he's converted his thrifting mania into a career. It's a job he loves, but he knows others groove on his thrift skills as well. "It's a pretty neat feeling to walk into a place after I've decorated it. I was waiting in the restaurant once and I saw a father come in carrying a child. They stopped and pointed to a lot of the signs and animals hung on the wall and the father was telling the kid about the decorations. I thought, 'Wow, here I bought this stuff and put it up there, and it's made such an impact that this father's taking his little son around to show him all the items on the wall.' It was fun to see someone look at something I've done and appreciate it."

• • •

11 The Bar Area

ANYONE FOR COCKTAILS?

With so much barware available in the thrifts, you should prepare and serve drinks with the intended equipment and specific glassware. Here's the minimum you will need:

For Measuring: A teaspoon and a tablespoon (get the measuring kind, not just any old spoon, which can be inaccurate). Thrift a large shot glass that lists measurements in half ounces.

For Mixing: A cocktail shaker with top. (Having trouble getting that metal lid off? Run the lid under hot water. If that fails, try a little penetrating oil.) Shakers without lids can be used for preparing cocktails that only need stirring. They're also swell for storing your swizzle sticks. Have a bowl or bucket handy for ice. Don't forget the strainer.

For Fussing with Ingredients: Bottle and can openers, lemon/lime squeezer (this is not your hand, it's a metal vise thing), a paring knife for making peel bits, and toothpicks for olives and onions.

For Serving: Bar towel, tray, coasters, napkins, straws, and swizzle sticks.

For *Really* Mixing It Up: Ice crusher and blender. Dedicated tropical drink kings should seek out a juicer.

PHOTO BY VANESSA DOMICO

And Finally, for Drinking: A bar guide will instruct you as to which drink belongs in which glass, but any good home barkeep has the four basic glasses: an old-fashioned glass, a highball glass, and—the two pieces of stemware—a wine glass and a cocktail glass. (The stem keeps the drinker's warm hands away from the perfectly chilled drink.) Since glasses are so gosh-darn cheap in the thrifts, fill up your home bar with specialized glassware—champagne flutes, beer mugs, liqueur glasses, shot glasses, pilsner glasses, brandy snifters, and sherry glasses. Too bad you can't thrift the booze . . .

Mixology—The Lost Science

Time was when every gentleman could be expected to whip up elaborate cocktails on demand for guests. Should he not know how to mix a "Ward 8" or a "Millionaire No. 2," he consulted his handy bar guide. No aspiring mixologist should be without one. Nor should any established mixologist be dissuaded from purchasing several bar guides. Bar guides were often issued by feuding famous bartenders, and they feature ever-so-slight variations on cocktails. As any mixologist knows, it's the barely perceptible variations that distinguish a perfect cocktail from a merely acceptable one. Like any science, the practitioner must continue to research and experiment. Fortunately, a lot of bar guides go to the thrifts.

WHATEVER HAPPENED TO "FUN" DRINKING?

Drinking alcohol to excess is no longer considered funny. I am fascinated by the fact that such behavior *used* to be considered hilarious. A huge cultural shift since the 1970s has changed the way our society views drinking. Once there was no shortage of drinking paraphernalia to suggest how fun excessive drinking was or how amusing blotto people were. The jokey drunk merchandise has now been relegated to odd venues like mail-order catalogs that sell stuff-that-time-forgot, or low-class items like those tacky T-shirts you can buy on Spring Break ("Jack Daniels Field Tester"). But the "dregs" of this previous culture are still available at the thrifts. Joke liquor items are often found in good shape (many are undoubtedly unappreciated gifts). Sure, you can mix up Manhattans with plain barware, but why not have the crazy stuff on hand to remind you of the fun you're meant to be having? All the accouterments listed below can also be enjoyed with any non-alcoholic liquid.

Mixing: Look for a cocktail shaker with cartoony jokes. I've got one with a bunch of drunk firemen hanging off a racing fire engine. Not sure exactly what it's meant to convey, but it *seems* fun! Stirring should be done with naughty swizzle sticks, like the naked drunk girl tumbling into your glass "bottoms up"!

Booze dispensers: Make drinking more fun by having it dispensed in some hilarious fashion. There are two in my collection: the bowling ball that spews drink and the IV drip. Another common "howler" is the little-boy-peeing-booze-into-a-glass dispenser.

The swizzle stick is called "Harry Hangover."
PHOTO BY VANESSA DOMICO

Decor: Look for bar lamps—the classic is the drunk clinging for dear life to the lamppost—and funny wall plaques ("A camel can go 8 days without a drink, but who wants to be a camel?").

Other drinking humor can be found on glasses, shot glasses, coasters, snack trays, drink trays, ashtrays, ice buckets, and cocktail napkins—"That last drink made a new man of me. Get that new man a drink." And check the linens section for jokey bar towels and aprons. These items suggest only a few problems associated with overconsuming, and you'll note that most are temporary and all are

---

COMMON FUN DRINKING MOTIFS

- **Pink elephants**
- **Images of prone or crawling drunks**
- **Women with mussed hair and dresses slipping off**
- **People *in* drinking glasses**
- ***X*s for eyes, popping bubbles around the head, and tongue lagging out**

Here's a weird transitional piece. Funny, but this is pretty black humor. The glass lists many ills of the 1970s—generation gap, drugs, litter, overpopulation, famine, discrimination, etc.—in stark black and white text. Around the top of the glass in red, it says, "Drink for a Reason."
PHOTO BY VANESSA DOMICO

considered amusing—falling down, driving erratically, losing your wallet, hat, tie, or keys, being too drunk to open your car or house door, mistaking your wife for a good-looking woman, forgetting to go home, speaking in an amusing fashion with law enforcement officers, hugging lampposts, wearing lampshades, and singing loudly. Of course, the Number One Problem—The Hangover—was never forgotten, but there were no end of suggested cures, most involving another drink.

Some Guidebooks for Fun Drinking

Ed McMahon's Barside Companion (1969): Penned by the "celebrated elbow-bender of Television Row," this book covers "the gentlemanly art of drinking." Essentially a guide on how to *be* a fun drunk—tricks and games you can play with your glass, the ice cubes, the straw, the olive toothpick, cigarettes, and coins. Sample chapter heading: ".003 Isn't Much, But It's a Start!"

Here's How! A Round-the-World Bar Guide by Lawrence Blochman and Members of the Overseas Press Club (1957): I lived in Press Town U.S.A. (Washington D.C.), and the consensus is old-time press guys *do* know the best bars and drinks! Let the book tell you why: "The foreign correspondent knows that certain well-known and well-frequented bars of the world's capitals are far better news sources than the anterooms of the world's chancelleries."[1] Best drink names: No Comment and Foreign Office Pick Up.

Cheers! An Informative and Entertaining Guide Through the Intoxicating World of Liquor by James Collier (1960): A semi-seri-

---

THE BY-LINE COCKTAIL FROM *HERE'S HOW!*

2 parts cognac
2 parts sloe gin

Stir with ice, strain and serve with a twist of lemon peel.
As every newsman knows, a by-line is reserved for the elite and should be given sparingly. The same applies to the cocktail.[2]

ous attempt to discuss alcohol, its social history, and physical effects, but any seriousness is belied by chapter titles like "The Martini and Other Friends" and "How to Appear Sober When You're Not!" Suggested Happy Hour intake: 4 cocktails, a dozen cigarettes, and some salted peanuts. Go easy on those peanuts, they're fattening.

PHRASES TO KNOW
Say when
Fill 'er up
Thanks, I *will* have another
One for the road
Just one more
Bottoms up
Bartender!

ACCESSORIES FOR SMOKERS OR NONSMOKERS

You can't convince anyone anymore that smoking is glamorous, except impressionable fifteen-year-olds who wonder what cool place it is Joe Camel does hang out. But smoking *used* to be glamorous! Sophisticated, fun, even good for you (it reputedly aided the digestion, slimmed the figure, and calmed the nerves). But as any child can tell you, now cigarette smoking gets some of the worst press around. The health of the nation notwithstanding, the upside of the smoking downswing is that the thrifts are filled with the discarded accouterments of cigarette-happy days. You hardly have to be a smoker to enjoy some of the leftover glamor. Most smoking accessories are priced very cheaply, mainly because of their great availability and consumers' lack of interest in them. Contemporary smokers don't want fussy things like refillable lighters and cigarette cases.

The Humble Ashtray

Thrifts are stocked with an endless variety of ashtrays. Immediately disregard the dull, plain ones—the clear glass, the cheap plastic, and the colored aluminum. There's too many cool ashtrays out there to waste time on blah items. Decide whether you need a handful of small ones (pick a theme, shape, color, or style) or a gigantic twenty-smoker coffee table model. Most ashtray stands take a standard shape ashtray, so don't sweat it if the ashtray is missing. Look for promotional ashtrays from a variety of restaurants, nightclubs, bars, hotels, motels, gas stations, businesses, and even hospitals. They are an easy and cheap source of genuine American retro-charm. Some have the best 1950s outer space googie graphics and great slogans ("Orbit Motel—Easy to Find, Hard to Leave"). Older ashtrays are easily identified by having the fewer-than-seven-digit phone numbers or phone numbers that include letters.

If You Smoke: Any smoker knows you can never have too many ashtrays. Stock up at 50 cents each and puff away! You'll enjoy that smoke more if you're using a pink and black '50s boomerang ashtray rather than that cheap glass ashtray you lifted from the Happy Hour bar.

If You Don't Smoke: An ashtray is a basic utilitarian shape. They are perfect for holding soap, paper clips, candy, small snacks, marbles, keys, thumbtacks, pins, nails, screws, bobby pins, earrings, etc. Any small thing prone to rolling around and getting lost is happier in an ashtray.

May I Offer You a Light?

Why even deal with those horrible cheap plastic disposable lighters? It's certainly more economical to thrift one good lighter and get a tin of lighter fluid. You will also keep disposable lighters out of the landfills. These days it's *easier* to operate an old lighter—the new childproof disposals require mechanical engineers to get a flame out of them. Lighters didn't used to be the generic plastic things we have today, they were carefully selected to reflect the owner's personality and style. Why should you settle for anything less?

A "hippie-style" fake Zippo, a promotional lighter from The Tender Trap, and a matched set of ladies' smoking accessories—lighter and cigarette case.
PHOTO BY VANESSA DOMICO

Most lighters won't work in the thrift store (even if they let you test it) because there is no fluid in them and/or they need new flints. When examining a lighter, eyeball it to see what kind of shape it's in—it shouldn't be cracked, and the lighting mechanism should look intact and not all twisted up. Flints and fluids are very easy to replace. (I've seen so many great old lighters sold for pennies because "they don't work," when all they needed was fluid or flint).

Most of the lighters for sale are men's lighters. They are larger, heavier, and tend to have "manly" designs (geometrics, company insignias, etched deer horns.) Ladies' lighters are generally long and slim and may have a more feminine look, like a metal brocade overlay. You see the occasional odd ladies' combo-lighters—a lipstick holder with a lighter or lighter on a necklace. Why are there fewer ladies' lighters? Men smoked more than women. Also, men were

Tabletop lighters are not as common as pocket lighters. They are so out-of-date that I've seen shoppers mystified by them in the thrifts, wondering what on earth they were. The tabletop models were big—but hopefully attractively designed—lighters that sat in the middle of the coffee table. I've seen some so enormous that they require two hands to operate. They hold a lot of fluid, and they ensure that everyone will have a guaranteed light throughout the party.

the recipients of those promotional lighters. Or was it simply that a woman knew some chivalrous man would always dash forward to light her cigarette? Naturally, there's no difference in the function between lighter sexes, so buy the one you like the look of.

If You Smoke: Travel in style! Keep plenty of flints and lighter fluid on hand. Never leave the house without one or two of your best lighters. Match them to your outfits and occasions—a sleek silvertone for drinks with the boss or a promotional nightclub lighter for a swingin' scene. Show your class by snapping open your flame the instant you see a smoker fumbling for a light.

If You Don't Smoke: You can still be a help to other smokers, even if you don't smoke yourself. If smoking is anathema to you, remember that a lighter is just a contained flame and can be useful around the house in place of matches. Lighters are cute little *objets*. Stash a couple on a shelf and marvel at how nicely designed the most basic things used to be.

Pocket Cigarette Cases

The cigarette case is a lost item, as is the art of gracefully snapping open your sleek little case to offer a cigarette. Cases protected your cigarettes from getting crushed before the hard cardboard pack had been developed. Like lighters, cigarette cases were designed by gender, though many abstract patterns are unisex.

If You Smoke: These are still available at the thrifts (and screening a few old movies will instruct you in technique). Most only hold about ten cigarettes (so if you're a heavy-duty smoker you'll need to carry refills), and many were designed to hold filterless cigarettes and are too short for today's smokes.

If You Don't Smoke: Most cigarette cases have a springloaded internal arm, which makes them ideal for carrying small flat loose things like business cards, stamps, odd scraps of paper, a few tissues, etc.

Cigarette Boxes and Dispensers

Nice homes had pretty little boxes for keeping cigarettes. One might have had several around the house, but certainly there was one on the coffee table for guests to draw from. Even though the box may be shaped just like the cigarette packet, you should remove the cigarettes from the packet and store them loose. Not as commonly found, but way cool, are mechanical cigarette dispensers.

PHOTO BY VANESSA DOMICO

While the Cold War was still on, I bought this cigarette dispenser/music box at a Maryland flea market for $3. When the "books" are opened, the cigarettes are displayed while a waltz plays. The lettering is Russian and, loosely translated, the books commemorate the Soviet space flights of 1957, 1961, and 1966. A truly odd piece, it has no markings whatsoever. While it's pure capitalist kitsch, I can't imagine an American manufacturer making such an item at the height of the Space Race and Cold War. Some recent books on Soviet Space Race memorabilia at least confirmed that the Russians did in fact produce their own share of kitsch items related to space exploration (e.g. Sputnik toothpaste), but this item's provenance remains unknown to me.

If You Smoke: Your guests will be impressed when you proffer a cute little tabletop box and invite them to extract a cigarette. It's certainly classier than just leaving the paper pack lying around. Beware of older boxes and dispensers that held unfiltered cigarettes: the storage area will be too short to hold today's filter-tipped cigarettes.

If You Don't Smoke: If they're the basic box design, they can hold anything small—earrings, cuff links, keys, etc.

For total smoking enjoyment, men will want to thrift a smoking jacket. A smoking jacket is usually styled like a bathrobe but hangs only as far as the upper thigh. They are fussier than bathrobes (dare I say more feminine?) and often made from colorful Oriental-style fabrics with grosgrain lapels and tasseled belts. Others are cut closer to a blazer but are no less ornate. Store your smoking jacket in the Manly Den (see chapter 7).

12 The Library

Most thrifts stock a selection of books as lively, if not more so, as any bookstore. Everything from the world's most popular books (The Bible, *The Guinness Book of World Records*, *The Firm*), to the most misguided and unappreciated publishing venture. The stock is kept in flux by the disposable nature of books. There are book hoarders (and I'm one of them) who must agonize for years whether to throw a book out, but most book readers return a fair number of their books to the marketplace. Whether you hoard or dispose, thrifting books is good for all. Bibliophiles will amass gigantic collections for mere pennies; read-and-move-on types will appreciate the low-budget, almost rental quality of thrift book-shopping—buy cheaply, read, and return to thrift.

There are so many books in thrifts that I'll leave it up to you to pick out what you want. Nonetheless, here are some thoughts on perennial thrift books, some book-buying schemes you may not have thought of, and some other suggestions for your home library.

WHERE DO I PUT ALL MY BOOKS?!

Shelves are rarely for sale at the thrifts. They're too useful to everybody and don't get donated as often. And, unlike a chair, they don't really go out of style. A shelf is a shelf, and usually, if stuff is piled on it, you can't see the "style" anyway. They're so handy that when shelves *do* come into the thrift, the thrifts keep 'em and use 'em. I need shelves in my life more than anything else! Why can't the thrifts institute some kind of Frequent Buyer Policy, where if you buy, say, five hundred books (which I can do easily), you get a free shelf?

Even a small shelf is better than no shelf. Shelves designed to hold videotapes are a nice size. Bathroom wall shelves also work. They don't hold many books, but you can get a *lot* of little shelves and they'll fit in odd wall spaces. Often stashed under piles in thrift stores are these little metal V-shaped racks that sit about two to three inches off the floor. They can hold one or two dozen books, have the advantage of mobility, and fit in hard-to-use areas such as under chairs and behind doors. Keep them out of the way of foot traffic though; they are very painful to walk into.

BOOK PRICES MAY VARY

One of the most inconsistent areas of thrift-store pricing is books. The identical paperback book in different thrifts (or in the same thrift, but on different days!) may be priced anywhere from 25 cents to $3.50. Let's look at the various book pricing structures used by most thrifts and sort out the advantages and disadvantages of each.

Flat Price: The simplest pricing scheme. All books are 99 cents. Besides the obvious ease of this system for both store clerks and customers, the big plus is snapping up expensive hardcovers such as photographic art books for 99 cents. The downside is that 99 cents might be a bit too much to pick up a book on a whim—kooky subject matter or flashy cover—when you know you'll never read it.

Individually Marked: Here you're at the mercy of the store employee who priced the book. Does your value system match his? Generally speaking (and is it ever hard to make generalizations about thrift-store pricing!), the more recent and the larger the book, the more expensively it will be marked. So this might not be the store in which to pick up the new Michael Crichton paperback at $2.50, but a lovely old hardcover of *Great Expectations* or a 1950s decorating guide might only be a quarter.

Based on Original Price: This is by far the trickiest pricing structure. And to complicate book buying further, this pricing scheme usually only applies to the paperback books! The theory is that the most recent (and we can assume most coveted) book will have the higher cover price and the thrift will reap a larger profit, secure in its conviction that the book is contemporary enough to be desired.

This system has several flaws:

1. The newness and costliness of a book don't necessarily equal desirability.

2. It is not unusual to find several copies of the same book—say a popular mystery like Agatha Christie's *Murder on the Orient Express*. Since this book has been consistently published over sixty years, thrift prices will vary. Based on one thrift's sliding scale, a copy of *Murder on the Orient Express* from the 1940s, 1950s, or 1960s will cost a quarter; the 1970s, 45 cents; the 1980s, 95 cents; and a current paperback version, $1.45. Talk about shifting value—just what is this work worth?

3. Checkout is a nightmare. Whoever thought up this pricing system obviously never consulted with the clerks who have to negotiate it! Each book must be inspected and fumbled about while the clerk seeks the original price. Remember, the prices on books are printed very small and in strange places. Once the clerk finds the price, she must then look it up on the chart and punch in the corresponding thrift price.

4. When paperbacks were first introduced in the 1940s, most did not list a cover price. A paperback cost 25 cents and everybody knew that. Paperbacks remain so priced well into the '50s. Try taking one of those paperbacks up to the counter for checkout pricing. After an excruciating minute, while you watch the clerk turn the book around and around, you helpfully say, "Uh, the book price is 25 cents." "Oh no dear," she says, "the price is based on the cover price." "I know that," you say. "The book used to cost 25 cents." "Oh, do you see the price on here?"—as she hands you the book and hopes that you'll point it out. "No, the price isn't listed on the book—it's just that they *all* used to cost 25 cents."

Proceed to:

Ending A: An obliging or could-care-less clerk who rings up the book at the 25 cent rate.

Ending B: A rule-happy clerk who takes the book away from you and says, "We can't sell this if it doesn't have a price."

Ending C: A cautious clerk who gets a manager for a price check. The entire looking-for-price scenario is repeated with the manager, who then either does A or B.

   As someone who is apt to buy a dozen books at a time, I can only stand by baffled at this curious pricing procedure. There are two advantages to this system, though. If you like to buy old paperbacks—to read or just groove on the outrageous covers—they're a bargain at the cheapest rate. (Ironically, of all the paperbacks a thrift might have, these are where the high-priced "collectibles" are. Most thrifts remain oblivious to the pulp paperback collectibles market.) Also, for a perennially published book, you can select the *oldest* copy on the shelves and pay less.

LOOKING FORWARD TO READING LAST YEAR'S BESTSELLER!

I like a good four-hundred-page legal thriller or Hollywood rags-to-riches story as much as the next person, but I never ever buy the big "beach books" new! It's one of the few thrifting guarantees. If a book sells a gazillion copies, generally twelve to eighteen months after the everybody-is-reading-it time, the thrifts fill up with multiple copies.

   PRO: Considerable savings. Compare 50 cents to $6.95. For 50 cents, the book is just as thrilling.

   PRO: After spending over $7 for a book, you might feel obligated to keep it around for a while. These books are thick and take up valuable shelf space. However, the used copy is easy to ditch back at the thrift once you get your 50 cents' worth.

   CON: You have to wait till everybody else is done reading it.

   CON: People keep asking you if you've read it.

   PRO: You're spared the idiotic water-cooler conversation about this year's hit book. By the time you get around to reading it, nobody wants to talk about it any more.

   CON: In the babble surrounding the book *du jour*, you might overhear key plot elements.

   PRO: Not to worry. It'll be another year till you actually read the book and you're apt to forget some plot twist of a book you haven't even read. And with many of these books, it is already startlingly obvious what is going to happen anyway. Oh, the upstart young lawyer with a conscience wins the case?

BIOGRAPHIES OF THE FAMOUS AND NOT-SO-FAMOUS

No famous person has truly "arrived" without at least one biography (or autobiography). It hardly matters anymore whether the individual actually accomplished anything real or did anything interesting—the hackneyed "fifteen minutes of fame" is the only

---

WE CAN'T QUITE GET A HANDLE ON THESE PEOPLE . . .

Some celebrities shift into a very special class of biography when even a dozen books can't answer the question "Who Was He/She?" Multiple biographies of the following people are readily available in any thrift and will need their own shelf:

- Marilyn Monroe

- Elvis Presley

- Richard M. Nixon

- Her former Royal Highness, Diana, Princess of Wales

- John F. Kennedy (and related conspiracy books)

- O. J. Simpson (and related trial books)

- New Kids on the Block

---

prerequisite. And since quickie bios and fringe bios have a very short shelf life in a real bookstore, the thrift store is the best place to find them. A shelf of celebrity bios is a nice "literary" addition to any pop-culture home. With books like *Emcee Monty Hall* and *Vanna Speaks*, you can quickly put together a shelf that's the literary equivalent of the Hollywood Squares. Don't overlook compilation bios either. There may not be enough material on one individual to merit a biography, but several lesser people can be totaled up to equal an impressive biographical work like *Rock Star Wives*.

Way out past the celebrities and semicelebrities are the hangers-on. These are the former friends, the assistant press agents, the woman who lived next door to the serial killer, the bodyguard, or the I-promised-I-wouldn't-tell one-night-standee. We are waaay out on the edge of the media event, but I personally like the views you get out here. Thank goodness people do have the chutzpah to cash in on their quickie minutes of fame and dash out autobiographies. Without their foresight, these tiny, oh so tiny, pieces of history would be lost forever.

APPEARING ERUDITE IN JUST <u>MINUTES!</u>—THE INSTANT CLASSICS LIBRARY

I'm shallow, I admit it. I'm prone to making snap judgments about people based on the objects they choose to surround themselves with. If I visit your pad, the first place I'll check is your bookshelf.

And listen, buddy, just because all I read anymore is trash, that doesn't mean I don't know a "good book" when I see one!

But who has time to read anymore? And it seems *especially* hard to make time to read something like *The Portrait of a Lady*. In the thrifts sits the entire canon, and then some, of the World's Great Literature—Greek tragedies, cryptic Middle English, poetry, Shakespeare, French restoration comedies, sprawling Victorian novels, the complete works of Herman Melville . . . and priced to move! The thrift may mark up last year's Scott Turow thriller, but eight hundred paperback pages of *Vanity Fair* is some bargain at 50 cents.

It's not only which works you have (though a well-rounded collection is a plus), it's the *shape* they're in. Specifically, do the books show signs of having been read, *vigorously* read—dog-eared pages, coffee stains, and taped-over cover tear? The book's spine should show evidence that *every* page was turned and read. (Next time you're in the thrift, take a look at some forlorn classics regularly assigned to high school seniors, you'll see spine wear and margin notes that only extend to the third chapter.) You need to foster only the *illusion* of having read the classics, not actually pore over them yourself. The chances are slim to nil that any visitor will ask you about your Thomas Hardy shelf. If queried, say the book is "one of my favorites" or "an amazing work."

You can also build equally impressive libraries of historical, sociological, political, and cultural works or some other substratum of higher learning. Don't go overboard by thrifting every subject—create the impression that you have an "area of interest." Hard science books are not as widely published, and if visitors see too many, they may ask you to explain something quantitatively like how come frogs don't drown. It's easier to stick to the more subjective arts-and-letters disciplines. Remember, there is no right answer to whether Milton was a great poet. That's only someone's interpretation and it's open to discussion.

You say it seems unethical or wrong to cram your shelves with classics you haven't read? Not at all. Who's to say you won't get around to reading them one day? Certainly, purchasing them first is a step in the right direction. Second, if you do not draw attention to this shelf and yet a shallow visitor such as myself makes the assumption that you have indeed read these books, is that *your* fault? I think not.

Instant Classic Library on the Go

Pick up a classic work for 50 cents and carry it around with you. Don't be too hip. No pretending to read while walking down the street or sticking it in your blazer pocket. Stash it discreetly in your briefcase or knapsack. Ironically, modern life is so wearisome that while waiting for the bus, stuck in a traffic jam, or bored to death over lunchtime Big Macs, you may actually end up reading it.

SHOPPING FOR THE CLASSICS: SOME TIPS

- Many paperback houses (Penguin, Bantam, Signet, Dover) have been publishing budget versions of the classics for years. Most editions are conveniently labeled "classics."

- Learn to recognize the spines of the highbrow houses. Anything that says "University of Such-and-Such Press" is a good tip-off.

- The King James Version is the "classic" Bible; *Good News for Modern Man* is the latter-day "travesty." A Bible in Greek or Latin is overdoing it.

- Any paperback with a cover featuring a Greek or Roman statue, an oil portrait of some long-dead nobleman, a watercolor of the market square, or an old map is probably a "classic" work.

- Cliff's Notes are not now, nor have they ever been, "classics," or considered acceptable substitutes for classics. If you must buy them, keep them under your bed.

WHY THERE ARE <u>HARDLY</u> <u>ANY</u> ROMANCE NOVELS IN THRIFT STORES

Ahhh, love . . . if you can't be in it, why not just read about it? I bet there isn't a thrift around that doesn't have at least three dozen romance novels sitting on the shelves, and most probably have tens of dozens. You know which books I mean—the slim numbered series, often referred to by an incorrect generic term, "Harlequin romances." The correct term is "romance fiction." In truth, I'd never paid any attention to romance novels before except to curse their presence and skip over them while looking for other books. But there are too many in the thrifts to ignore, and once I started investigating, I grew quite fascinated with them.

The granddaddy of all romance novels is Harlequin Enterprises, a Canadian company. Since 1964, it has published only romance novels. Harlequin thought up the contemporary narrative formula, packaging, and distribution of romance novels, and other publishers have paid Harlequin the highest business compliment by dashing right out and imitating it. The omnipresence of romance novels that we know today is attributed to one man, W. Lawrence Heisey, a former Proctor and Gamble salesman. It was his genius to emphasize the *brand name* of the book over the title or author. He also gave the books an identical look—a shopper can instantly recognize a Harlequin by the smallest bit of spine.

Early on, Harlequin isolated a preexisting and very viable group of consumers—avid women readers—and conducted extensive research to find out what they wanted to read. Once pinpointed, the product was developed and delivered cheaply and easily through everyday convenient places like supermarkets, drugstores, and mail order subscription. Bingo! The books sold and sold and sold. In 1990 alone, Harlequin sold 194 million books.[1]

Because they are replaced monthly, the books have a short retail shelf life. Harlequin employs about a thousand writers generating sixty new novels a month.[2] Why publish so many? Look at these numbers from a 1981 study of romance readers: 33 percent of the women read five to nine romance novels a week! Another 55 percent read one to four a week.[3] That's anywhere from 52 to 468 per year per reader for 88 percent of romance novel readers! The reader at the high end of that equation is actually reading forty novels a month.

The more I researched romance novels, the more stunned I was at the disparity between this gigantic, profitable market and the way most media and popular culture sources utterly disregard it. (The one exception is academia, where several studies of romance fiction and its readers have been published.) In 1992, romance fiction accounted for 35 percent of *all* paperbacks sold![4] I'm a sucker for the underdog. And while in a financial sense, romance novels do just fine, they are ignored, sneered at, and not allowed to play in the yard with the popular kids. People are snobby about them. They turn up their noses in disgust at formulaic romance fiction—but what about other formulaic crap designed for mass-market entertainment (these books are, after all, presented as entertainment, not as great literature) that gets oodles of attention?

So, now we come back to the original question: "Why are there so many romance novels in the thrifts?" Given the staggering numbers of romance novels published, sold, and read, I say, "Why aren't there *more* in the thrifts!?!" After the math of production and readership, compared to all the existing books (or even just existing romance novels), there really aren't that many at all in thrift stores! I still don't want to read them, and they still get in my way at the thrift, but I now have a new respect for this colossal amount of stuff traveling around seemingly unnoticed in its own orbit. It's like discovering there's a whole other race of people living beneath the city!

I would, though, like to commend the thrift stores that put all these books in one place on the same shelf. It's win-win. Those who are looking for them can go right to the source. Those who are not can book-browse in peace without hitting a romance novel every three books.

JUDGING BOOKS BY THEIR COVERS

Old paperbacks are becoming collectible, but you still have one advantage over the collector. Many of the old paperbacks that show up at the thrifts are in less than perfect condition. Lucky for us, the collector hasn't much interest in books with cracked spines, small tears, flaking on the cover, and a million other sins. You don't have to be so fussy. If it has a visually interesting cover and it's priced to move, get it. It's just a cheap paperback book, not the Gutenberg Bible.

The downside of buying books for the cover is in the display. There's little point in shelving them and then staring at their rather ordinary spines. Prop them up around the house so you can enjoy the art. If you're the handyman type, hammer some rails on the wall so that a whole row of covers can be displayed at once. If you have a lot of books-for-

PHOTO BY BILL O'LEARY

the-covers, rotate the selection every now and then so you and your guests can appreciate them all. I pick a theme for the temporary displays (like women in underwear holding guns or death scene covers featuring pins and needles).

∗TIP∗ After buying a book for the cover, try reading it. Beneath many lurid covers are long-since-forgotten but not-half-bad stories. I've been pleasantly surprised to find a sensitive portrayal of star-crossed love under a garish cover of a man throwing a half-clad woman down the stairs.

13 Bed and Bath

THE BEDROOM

Your body will be just as close to bed linens as clothing, so you'll want to thrift the fabrics you like. Refer back to chapter 5 if you need to brush up on fabrics. Linens must be labeled for content under the Textile Fiber Products Identification Act, but linens manufactured before 1960 may not be labeled or the label may be missing.

Always take a minute to *completely unfold* any bedding before you buy! Check for stains (both sides of a thick, opaque item like a quilt or blanket) and holes. If it's something you really love the look and the price of but it's got a big tear or some other defect, consider using it as a beach or picnic blanket, as a pet bed, or in some other it-will-just-get-dirty-anyway place like the front porch sofa. Also, depending on the size and location of the defect, you may be able to salvage it by cutting it up for curtains or making a king-sized piece of bedding twin size. Unfolding also gives you a good gauge of the size. Some older bedding is not marked "twin" or "queen" and you just have to eyeball it. You'll see that a twin bedspread that's designed to hang down both sides of the twin bed will still be wide enough to cover the top of a full- or queen-sized bed nicely.

Bedding is awkward and heavy to carry around the thrift, so get a cart and put the big blanket in it immediately! I lost the best chenille bedspread I ever saw because I was too lazy to get a cart or to carry it around while I continued to shop. An empty store in a small, very nontrendy town, but it was gone five minutes after I decided not to carry it.

CLOTHING FOR YOUR BED

Sheets

Do you ever notice how many orphaned sheets and pillowcases there are at thrifts? An ideal set should have the bottom sheet, top sheet, and one or two pillowcases. Do people donate one sheet at a time or do they get separated and mixed up in the thrift sorting room? Another odd thing is some thrifts will hang the three pieces separately, one

So far I've only found one pillowcase in this rockin' set of bedsheets.
PHOTO BY VANESSA DOMICO

sheet per hanger, instead of hanging the whole set together. This contributes to the single-sheet problem if a shopper should, for whatever reason, just buy one sheet. If all the parts are hung together, no problem. Common sheets you can buy singly as you see them and put the set together gradually. (If you spend enough time in the linens department, you will come to recognize common sheets.) I'm fond of polka-dotted sheets and will buy them singly. A bed with a pink polka-dot bottom sheet and a green polka-dot top sheet looks rather cool.

TIP All the kookiest sheets are usually children's sheets and twin-sized. If you have a full-sized bed and you can't sleep without Dukes of Hazard or Smurf sheets, consider thrifting four matching twin sheets and sewing them together to make two large sheets.

Most sheets in the thrifts are a polyester/cotton blend. (The selling advantage of the poly blend is, believe it or not, that you don't have to iron the sheets! They don't get as wrinkled in the wash.) Newer sheets will have a tiny label somewhere along the seam if you want to check fabric make-up. With all-cotton sheets, the higher the thread count, the stronger the sheet will be and the softer it will become over time. The Dream Sheets for me are pure linen sheets! Hundreds of dollars new, but one day I will find them! Ironically, a *new* linen sheet is not that comfortable. The fabric can be rough and stiff. But they age beautifully, becoming softer and softer, and they'll outlast any cotton sheet by years.

Blankets

Blankets are made from wool, cotton, synthetics, and various combinations of those three fabrics. Wool blankets are the coziest, but if they're dirty, it's a big chore to wash them! A nice wool blanket in a good color/pattern and in decent shape is a good investment, though—they'll easily outlive cotton and synthetic blankets and they're warmer. Unfortunately, since its invention in the early 1950s, acrylic fiber has dominated the blanket industry. You can get lucky—they do make blankets out of lovely soft wools like cashmere and mohair.

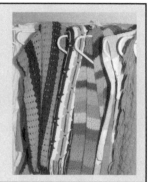

By far the most common item in the linens section is the knitted acrylic yarn afghan in rainbows of colors. I never see anyone buy one. I'm perplexed that there are so many—do people spend weeks making one, then donate it to the thrift? Or do they keep the one they just made and donate the one they made last month? Does Grandma know you ditched it at the thrift?

PHOTO BY AUTHOR

Quilts

I am always mystified that people give quilts to the thrift store. They represent so much work—even the poorly done or less elaborate ones. (Finding quilts may be a factor of where you live. I see lots in the Midwest, but pals in California say they never see them.) Quilts should be checked carefully for torn seams. Quilts are nothing but a mass of seams held together by tiny scraps of fabric. If they're in my price range, I'll buy a quilt with some small tears, especially if it's got an interesting design or is made from old patterned fabric. Some can be repaired (I think about it, but never do it). I don't mind a few small holes or tears—it's part of the quilt's charm. I don't know what bright person started the trend of quilting with double-knit polyester—these quilts look cheap and shabby no matter how carefully somebody sewed them. The plus is that the fabric colors stay bright and they don't tear as easily. But while a cotton quilt can be quite a pleasant covering on a warm summer night, can you imagine being trapped under a polyester quilt in July?

Quilts are where you see some ingenious thrifty sewing. I've seen quilts in the thrifts made from ties, squares of men's wool suiting (probably from a fabric sample book), curtains, upholstery fabric, dish towels, and sheets. When a pal thrifted the most fabulous quilt made from 1940s and 1950s patterned fabric, I seethed with jealousy and decided to retaliate by making my own. (The sewing part took years—I don't even want to talk about it.) The *fun* part was discovering that the linens section of the thrift was the best source of odd bits of cheap old fabric that could be cut up into squares. I bought up '50s cotton aprons (so many unworn!), dish towels, tablecloths, napkins, stray curtain valances, and scraps as long as they cost less than a dollar. I must say, apart from the amateur sewing, the completed quilt is quite "authentic 1950s" looking. You needn't be so ambitious, but it's one way to use up all those aprons nobody ever buys.

Chenille bedspreads are those grandma's-house-looking bedspreads with raised fuzz patterns. The original chenille bedspreads were a nineteenth-century Southern handicraft called "turfin'." To disguise holes and mending in existing bedding, women would bunch up threads, fluff them up, and cut them off, leaving a fuzzy little pattern behind. Turfin' progressed from mending aid to art craft and finally to machine-made bedspreads. In 1941, an eighteen-needle machine was invented that could "turf" as fast as three hundred hands. (This machine was the forerunner of the one that gave us shag carpeting.) Mass production of chenille bedspreads meant that the raised patterns became more elaborate, but the bad news was the threads used were generally monochrome. When thriftin' for turfin', check how fluffy the pile is and look for areas of missing fuzz. The better chenille spreads are cotton; the acrylic ones look and feel pretty yucky.

Bedspreads

Brighten up the drabbest room and draw attention away from an ugly bed with a colorful bedspread. A bedspread is a big eye-catcher and hopefully will keep visitors from noticing that pile of underwear or the bedside Jackie Collins novel you're secretly reading. Plenty of selection in the thrifts. It's smart to go with a washable one. Check out kids' slumber bags too! You'll find them in polyester, cotton, and flannel and with the craziest graphics! Shoppers are reluctant to buy them since they're an odd size with a seemingly specific use (kids' slumber parties). Crawl right in one during your own slumber party. Cocoon in it while watching TV or reading. Unzipped (and if you like, cut off the zipper) and unfolded, they make a handy bedspread or watching-TV blanket.

THE BATHROOM

You do have to buy a number of new things for the bathroom—toiletries, for instance. (Have you ever seen anybody buy those bags of half-used shampoo and dried-up little motel soaps at the thrifts? I just can't even imagine

> **S**oap dishes are unbelievably dull. Use a cool saucer or ashtray instead. Anything ceramic is far better than those cheap plastic soap dishes they sell new.

who would think to donate a half-bottle of shampoo in the first place!) The bathroom is also a good place to experiment with a theme room or matching motif. It's so small and doesn't need loads of stuff like a living room.

Big Hair—Now Available Cheap!

Once only professional hairdressers wielded the blow dryer . . . then came the Big Hair Seventies. Women had always spent hours pumping heat onto their heads to achieve desired hair styles, but during the 1970s, the blow dryer went unisex. It was OK to have longish hair, but it had to be neat and styled. Men reached for the Son of a Gun and wasted another half hour (at least) getting ready to go out. Equality is won in small steps. Blow dryers are now thrift-store regulars! There's always one and sometimes as many as two dozen. I like to think that folks have wised up and realized that a gigantic head of hair doesn't necessarily guarantee social or economic success and that hair dries quite nicely on its own. The trend back to shorter hair surely caused people to ditch the blow dryer. Or maybe they got tired of standing, arms raised, first thing in the morning with jet-propelled hot air roaring in their ear?

TIP I've never seen anybody buying a used contemporary blow dryer, but I knew a guy who bought up the old metal ones (they came in great pastel colors!), and he used them as wall decorations for his bathroom.

How Will I Look at the Office?

If you really want to maximize your mirror time, consider thrifting an electric mirror! These mirrors (first put out by Clairol in 1968) are surrounded by lights whose glow can be adjusted to simulate "real world" lighting like indoor, outdoor, and fluorescent. Some electric mirrors have more evocative settings like "sunlight," "office," or "candlelight." The mirrors were sold to women so that before they left the house they could adjust their makeup to complement the light where they were going. Clever, huh?

Don't Forget to Dry Off Before You Step on the Scale!

The small stand-upon weight scale was first sold as a housewares item during the health craze of the 1920s. You're probably wishing

some member of your family bought those stocks, since manufacturers of home scales have never looked back. Americans have only become more and more weight-obsessed. I refuse to step on a scale, but I think some of the old ones look kind of homey parked under the sink. There has been no shortage of styles and colors over the years—they even made one that yelled at you (as if stepping on a scale isn't traumatic enough!). Scales can become uncalibrated over time and lose their precision. Thrift one that consistently underweighs. You'll feel much better about it.

The glass with the what-you-weigh line on it is missing, so in theory this scale gives you a range of 30 kilograms (or 66 pounds for those who can't Think Metric) to pick from.
PHOTO BY VANESSA DOMICO

Bath Linens

Luckily, most of the rugs available in thrift stores are bathroom rugs. Make sure they can go in the wash! Brave sorts might even want to check out the toilet rugs—the U-shaped one for the base of the toilet and the rug for the lid, but for obvious reasons, most shoppers are leery of shag that has been that close to the commode. Guys, you know . . .

The more towels you have, the less often you have to wash them. Just keep reaching for a new one from your towering stack. And at a couple bucks each for big, thirsty, colorful towels—stock up. I like the big fluffy two-color ones with the name of a fancy hotel on it. I'd never dream of stealing one from a hotel (like I'm ever in a fancy hotel anyway . . .), but I take advantage of the fact that *other* people steal 'em and then give them to the thrifts. Hotel towels are not so common anymore. Most hotels have probably abandoned the two-tone hotel towel because plain towels are cheaper and guests may be less likely to steal a plain towel as a souvenir. For years I kept a small blue and white bath mat in my bathroom from the "Hotel Colon"—Get it? Colon? Bathroom? I thought it was pretty funny (and an unfortunate name for a hotel!) till somebody told me that "Colon" is Spanish for "Columbus," as in Christopher. I was disappointed, but we all have to grow up.

Step from the Shower in Style!

Probably half the bathrobes in the thrifts are missing the matching belt. If the bathrobe is otherwise cool, in good shape, and priced right, just improvise a belt. Get a tie, a long thin scarf, or a piece of drapery cord and use that as a belt. Thrift a giant brooch and use that to hold the robe together. Much more attractive than a safety pin, but it serves the same function. And men! What about one of those terry-cloth skirt things for *apres* bath? I see them all the time, does anyone wear them?

Toilet Paper Dolls and Other Bathroom Crafts

You're free to decorate your bathroom any way you choose, but be alert for a substratum of crafts designed for the bathroom. Actually, they're designed to *disguise* your bathroom—to hide all the unmentionables that you might have to keep in there! These bath-crafts are often knitted or sewn. All err on the side of cloying and cute—cats, poodles, dolls, angels, and other whimsy prevail. When I first started coming across these things in thrifts, I couldn't figure out what they were. What is this circular can-shaped fabric thing with a doll's face on it? I bought it because it was weird. How was I to know it's meant to cover a spare roll of toilet paper!? Imagine your guests' shock if they see an exposed roll of toilet paper! It's easier to imagine their dismay when they can't *find* the spare roll because they'd never think to look under that doll's skirt for it!

THINGS IN YOUR BATHROOM THAT SHOULD BE COVERED

- **Spare toilet paper roll(s)**
- **Toilet brush**
- **Tissue paper box**
- **Cans of hair spray**
- **Toilet lid**

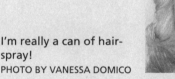

I'm really a can of hair-spray!
PHOTO BY VANESSA DOMICO

14 The Entertainment Area

MUSIC FROM THE MASSES

There has been a good deal of wailing among thrifters lately about the dearth of good thrift-shop records. Since the publication several years ago of the *Incredibly Strange Music* books, oddball old records are now promoted extensively in zines, on Internet groups, and by big media like *SPIN* and the *New York Times*. Music companies have dug down deep in their vaults and reissued long-forgotten material like exotica, cocktail music, forlorn celebrity vocalists, lounge singers, and old comedy acts. Each new reissue or compilation CD inspires even more interest in the original dusty vinyl.

Part of this moaning is pure sour grapes on the part of early collectors, who benefited from the lack of interest in quirky old vinyl, and this is understandable. Every one of us has had a pet collection of completely unwanted stuff that suddenly got rubber-stamped "collectible" and touted in the mainstream media. Not only does such attention dry up your previously untapped and ignored sources, but there's the added emotional cost of having your uniqueness made standard. All thrifters have at least one thrifting buddy who for years bored us silly with his extensive weird record collection—now *all* thrifters and alternative types are expected to be purchasing the same. What once defined you or your friend now defines everybody.

Nonetheless, there are *still* fun pieces of vinyl out there and available for thrifting. Barring any set-asides going on in the sorting room, the chances of you finding a now-everybody-wants-it-artist like Esquivel are often dependent on sheer luck. Who is in the thrift when it hits the floor? More competition means that this record won't sit around for six weeks waiting for *you* to buy it, but it is still in circulation.

Keep in mind, there were a bazillion records made. While the merits of a few rediscovered artists may be legitimate and the subsequent interest has indeed reduced the supply of those records, there are so many more unwanted records that may hold real charms for you. If you seek weird sounds, schmaltzy music, bad singing, foreign music, reactionary spoken word, religious oddities, good, bad, or both cover graphics, there's buttloads of it out there. Hopefully, your thrift isn't charging sky-high prices for vinyl, so just take some chances. Buy something that looks fun or odd. This is how all the currently trendy vinyl records got "discovered." Somebody just bought them as a lark and then discovered they liked 'em. In sum, don't be negative about what's already gone. Be positive about what you've yet to find.

How is it that you can just *sense* a record collector? The minute they approach the bins, some internal "uh oh" radar goes off. They emit an anxiety that's almost palpable—and that frantic way they flip through the records! If there's several rows or stacks of records, you can bet they'll be hunched over them arms akimbo so that you can't even get near. I've seen guys (and truly, they're mostly guys) sprawled out across several stacks. I'm no longer intimidated by these pathetic types. I barge right in and say "excuse me" enough times till they move over already!

If there's only room for one person to look at the records and you're there first, they stand right behind you and bore over your shoulder as you flip the records *for them.* You can sense their muscles coiling, ready to pounce when *you* unearth the record *they* want. They can't even grant you the courtesy that you probably aren't even looking for the same records! If you haven't got the nerve to turn around and tell 'em to scram, try freezing. Just stop in midflip and stare intently at any old record. Don't pick it up, just stare at it. Hold this pose long enough and they'll get frustrated and go away. If they deign to speak to you and ask if you're still looking at the records, say "yes," and flip over the next record. Stare at that one until they go away.

I walked up to a thrift vinyl bin once *just seconds* before one of those sweaty collector-types you can spot at a hundred yards. And *I* pulled the 50 cent Esquivel record out of the dross. He probably wouldn't have wanted it anyway since it was a library copy (it hadn't been checked out since 1967!) and the cover had been all cut up and reinforced with extra cardboard. That's OK by me—the vinyl was intact and all I wanna do is play it, not worship it. The "price" I had to pay was standing in an endless checkout line with this perspiring guy behind me, audibly breathing down my neck.

Vinyl—The World's Most Precious Substance?!

To me, the critical problem is that thrift stores are now regularly charging upwards of $2 and $3 for *any* vinyl record. Some vinyl isn't worth a Fig Newton, either because it truly has no redeemable artistic, aesthetic, or even camp value or because of its unbelievable availability. Don't people who work in thrift stores notice how many Herb Alpert and Billy Joel records stroll in and sit unsold for weeks?! Are these inflated prices the result of information about high-priced "collectible" vinyl filtering down to thrifts—or is it the very erroneous assumption that since vinyl record production has all but ceased, *all* vinyl is instantly collectible?

Eight-tracks, by this argument, would be far more valuable, since production *absolutely* stopped (with no discussion of putting out a few albums on 8-track for the audiophile analog-snob market), and it ceased much earlier than vinyl. But 8-tracks remain the ugly child of the analog family and are usually priced significantly lower than their vinyl counterparts. The leftover bad image 8-tracks have causes their devaluation. It's not for lack of available equipment. I see more functioning 8-track players in thrifts than turntables, but 8-tracks took a bad social hit in the early 1980s when they were widely dismissed and ridiculed. Some thrifts are so confident of this scourge that they don't even put 8-tracks out on the floor anymore. The overinflation of vinyl prices is one of the reasons I settled my twenty-year feud with 8-tracks. Why spend $2.50 on a Grand Funk LP you kinda wouldn't mind having but it's not an urgent matter, when you can pick up the same tunes for 49 cents on 8-track?

TIP **If the 8-track you want doesn't have a cardboard sleeve on it, take one from another 8-track you're not buying. Don't worry if it doesn't match the label or color, it's just to protect your 8-track.**

CDs—More Precious Than Vinyl?!

I'm also annoyed at thrifts for their CD pricing. Because CDs now cost more new than vinyl ever did, thrifts feel justified in charging more for them. Most are in the $4 to $8 range (precisely what vinyl used to cost *new*!). And the truth of economics is, it didn't really cost the manufacturer that much more to produce this item (the cost of producing a CD has become comparable to the cost of producing a vinyl recording). Just because the public has been suckered into paying more for the new format doesn't actually mean it's truly *worth* that. To me this overcharging is analogous to the occasional thrift overpricing you see on designer clothing.

Outrageous CD pricing has wiped out what was once the great advantage for music fans who shopped for tunes in the thrifts. You didn't have to pay the full price for a piece of music that you sorta wanted (but not enough to pay retail for), because you could be reasonably confident that any popular album would eventually filter down to the thrifts and you could pick it up cheap then. The lower price also meant that you could take the "50 cent chance" on a piece of music you weren't even sure you'd like. You wouldn't wager $7 on it, but for 50 cents you were willing to gamble that it might be something you liked. Or, if you only like one song on the album, 50 cents is a fair price to pay, but $5 is a lot to pay for a single.

CDs take up more room than vinyl and are harder to display. (Right now it seems thrifts keep 'em up in the front counter, but between the CDs, the scraggly Barbies, and the McDonald's glasses, something's gotta give!) I'm hoping future gluts of bad unsold CDs will force the thrifts to reevaluate their pricing structure. I'd buy a CD for 50 cents. My worst fear (and this is more likely to happen) is that some *other* music format will come along, the manufacture of CDs will ceased and they'll all be instantly collectible!

LPs AS WALL ART

Album covers make great wall art, and it's a swell way to deal with all those stacks of crappy tunes with fabulous covers. Quick decorating means just propping the LP up against something. You might be lucky enough to live in a pad with a built-in picture or plate rail—perfect for displaying LP covers. (Handymen will note that it is relatively easy to build your own picture rail. Lumber stores sell long strips of decorative wood trim that already have a handy groove carved in them.)

If you're willing to make tiny modifications to the jacket (thereby reducing the value! oh no!!), there are a couple of other easy ways to display the covers. (All these involve storing the vinyl disc somewhere else.)

1. Affix a sticky picture hook to the other side of the cover, then hang as you would a picture.

2. Thumbtack to wall. Put the thumbtack on the *inside* of the sleeve.

SOME IDEAS FOR AMASSING LP COVER ART

- Pick one well-covered work of music (like *The Nutcracker Suite* or *Danse Macabre*) and seek out as many different renditions and covers as possible. Line 'em up.

- Pick one popular record, set a low price limit, and buy as *many* copies as you can.

- There's a 101 million different *101 Strings* records—how many different ones can you find?

- Decide on a visual theme and purchase those covers—e.g., red background, blonde women, boats, or people drinking.

- "Music to Verb By": I still see lots of these. They're generally compilations of selections from the record label's catalog. The funniest titles come sponsored by a product like *Music to Recline By (in a Berkline Chair)*. The related category is "Music for Verbing" like *Music for Cooking with Gas* (sponsor: Caloric stoves.)

---

3. Poke a small hole in the top corner of the sleeve (or two if necessary—some LPs have the opening at the bottom of the cover image). Using a needle, run a bit of heavy thread or fishing line through the album sleeve and hole. Tie the two ends together and hang from a hook or nail. Hang *several* LP covers along a taut straight piece of string.

Records for Humming Along With

The 1980s will be back any minute now . . . Seems like a lot of people have been dumping their '80s "fun rock" collections *en masse* at the thrifts—lots of lite new wave like ABC, Duran Duran, and Kajagoogoo; just-got-lucky bar bands like Huey Lewis, Bryan Adams, and INXS; and big-hair rock like Poison, Bon Jovi, and Ratt. Maybe it's where I live, but I don't see much '80s rap, soul, or country being dumped, but the bins are packed with the MTV darlings. This could be the time to make peace with the '80s. Stock up now before somebody charges $20 for that Haircut 100 LP. And of course thrifting a cache of bad '80s records is the perfect excuse to throw an 1980s Retro Party. (See chapter 6.)

You Are the DJ

One of the great pleasures of thrifting any old record is making wacky compilation tapes. Tapes are a super way to hear a bunch of your fave tunes from vinyl in one easy package, rather than having to get up and switch the records. It's also a great way to salvage just the one or two good tunes on the record. And there's no limit to the clever tapes you can put together—juxtaposing military speeches with Hank Williams tributes and former drug-addict choirs with mambas.

MUSIC TO DRIVE PEOPLE NUTS BY

- Why don't they make phony "sounds like" records anymore? You know the ones: in fine print under the big words "Johnny Cash," it says "as performed by The Country Road." What if you had an entire collection of those and baffled your friends by only playing the bad sound-alike versions?

- The subcategory of the "sounds like" records are the "string alongs," where a cheesy orchestra plays today's top hits (*The Manhattan Strings Play Instrumental Versions of Hits Made Famous by The Monkees.*) You can really drive your rock-n-roll purist friends nutso with these tunes!

- Thrift some monaural classical music. Hear why the introduction of stereo was such a big deal. Spin these discs to drive visiting audiophiles crazy.

✳TIP✳ Always always always take a look at the vinyl *inside* the jacket (unless you're buying purely for jacket alone). While some buyers might want to ascertain what shape the vinyl is in, I recommend this simple procedure just to see *what* record is inside the jacket. Why is it that I can *never* remember to do this in the store and I always get home and find a Donna Summer 12-inch inside the Skeeter Davis jacket?

WHAT ABOUT HERB ALPERT?

When *New York Times* columnist Maureen Dowd wrote an op-ed piece about finally ditching the clutter of her life, she not coincidentally titled it "Adieu Herb Alpert." She must be the last person on earth not to have already donated their Herb Alpert records to the thrift stores! Anecdotal evidence shows Herb Alpert records (with *Whipped Cream and Other Delights* coming in #1) to be the Most Donated Records Ever! *Whipped Cream and Other Delights* was certified gold (sold at least 500,000 copies). Doesn't it seem to you that you've already seen each and every one of those? From the sheer numbers I see in thrifts, I would have guessed that record had sold over a billion! I have a new theory that maybe these 500,000 or so copies of *Whipped Cream* are just circulating around the thrift stores and that none of these copies exists in original homes anymore.

How can we get this record out of the thrifts? What can be done with it? I polled some fed-up thrifters for suggestions:

- Give everybody you know a copy for Christmas.
- Replace tiles on space shuttle (maybe they'll fall off in outer space and become another galaxy's problem).
- Repair potholes.
- Use as prom decoration. Isn't "Whipped Cream and Other Delights" a great prom theme?
- Use as ceiling tiles.
- Use as CD and computer diskette mailers.
- Donate to former Soviet Bloc countries desperate for American culture they missed out on.
- Return them postage-due to Herb. Let him keep them.

I ♥ K-TEL RECORDS

The word "K-tel" is practically synonymous with a twenty-hit compilation record with a silly generic name and bad cover art, but all comments also apply to the lesser-known compilation labels like Ronco and Adam VIII.

My favorite records of all time are still the K-tel compilations of the 1970s. I realize the word "K-tel" is a punch line, but I'm not ashamed. I love K-tel. I was *the* Top 40 expert throughout the '70s. And I knew all the tunes—name a '70s Top 40 song and I can recite most of the lyrics, tell you who sang it, what city they came from, what their less-successful follow-up hit was, and how high it charted. I'm not gonna even try to list all the songs and artists I liked—or *defend* them. Suffice it to say that I was at a simpler age and I liked virtually anything—pop, bubblegum, rock, soul, funk, oldies, country-pop crossovers, disco, etc.

K-tel records entered my consciousness in the mid-1970s, when we got—tah-dah!—the TV! I *adored* the K-tel TV

> **A CLEANER SOUND**
> Records were made from vinyl, and while it doesn't like to be grabbed with sticky fingers or skittled across the floor, it's not so fragile you can't clean it up a bit. Try a little soapy water and a soft sponge—just wash the black part, not the paper label. Rinse clean—you don't want any dreaded soapy residue. A light cleaning will cut down on the background noise of old records, but you'll just have to learn to love those permanent scratches and skips.

FUN FACTS ABOUT K-TEL

- K-tel started business in 1962 selling Teflon-coated frying pans on TV.

- First K-tel compilation was *25 Polka Hits* (1970).

- K-tel's bestseller *Hooked on Classics* (disco versions of classical themes) sold nearly 10 million copies.

- Contrary to the myth, K-tel records always were and still are sold in stores.

---

commercials. They'd take thirty-five minutes of mixed-up Top 40 music and condense it to a sixty-second advertisement. They would play a teasing snippet of my favorite song, followed in five seconds by another and another and another. As the names of songs and artists scrolled by, I drooled—all my favorite songs on *one* record! Everybody remembers K-tel's TV ads—the "announcer voice" ("twenty-two FAN-TAS-tic hits!"), the cheesy graphics, hoary sound effects (whoosh), and the key closing phrase—"Available through this TV offer."

Well, that was it for me. "Available through this TV offer." They were unattainable to me. There was that adult-obstacle of "check, money order, charge card, or C.O.D." I longed for all those records—they were an in-hand distillation of my Top 40 obsession. However ethereal the radio was, the right K-tel compilation would preserve that crazy selection of Top 40 hits from the summer of '74 forever.

I acquired my first K-tel record in 1975 (borrowed it and I'm sorry to say I still have it). By 1981, I was finally purchasing K-tel records, not "through a TV offer" but *at thrifts*. That's right, I just regressed on the spot and bought up every K-tel record I'd ever seen advertised. What a bargain—no more than 50 cents and *cash only*, please. Today I have a huge stack. I am increasingly partial to the K-tel 8-tracks, which play on and on like the radio, repeating the same twenty songs again and again.

It's no coincidence that as I began to buy up K-tel compilations in earnest, our culture began to lose Top 40 all-purpose radio in favor of more streamlined, market-driven niche formats. My K-tel buying spree now is not just to reclaim my youth and all the records I couldn't buy, but also a fuzzy nostalgia for that lost format, Top 40, with its kooky mix of tunes.

Of course, I'm not blind to problems with K-tel records. Here's a list of PROs and CONs to consider when thrifting for them.

PRO: The 1970s collections are deliciously unformatted and provide a great mix of sounds—bubblegum, rock, soul, instrumentals. (By the 1980s, K-tel was more in line with contemporary radio and releasing formatted packages, e.g., *Rap: Straight Outta the Ghetto*.)

CON: The higgly-piggly nature of K-tel compilations provides some alarming juxtapositions. Dig these adjacent tracks: "Theme from 'Roots'" (Quincy Jones) and "Hard Luck Woman" (KISS) or "Carwash" (Rose Royce) and "Lucille" (Kenny Rogers).

PRO: They make a great gift. Buy it for your Gen-Y nephew—the year he was born! Much more fun than the *New York Times* front page. Bring it to the high school reunion. Hey, the summer we graduated! Fifty cents' worth of cheap nostalgia, they'll be crying in their Bud Lite all night.

CON: Really bad cover art. Even the "quantity makes it cool" argument doesn't work here. Thirty K-tel records lined up still look bad.
PHOTO BY VANESSA DOMICO

PRO: Because they were issued so frequently, K-tel records contain all the great one-hit wonders. A super way to retrieve them! You can look for years and never find the free-standing 45 or LP.

CON: There's always one completely unknown never-ever-heard-before song. (And there's usually a good reason why you never heard it: it bites.) "Coal Town" by The Stanky Brown Group? "Risky Changes" by Bionic Boogie?

PRO: Get a copy of the song you secretly liked and are *still* too embarrassed to buy. Sure, the *Fantastic* LP has your guilty pleasure "The Night That the Lights Went Out in Georgia," but you can tell pals you bought it for the rare U.S. release of Gary Glitter's "Rock 'n' Roll, Part Two."

CON: There have been allegations that K-tel used "soundalikes" or something less than the "original recording, original song, original artist" on some of the tracks.

PRO: Can you find these tracks? Can your smarty-pants recordhead friend who claims to know everything? What fun!

CON: The songs are edited down.
PRO: The songs are edited down.

CON: Recordings have that faraway tin-can sound, and thrifted K-tel records are apt to be badly scratched.
PRO: Poor acoustical qualities recreate that late-night AM radio feel. Besides, this "lo-fi" trend is hot.

PRO: What other label was cool enough to have its own board game? You know it—K-tel Superstar Game, 1973. One day, I will find this game, too . . .

PRO: Great album titles—the simplicity of *Disco Nights*.
CON: Stupid album titles—the meaninglessness of *Disco Fire*.
CON: Due to the generic nature of the titles and the cover art, you can accidentally buy several copies of the same album. (Do I already have *Hit Machine* or is it *Music Machine*?)

PRO: Buy back your youth. All those tunes you loved and never got around to buying—now you can buy them by the fistful.
PRO: Buy back the youth you *wished* you had. It stuns me to see an ad for a $16 CD of "bad" '70s songs. No reason why you shouldn't want these tunes. It's just dumb to pay nearly twenty bucks for a "compilation CD" when the thrifts are packed with the original "bad" '70s compilations—K-tel records! Same difference, less $$. And digital schmigital—go authentic—we didn't have "digital sound" in the 1970s. (And by the way, for the cost of one CD you can thrift a record player and/or 8-track player and a starter set of K-tel compilations.)

PRO: K-tel records are plentiful. They turn up regularly at thrifts.

PRO: They're cheap. Even in the thrifts that price records individually, you'll find your K-tel records priced to move! And as far as I know, they haven't been made "collectible"—so buy low! ALL the BIG hits! One LOW price!

DISCO FEVER

When we say "disco" we might just mean "dance music of the late 1970s," but the big disco picture was another kooky fad. Disco grew out of the gay and ethnic urban clubs of the mid-1970s. These vibrant subcultures had been boogying for years, and from them much of the groundwork was laid for the disco craze—the music, the bands, the clothes, the

A local thrift recently unearthed this T-shirt. If that message isn't strong enough, note that the word "DEATH" is in red, "BEFORE DISCO" in black.

PHOTO BY VANESSA DOMICO

exclusive club feel, and the all-night, go-for-broke weekend lifestyle. The disco trend spread to other urban pockets and a casual feature story in *New York* magazine about a group of Italian guys in Brooklyn who were stars of their local disco exploded the new fad. The article (with the rather cumbersome title of "Tribal Rites of the New Saturday Night") became the basis for the film *Saturday Night Fever*. *Saturday Night Fever* came out late 1977—and the rest, as they say, was disco history.

Disco is better remembered now for the broadside backlash it got rather than for the fad itself. Its true fad-time was pretty short. The timeline is fuzzy since the disco experience existed for several years before *Saturday Night Fever* and it lived on in various areas well into the 1980s (though usually disguised as a "dance club"). The change in nomenclature was almost imperative given the fierce antagonism to disco that occurred soon after the fad broke.

The "disco sucks" movement got as much hype as the fad. In the summer of 1979, Steve Dahl, a DJ from a Chicago radio station, staged a successful (that is, it got marvelously out of control) disco record-burning at Comiskey Park. Music critics wailed that the death of rock and roll was upon us—that we'd all been reduced to boom-boom-boom synthesized beat slaves, muttering repetitive lyrics over and over. (Much of the gnashing of teeth was brought about when even dinosaur rock acts discofied their new tunes.) Major performers and impresarios who had ridden the disco wave (Donna Summer, Bee Gees, John Travolta, Village People, Robert Stigwood, Giorgio Moroder) found themselves cast out of Eden, and many disappeared or wrangled with excruciatingly long comebacks. The clubs closed, the dance instructors went broke, the all-disco radio formats went back to Top 40 or sided with the enemy and went all-rock.

But backlashes happen, fads die, stuff gets dumped at thrifts— and years later, we get to go retrieve it and have a big ole party with it. It's safe now to return to the disco lifestyle even for just one glittery evening.

Let's Boogie Down, Shall We?—Throwing a Disco Party

Records: While decor, atmosphere, and appropriate clothing are important, the key element of any disco party is the music. It takes a *disco* record to make a *disco* party. This is the time to carefully examine all those 12-inch singles you usually skip over. Delight partygoers with your arcane knowledge of New York City special mixes. If you're unsure what constitutes an authentic disco record, have no fear. The record industry put out plenty of albums just for you. Let's start with the basics—any record that says "disco" on it is probably a disco dance tune. K-tel and Ronco released several compilation albums of popular disco hits. Nearly everything on the Casablanca label is dance music (KISS excepted!). In the very-unwanted-vinyl bins, you'll also find three marketing horrors of the disco craze:

1. The discofied-other-type-of-music, like *Hooked on Classics* or *Disco Christmas*

2. crappy soundalike bands like the Disko Band and

3. novelty disco like *Sesame Street Fever.*

While not *verboten* outright, these types of disco should be approached cautiously and used sparingly. Your guests will flee in disgust if you play the entire *Mickey Mouse Disco* record. Unless you're using 8-tracks or stacking vinyl on a record player, better to prerecord your party tunes on cassette tape. The music should be nonstop. No parking on the dance floor, baby.

Books: Disco was hardly a literate craze—even the song lyrics were cited for their mind-numbing banality. Still, every fad has its share of quickie books, and disco was no exception. There's a handful of instructional dance books. Stock up on rush-to-print bios of disco celebrities (John "From Sweathog to Superstar" Travolta, the Bee Gees, Andy Gibb, Donna Summer) and novelizations of hit films (*Saturday Night Fever, Thank God It's Friday,* and *Can't Stop the Music*). Give these away as door prizes.

The Party: There were different strata of disco—the suburban chain disco, the kiddie rec room party, but the headiest disco experience was the trendy Manhattan nightclub scene. The trappings for the white-hot nightclub may be harder to come by, but you'll love the sophisticated dressing. Let your guests know about this party early! They'll want a lot of time to thrift just the right ensemble.

Decoration: The interior of the disco nightclub is pretty basic—just three colors—black, silver, and flashing lights. Keep the room as bare and as dark as possible. Hang dark sheets, curtains, or shades over the windows. Move all your furniture (and rugs) elsewhere to create maximum dance space and to approximate that downtown warehouse feel. If you need one or two chairs, thrift cheap bad airport plastic chairs and spray-paint them silver. Hang as many mirrors as you can. This is a narcissistic scene; everyone should be able to watch themselves dance. Mirrors also help your "space" feel deeper and bounce your flashing lights around.

Lighting: Appropriate lighting is important. If you're lucky enough to have thrifted a strobe light, then plug it in! Ditto with a mirror ball. (I had a confirmed thrift sighting of one of these, so it is possible.) Hang strings of Xmas bulbs (the small white ones are classier), and set them to blink. If you're forced to make do with regular lamps, at least use colored bulbs (blue is good, it gives "cool" light).

Gimmicks: Studio 54 used to have a fake snow dispenser—geddit? Other discos had bubble- and glitter-dispensing machines. You can approximate this by tossing handfuls of glittery confetti in front of a fan. Make sure beforehand that you've thrifted a good vacuum cleaner. A cheap piece of red carpet and/or rope (look in the drapery section for those satiny braided cords) outside your door will give your party that exclusive feel.

Dress: The disco lifestyle is not about the supercasual 1970s. It's a dress-up affair, but there's a wide range between the ready-to-play, I-love-my-body sex slave look and the I've-just-come-to-unwind-after-the-opera look. Remember that the point of the party is dancing—lots of physical activity—so dress for comfort *and* style (though with any nightclub scene, it's perfectly reasonable to err on the side of style and not comfort). The ultimate look is something sophisticated and shiny that looks great when you're twirling, but feels good too. Mix and match your outfit from the disco scene staples below. When in doubt, it's better to be more outrageous than too dull. The *worst* crime you can commit is to look like a Travolta clone—no white three-piece suits!

Guys: The I-Love-My-Body look can include satin boxer shorts, skintight T-shirt or tank top (look for those really low-cut tanks!), or no shirt at all (but only if you're buff—this is a trendy nightclub,

Hard not to plan a whole party around this shirt! PHOTO BY GORDON SIMPSON

not a truck pull). For the more inhibited, get dolled up in dress shirts or loose blouson-style shirts for easier movement, designer jeans, dress slacks (tight around the waist and butt, but with wide legs), a loose blazer with the sleeves pushed up or something kooky but modest like a paratrooper jumpsuit or mechanic's coveralls with a cinch belt! Footwear includes cowboy boots (tuck your designer jeans into them), clean, expensive athletic shoes, or high-heeled loafers. (The disco platforms occurred early in the disco scene and were pretty much over in sophisticated discos by the late '70s.)

Hit the jewelry display case at the thrifts. Get a fake gold chain and look for these medallions to hang from it—fist, Hawaiian hang-loose two-fingered fist, coke spoon, zodiac signs, religious medals, ankh (King Tut was big then, too). Too many chains and puka shells are a little down-market, so use sparingly.

Gals: Fortunately, it's easier with women's clothes to combine sophistication and sex appeal. The ultimate disco outfit was the slinky shimmering Qiana dress, with slits up the side, spaghetti straps, and worn with a skinny snake belt. Designer jeans (as tight as possible) look good with a loose shiny blouse tucked in. If you can thrift satin or clear vinyl jeans, go for it! Those who are superfit can hit the floor in satin boxer shorts (yes, these are unisex!), tiny tank tops and tube tops, spandex pants, and leotards. See-through anything is good, and if you must wear underwear, make sure it doesn't show. Shoes should be as high-heeled as possible—the disco shoe was a strappy, narrow-heeled sandal or mule. Black, gold, silver, and red are all hot colors. Wear nude pantyhose, sparkley tights, or no hose at all. Roller skates (not blades!) optional.

Accessories for the ladies: A disco purse is a teeny tiny glittery purse with a long strap you wear across your body while you dance and holds just lipstick and mad money. Silk flowers may be worn in your hair on combs or pinned to your belt. If you're lucky enough to score light-up jewelry and clothing—wear it! Otherwise, thrift a few gold chains and look for those dangling charms that say "Foxy," "Lady," "Bitch," or "Disco." Sure, they're a little slutty, but it's part of the charade. Avoid big clunky jewelry that will get in your way when boogying. Heavy make-up is a must—paint on obvious blush lines over your cheekbones. The frizzier you can get your hair the better! Luckily the thrifts are filled with ditched hair crimpers that will make even the limpest hair go all Bride of Frankenstein!

Dancing: It's about *you!* No need for partner dancing. Show everybody *you're* the greatest dancer! The party host should have towels on hand for mopping up the dancers.

Contest: Award a prize to the individual with the most attitude. Bonus points if a guest arrives in a limo.

Libations: Brush up on mixing swinging 1970s cocktails like tequila sunrises, Harvey Wallbangers, White Russians, screwdrivers, and wine spritzers. If you've got a blender and time, those frozen concoctions are big hits—margaritas, piña coladas, and fruit daiquiris. Serve the "classy" beers of the 1970s—Löwenbrau, Heineken, and St. Pauli Girl. For nonboozers, supply Perrier. Don't worry about food—it's a nightclub, not a restaurant. People should have eaten before they came.

Staff: Having minimally dressed bar staff is also fun. Men should be topless, well-muscled, and sport a black bow tie. For women, tiny skirt or shorts, tank or halter top, and the requisite black bow tie. And definitely appoint somebody bouncer/doorman. Even if they let everybody in anyway, your guests will thrill to being "picked."

15 The Game Room

The following section discusses toys and games that are apt to have appeal for adults, especially those interested in the intersection of toys and popular culture. This does not mean that toys in thrift shops should be reserved for ironic twenty-somethings who need a Sylvester Stallone arm-wrestler action figure to complete their at-home diorama of a Planet Hollywood opening. Most of the toys in thrifts were designed for children to play with and while I will not cover the very complex and often-misunderstood process of buying toys for kids, I certainly encourage you to do the obvious. If there are children in your life, when hitting the toy section at the thrift, keep them in mind too.

Sometimes it helps to *act* like you're buying stuff for kids. Toys are ever more collectible and I see no reason to alert thrifts to the fact that I'm buying certain toys for my own amusement. Not to mention how embarrassing it can be to explain why you're buying a bag of Legos for yourself. One time in an Akron Goodwill, while I was buying over one hundred puffy vinyl magnets with 1970s slogans on them, the clerk asked me if I was planning to give them to kids. (No way! At 1 cent each, these were all mine!) Embarrassed, I blurted out, "Church group!" The woman beamed. I guess she hadn't noticed the ones that said "Grass Is Where It's At" or "Women on Top."

Where Are the Holly Hobbies of Yesteryear?
During my last visit to a retail toy store, I was staggered by the bazaar of licensing. I could barely discern stand-alone toys but was

Nice things for kids to play with! PHOTO BY VANESSA DOMICO

TIP The toy section is where you find so much cool stuff in thrifts. It might be the toy you used to have, the toy you always wanted or *not a toy at all.* The toy section is one of the repositories of not-easy-to-classify merchandise at thrifts. *Always check it.* I have found: voodoo shrunken head swizzle sticks, tiki figures, gigantic masks, Panasonic kooky '70s radios, a Reaganomics dart board, Watergate memorabilia, and old wig heads.

able to wander through Barbie World, Power Ranger World, Lego World, and Pocahantas World. Toy licensing is where it's at! The benefits (should the license take off) are enormous. There's reduced advertising costs (one ad spot spills over onto all the products) and the built-in hype factor of unleashing a hundred similar products at once. Licensing contributes to substantial toy discard in two ways. The license doesn't "take" or the public's desire is overestimated—remember *Dick Tracy* 1990 or *Flintstones* 1994? Some of this merchandise gets dumped *new* at the thrifts. Alternately, when the appeal of a popular license dies, a tidal wave of matching crap hits the thrift! We are still digging out from California Raisins, New Kids on the Block, and Teenage Mutant Ninja Turtles.

AN ORPHANAGE OF DOLLS

Why do thrifts stock the most forlorn, scraggly-looking dolls? Those bins of broken, dirty, shapeless, naked dolls with matted hair and pen marks on their faces have a grim quality. Disturbing even, since most dolls are designed to look like babies or children. At the other end of the spectrum are the "behind the counter" ($20 and up) dolls, sal-

Explain *this* to your kids! In 1991, the Pee-Wee Herman phase was waning and the thrifts were filling up with a myriad of licensed Pee-Wee products—all marked for pennies and all collecting dust. Then Mr. Herman got busted for indecent exposure at an X-rated movie theater. When the howling of concerned citizens quieted down—lo and behold! the Pee-Wee Herman stuff had been stamped collectible! Not because the TV show no longer ran (it had, after all, *just* ceased), but because Pee-Wee had had his hands down his pants! I fail to see how being caught jerking off should rapidly accelerate the value of millions of pieces of cheap merchandise! And just what kind of message does that send to other has-been celebrities?

vaged from the dolls-near-death pile, to be sold to doll collectors (and this is a particularly rabid group!). Sadly, it seems none of the dolls will go to a good, loving post-thrift home—some sicko buys the damaged ones and does who-knows-what with them, and the "good dolls" are taken away to be put on a shelf or back in a box.

At least all-plastic dolls clean up with a bit of soap and water. The true horror of thrift-store dolls are the discarded Cabbage Patch Kids. Now they lie in piles at the thrifts ditched by "adoptive parents," their tiny smiles and bright eyes betrayed by their grimy rag bodies. What does it say about the so-called "adoption lessons" when these adopted "kids" are dumped *en masse* just as they are hitting their trickier adolescent years? This is a scene I missed in *Toy Story*—where hundreds of bitter, dirty, nameless Cabbage Patch Kids stalk Hollywood Boulevard at night.

No wonder this yarn doll is smiling. He's leaving the Pac Rat Palace in Rapid City for a good home!
PHOTO BY JULIE PEASLEY

Video Killed the Action Hero Doll: Sales of dolls-for-boys, or "action hero figures" as they prefer to be known, have declined steadily since video games cornered the boy-toy market. Many languish motionless on thrift shelves. The oddest of them are the action dolls that don't have moving limbs—inert pieces of plastic that you can only wave around in your hand. I'm stunned by the number of pro-wrestling figures that don't move. Come on! These are some of the world's most highly trained athletes! How come they don't move?!

ColecoVision, Activision, Astrovision, Intellivision... Uh, what *vision* was that again? Since toys have joined the microchip revolution, now much of the discard in toys is based on an unstable industry and obsolete technology. The company you bought the video game from last year went belly-up—say good-bye to future fun! Maybe you lucked out and bought from the still-stable company, but this year the game is in color! Or they changed the shape of the cartridge or added a new function button. Better upgrade. This is a bad development for thrifts. I foresee mountains of broken dusty decks and unusable cartridges without players. There's been a small revival of retro-gaming, but it doesn't seem to jibe with human nature that in a world of 3-D games, most people would rather be playing Frogger.

I Can't Remember *Who* I Am: Celebrity action figures are pretty collectible but only if they're still in the box. There's that box obsession angle that collectors have but I also think it's because the figures are so poorly designed that once they're missing the box and their costume, it's impossible to distinguish WHO they are anymore! Is it Cher? Brooke Shields? Brenda from *90210*?

Barbie: Groan. I'm bored with Barbie. She gets so much press and everybody fawns over Barbie. Barbie. Barbie. Barbie. The only Barbie doll that ever intrigued me was Earring Magic Ken with the purple fake leather vest and meshy shirt. But that Very Special Ken went quietly away to Fire Island or somewhere. OK, the big Barbie hairdressing heads are pretty cool. I use one for keeping all my hair barrettes on—she is the ultimate riot Brrrbie.

BOARD GAMES AND BORED GAMES

Want to know an easy way to weed out those stacks of 50 cent games you can't stop buying? Play them! Play at least one a week and you'll be horrified at how *bad* most of them are! You'll be running to give them back to the thrift! This is what is mind-boggling about the current sky-rocketing prices for movie and TV tie-in board games. Most are the dullest games—just variations of going

---

In the interest of saving you from paying sky-high prices for entertainment-related board games, I played some TV games and determined what easier-to-find game they were similar to.

- **Battlestar Galactica (Parker Brothers 1978)**
  Object: Be the first to capture the Cylon raider and bring it to your squadron launch pad on the Battlestar Galactica.
  What It Is: Checkers in Space.

- **Bionic Crisis (Parker Brothers 1976)**
  Object: Be the first to determine the right Bionic circuitry and restore Steve Austin's powers.
  What It Is: $6 Million Battleship

- **Charlie's Angels Game (Milton Bradley 1977)**
  Object: To gain points by trapping the villain with your team of Angels.
  What It Is: Backgammon in Bikinis

- **The Emergency Game (Milton Bradley 1974)**
  Object: Complete your team's mission first by traveling city streets.
  What It Is: Snakes and Ladders with Fire Engines

around the board but with the game pieces and names changed to reflect the appropriate entertainment tie-in. These games are escalating in price just because there's a picture of Henry Winkler on the box. Get in the habit of playing games you thrift and you'll find few you'll want to keep. This is the compromise solution because at least this way you still get to thrift all the kooky games you see, but with a few exceptions, you'll just be renting them!

With some board games it's no mystery why they're languishing at the thrifts.

How many times do you want to play a game called "Pass-Out"?

Pass-Out (1971): A drinking board game, though the instructions said, "Not be used with alcoholic beverages." I'm sure their lawyers made them say that, but how much orange juice do you have to shotgun before you pass out? We tested this game one night. It lived up to its name all right. I spent the night on the floor and at the first opportunity returned the game to the thrift!

The game is not in step with today's sexual mores . . .

Cruising: The Gay Board Game (1979): The object of the game is to move from "The Closet" to the post-coital resting area in a bathhouse. Game advancement is by picking the right tricks and avoiding vice cops, venereal diseases, and hustlers who are "Hung Like A Horse" (lose one turn while in the hospital!). Naturally I found this game with the other children's toys.

Wonder why this game didn't sell?

HMO: The Game (1987): Sample card: "Leave the emergency room after referring a patient to the appropriate specialist. Sues you for deserting a patient. It will cost you $4000 in legal fees." Fun fun fun.

Words of Advice about Mystery Dates and Mystery Games

BY LYNN PERIL

When I was growing up, I wanted nothing more than Parker Brothers' Mystery Date board game. Oh, you remember, the pink and white box, the little plastic door, "Will he be a dream? Or a dud?" Every birthday, Christmas, or other gift-giving occasion, I crossed my fingers before I unwrapped my presents. But there'd be a Twist-n-Turn Barbie or a Campus Queen lunch box, never The Game.

Of course, as soon as I hit adulthood, I started looking. But despite years of obsessive thrifting, the Mystery Date game is the one thing I never found. Trip after trip, I pulled all the games off the shelves only to be disappointed. Oh sure, there were plenty of wannabe dating-type games from the 1980s and 1990s—Heartthrob, Date Line, Girl Talk, Sweet Valley High, Perfect Wedding—but really, who cared? Not me. Only the original would do for Miss Snobby-Nose.

I can't quite remember how it happened. Maybe I was tired that day, or disappointed, or both, but I bought one of those pretenders to Mystery Date's throne. I brought it home, opened it up, and much to my surprise, discovered that despite the game's recent vintage, its philosophy was firmly rooted in the past: players rushed to get ready for dates with "dreamy guys" and sought to avoid dating disasters with dud-like losers. I was hooked, and a new collection took shape in my closet.

So take heed, thrifters. *Never* turn your nose up at the common stuff because you're focused in on the "holy grail." You might be missing a whole other realm of thrifting pleasure, not to mention that today's shelf-clogging crap is tomorrow's hard-to-find "collectible."

I Wanna Own It All!—Monopoly

Monopoly is probably the world's most popular board game. If that isn't a fitting tribute to smash-and-grab capitalism, I don't know what is. Is it any wonder Monopoly is popular—you can buy property for as low as $60! (You actually don't see that many Monopoly sets in thrifts, whereas the Game of Life is omnipresent. Is it that people tire of life but never weary of amassing property and screwing over a family member?) Monopoly is much more fun with the wooden houses. Your property seems more stable. In 1958, the wooden houses were replaced with plastic houses in the standard editions of Monopoly, though Parker Brothers always made "deluxe" editions that came with the wooden houses. An easy way to reclaim the wooden houses is to thrift one of the "deluxe" editions manufactured in 1985 for the 50th Anniversary of Monopoly. When I was a kid, I really enjoyed chewing on the wooden houses while playing. Not sure if that's why they discontinued them, but I sure miss 'em.

A further testament to the popularity and longevity of Monopoly is the whole subcategory of board games that are essentially Monopoly rip-offs or Monopoly-inspired. Every big U.S. city has a rip-off Monopoly game, usually named for the city. These games are little more than Monopoly with the street names changed. (The most pathetic Monopoly rip-off I ever saw was The Game of Greater Baldwinsville, N.Y. Makes Vermont Avenue look like a good buy.) Still, they can be amusing to play since you barely have to read the rules. Many of the games had promotional tie-ins with local businesses, and ten years later you'll be chuckling over how many long-gone restaurants and bars you're snapping up. Play Washington Scene and a mere $200,000 will get you either the Department of Defense or the Insurance Industry. Those are 1977 prices, of course.

Then there's the thrift store perennial Anti-Monopoly. In 1973, Ralph Anspach, a professor of economics at San Francisco State University, created and marketed a game called "Anti-Monopoly." In keeping with the spirit of the times, the object of this game was to break up monopolies, not create them. Almost immediately, Parker Brothers and its then-parent company General Foods filed a trademark infringement suit. They claimed the name "Monopoly" was theirs and was a threatened asset worth $60 million. In 1976, a San Francisco District Court settled in favor of Parker Brothers. Perhaps fortified by hours of playing his own game, Professor Anspach continued to fight for the right to sell his game. In 1980, an appeals court overturned the 1976 decision and returned the dis-

---

WHAT TO DO WITH INCOMPLETE GAMES

Often thrifts tape up board games or store them in bags so you can't check them for completeness. While it's always disappointing to return home and find an incomplete game, you can still salvage some fun. Missing tokens, dice, and spinners can be borrowed from other games. If the game is too incomplete to save, try these fun ideas:

- All the instruction cards are swell inserts in correspondence. Throw some of those value dilemma cards from the UnGame in with your utility payments.

- Bring a little amusement to a stranger's day. Leave trivia question cards tucked into bus seats and telephone booths instead of Jack Chick tracts.

- Reuse the tokens, dice, chips, and spinners in other games. Play Monopoly with the cast of Kojak cut-outs.

- Use game boards as wall art, an end table cover, or as a giant trivet for hot dishes.

pute to the lower courts. Production of Anti-Monopoly resumed. Parker Brothers continued to argue that their trademark was being infringed and that the entire Anti-Monopoly venture was hurting their business. Finally in 1983, the dispute was settled in the highest court in the land—the Supreme Court—in favor of Anspach.

JIGSAW PUZZLES

The first jigsaw puzzle is credited to an English mapmaker who in the 1760s (!) glued a map to a piece of wood, cut it along the country boundary lines, boxed it, and sold it as an educational aid. The grand heyday of jigsaw puzzles in this country occurred between the two World Wars. Improved die-cut processes (rather than the time-consuming task of hand-cutting puzzles) enabled the manufacturers to churn out zillions of puzzles. (During a mad craze for jigsaws in 1932–1933, 100 million puzzles were sold in just seven months.) Puzzles continued to sell respectably after World War II, though, like other older amusements, they took a hit from TV. And puzzle quality dropped—the cardboard became thinner, the nice details like "silhouette pieces" disappeared, and the same old "Snow Falling on Covered Bridge" scene got pretty tired. But in 1967, Springbok (now owned by Hallmark) issued puzzles in new shapes (circles, octagons), themes (reproductions of modern art like Jackson Pollock), and with new challenges (all one color) and spurred a flurry of re-interest in jigsaws. While there will never be a boom again like in the 1930s, jigsaw puzzles are still a healthy industry today, despite Game Boys and cyberspace.

Puzzles in the Thrifts

In among the hundreds of cheap bad landscape puzzles (these are like the Harlequin romances of the jigsaw shelf) are some real treasures. High Art? There's reproductions of famous paintings. Low Art? Sad-eyed waifs. Op Art? Escher-like images abound. Pop Art? The most! TV shows, movies, and other entertainment acts are well represented.

There are a few pitfalls with puzzles that predate the 1950s, but I think the fabulousness of these puzzles outweighs any small drawbacks. Some old puzzles came in an unmarked box and there is no representative picture to work from (though I enjoy watching a mystery image slowly emerge.) The word "interlocking" on the side of the box appears open to interpretation. To me, this means that two or more pieces fit together so tightly you can pick them up and they remain fused. Older puzzles were cut along gentler lines, not the severe "nub" and "void" of today's jigsaw pieces. The older pieces do not truly "lock" but more often slide next to one another and fit. The disadvantage is that you must start in one place and work only out from there, sliding the pieces next to each other and then regrouping them when you knock them with your elbow.

The fabulousness? Just the look of the old boxes themselves are great—old puzzle icons and retro puzzle names (Perfect Picture Puzzle, Tripl-Thick Miniature, Built-Rite). I see a stack of those old boxes and start plotting summer getaways to my fantasy 1930s Adirondacks cabin. The puzzles themselves have weird muted colors, similar to the tinting colors used on old postcards. The pieces are deliciously thick and the layers of cardboard

Don't overlook these flat frametray puzzles, usually found in the toy section. Some have "mature" images like this hot-to-trot 1940s cowgirl.

PHOTO BY VANESSA DOMICO

are densely pressed so that the piece has a "wood" feel and heft. Compare that with those flimsy bend-clean-in-half pieces from today's cheap puzzles.

Are all the pieces there? Who knows? Life is full of uncertainty. Oddly, newer puzzles are just as apt to be incomplete. (And if you're tackling an old puzzle, there is an added sense of amazement when the puzzle is finally completed in its entirety. What wondrous force of the universe keeps all those stray puzzle pieces together through decades of children, pets, moving—even that final traumatic voyage to the thrift store?) I buy loads of puzzles exclusively from thrift stores. Sure, it goes against every rule in the cosmos, but rarely is the puzzle missing pieces. I think that Man is Essentially Good and he does not stoop to throwing incomplete jigsaw puzzles in the thrift donation box. Still, the prospect of missing pieces hardly bothers me. You don't even know for sure that a piece is missing until you're at the very end, fitting the last piece in place—and then what difference does it make?

Completed puzzles can be converted to "art" and hung on your

Charley Lang of California glued 1170 completed puzzles to the walls and ceilings of his house. He bought most of them at Goodwill. "They're 79 cents," he said, "but I get a dime off for being a senior citizen."[1]

walls to be enjoyed. They sell a special glue for "freezing" completed jigsaw puzzles into shape. This bottle of glue costs three or four times the price of the thrifted puzzle. I found that covering the *back* of the completed puzzle with clear packing tape works just great.

- Hang it on the wall—art.
- Cover the entire wall—wallpaper.
- Cover the floor—linoleum.
- Affix to small tabletop—veneer.
- Pass on to another puzzler—friendship.
- Break up and put back in box to do again—endless fun.
- Return to thrift. (Seal up the box first! String is better than tape and note if the puzzle is complete. This will help the thrift resell it.)— good thrift karma.

Many unopened puzzles are no doubt gifts that were dumped without a thought at the thrift. You can reverse this process to your advantage. Still-sealed jigsaw puzzles make great cheap gifts, and they're especially handy for those ridiculous social occasions when you're expected to give a gift to somebody you don't know or like (think of the Office Holiday Gift Exchange where you draw the name of somebody down on the fourth floor). Jigsaw puzzles have been for years nice, polite gifts, and they're given regardless of whether the recipient enjoys them.

FIFTY-TWO PICKUP

A deck of cards, those fifty-two slips of paper, provides an almost endless amount of amusement. Most decks of cards in thrift stores are packaged in plastic bags—so even if you wanted to take the time to check for completeness, you can't get into the bag. If the cards have a cool back design or box, buy them if they're cheap. If you blow 45 cents on a dead deck, no big deal.

The Lost Social Art of Card-Playing

Social card-playing was once terrifically popular, and the thrifts are filled with the detritus of those days. If you play cards now or plan to take up card-playing in the future, why not enjoy the full experience of card-playing like in the good old days?

Playing cards is not as simple as dropping a deck of cards on a table. It's a social event and there are rules and appropriate accouterments. I have made a distinction here between genteel social

---

THINGS TO DO WITH AN INCOMPLETE DECK

- Enclose a neat-looking card in your correspondence.

- Hang from Christmas tree.

- Shellac cards onto boring card table to create fun *trompe l'oeil* effect.

- Use as bookmarks.

- Cut them in half and use the two matching pieces as tickets at your next party that features a raffle for door prizes.

- Make a mobile.

- Place cards on your forehead and use your ESP powers to guess which card it is.

- Pick up extra cash playing three-card monte with strangers at the bus stop.

- Some card games (like euchre or memory) do not require a full fifty-two-card deck. If you purchase a set of two matching but incomplete decks, you may be able to salvage one whole deck.

- Play solitaire till dawn with a deck of 51 . . .

---

card-playing (such as canasta or bridge) and the rowdier card games (such as poker or blackjack). You'll note that the accessories are different, but nearly all these items are easily thrifted. Most thrifts keep the card-playing supplies in those hanging plastic grab bags.

Furniture: A card table is a perfectly square table that folds up and away for easy storage. And no, they're not very sturdy, but they're just for playing cards around. There is a specific chair to use with a card table. It is a *small* foldout chair—not the big clunky metal folding chairs found in school auditoriums, but a daintier chair with a small seat. These are not necessarily comfortable chairs, but card-playing requires concentration, not a plush-lined, overstuffed stupor. Four *identical* chairs are used. Not only does this look nicer, but different chairs may place players at different heights and at various levels of comfort, which could affect play.

Card-themed glass fits neatly into a coaster/ashtray.
PHOTO BY VANESSA DOMICO

Equipment: You should play with the deck intended for the game; e.g., canasta requires two identical decks, bridge calls for two nar-

GROOVIN' ON OLD DECKS. . .

- Old souvenir scenes: A deck of souvenir cards is always a popular gift and was even more so when more people actually played cards. Lots of great images of Florida, Niagara Falls, and the western desert are waiting in the thrifts.

Check out old promotional decks. This deck from the Timken Tapered Roller Bearings of Canton, Ohio, looks deceptively like a basic abstract design, but closer inspection reveals a big ole roller bearing in the middle of the card back.

- The Lost Casinos: The Nevada casinos used to give away decks by the bucketful. They're tearing down some of the great old casinos to build family-oriented pyramids, but you can recapture the Rat Pack times with thrifted decks. A related pursuit would be playing only with decks of cards from airlines that are gone.

- Monogrammed cardbacks were popular: Look for your own initial(s) or try to thrift a whole alphabet's worth of decks. Complete sets of monogrammed cards still in a box make a nice stocking-stuffer for that person with the right initial (one initial is easy, three is tricky).

row contrasting decks. Inappropriate decks for social play include casino decks, children's decks, too-cute images (kittens), etc. The taste of the host/hostess is reflected in the choice of cards used. Playing cards today are made from plastic-coated paper. They're slippery, stick together, take ages to break in, and just don't *feel* good. What you want is an old paper deck with a linen finish. The score is kept on a small notepad using a fussy pen or pencil specifically designed for keeping score. The pen/pencil is shorter and slimmer than standard writing instruments.

You may want to invest in a shuffler. I've seen several models (including a battery-operated one). Most models draw from two stacks of cards and deliver a freshly shuffled pack to the table. It's a useful item when playing a two- or three-deck card game and for preventing card-mangling by not-so-dexterous human shufflers. Another item that contributes to the neatness of play is a molded tray that holds the draw and discard piles.

It is recommended that, no matter how old the friendships and how seasoned the players, an agreed-upon rule book be kept at the table. Eschew Hoyle's blah book for a zestier book, preferably by a president of a card club. (I use *Canasta: The Argentine Rummy Game* by Ottilie H. Reilly of the Regency Club, New York. In addition to the rules, Mrs. Reilly provides now-lost social advice such as: "A player should refrain from indicating in any way approval or disapproval of partner's call or play."[2])

Hosting the Genteel Card Party

Find a tablecloth with card-playing motifs printed or embroidered on. Make sure it's the right dimensions for your card table. Paper or cloth napkins are essential if you are serving "finger food" or greasy snacks like mixed nuts. (If they're card-related, great, but better to have plain napkins than none at all.) Most card hosts/hostesses serve small snacks during the game. Snack plates and candy/nut dishes are often found in the shape of suits. Be sure to have your "playing card" apron on.

You may occasionally see a small square tablecloth with strings or ribbons in each corner. Such a tablecloth is specific to card tables—the strings tie around the legs to hold the tablecloth in place.
PHOTO BY AUTHOR

Refreshments: Evening play often calls for mixed drinks. Highball glasses with card-playing motifs are appropriate for most cocktails. Swizzle sticks with the suits on the stem are quite common. (If card motifs are unavailable, try to provide a glass with a black or red design. Those stemmed coffee mugs with playing card faces on them are perfect for hot drinks.) Protect your table and play area by serving all chilled drinks on coasters. You may also want to impress your guests by using suit-shaped ice cubes! Look for the tray molds in the kitchenware section.

Who's in? Card Games with Bets

Poker, blackjack, and other gambling-intensive games were considered the province of men, and consequently the items related to play are different or even nonexistent. When the guys got together on Friday night to play poker, it was a respite from the fussy and cluttered female world, and the objects required often only meant deck of cards, flat playing surface, and cash. Still, men are not immune from being good hosts nor from enjoying a few specialized objects related to card play.

For manly hands, provide a sturdy deck. Use a basic no-nonsense deck like Bicycles or small check casino-style decks—no flowers or antebellum scenes. Now is the time to use that ribald deck with the Atlantic City showgirls on the back or the half-undressed women on the cardface. True card sharks will scorn the use of a shuffler or a molded discard tray. If you're gambling with chips, there are several options to look out for in thrifts. The most basic is a plastic bag filled with assorted chips. There's the upright spinning contraption with four to six slots that hold the chips vertically, or molded racks that store chips horizontally. I recently thrifted an intriguing set of soft plastic poker chips called Silent Partner made by Tupperware. And indeed, they don't make any noise at all when you throw them into the kitty!

If you need ashtrays, avoid the daintier card-related ones intended for bridge. Supply big basic ashtrays—or maybe an ashtray from your favorite casino. (Lots of casino ashtrays in the thrift stores—the heavy black glass ones are both functional and classy looking.) A lighter with a poker hand or Las Vegas image on it is a nice touch.

16 The Sports Room

7,000 YEARS OF BOWLING FUN

Those omnipresent bowling balls are probably the oldest, most consistent antiquity available for immediate purchase in the thrifts. Antiquity? You bet! Paleontologist Sir Flinders Petris unearthed an Egyptian bowling set (9 stone pins, 3 stone balls, and a marble wicket) that dated from around 5000 B.C.! Between proclamations, Protestant Church founder Martin Luther found time to get a few frames in. He even had his own bowling lane. It makes sense that as soon as some Early Man found or created a heavy stone ball, he threw it at something else to watch it fall over. This "sport" must have been institutionalized almost immediately!

The bowling ball has remained basically the same item all these centuries. (The big changes were with the pins: number, size, design, placement, and the automatic pin setter.) The ball material evolved from stone to wood, and then, earlier this century, to hard rubber. Changes in the finishing technique of the lanes (new shellacs and lacquers) affected the performance of the rubber ball, and new plastic materials were utilized to make better-behaved balls. The first plastic bowling balls were made from polyester, and then in the 1970s, a high-performing polyurethane ball was developed.

But ball material is just one factor in ball performance—the porosity (or texture) of the ball surface, the finish of the lanes, the internal ball weights, and the location of the finger holes in relation to the internal weights all affect play. Bowling expert Fred Borden

I confess that I don't move around much, especially when moving involves chasing a ball, but that hasn't prevented me from noticing quite the selection of sports equipment in the thrifts. Thrifty athletes should stock up on:

- Baseball mitts and bats
- Basketballs, footballs, and soccer balls
- Tennis and squash racquets
- Swimming flippers
- Skis and ski boots—I never see many poles.
- Golf clubs—I see beautiful old leather golf bags. When you consider that President Kennedy's *used* bag and clubs went for over $700,000, a couple of bucks is a steal.
- Hockey parts—sticks, pucks, gloves, face masks, goalie-wear.
- Ice skates and roller skates—and coming soon, plenty of in-line skates.
- Old skateboards—astound your thrasher friends with your wooden sidewalk-surfer!

A photographic early fiberglass skate-board from the 1970s
PHOTO BY AUTHOR

describes twenty-seven possible lane/ball conditions and suggests that, in a best-case scenario, the serious bowler might have twenty-seven differently configured bowling balls.[1] (Well, there's another game right there—thrifting all twenty-seven balls required!) Most bowling pros travel with about ten balls, and given the availability and low cost of bowling balls in thrifts, there's no reason you shouldn't stock up on balls too. Ball color does not technically affect play, but why not have a variety of colors? *Bowling for Women* (1964) recommends owning several colored balls to match your different outfits.

Besides being historic, why are bowling balls so cool? They are close to indestructible. They come in great colors, even marbleized and two-tone swirls. They have a nice all-American retro look without being too cute or obvious. They have handy holes in them so you can move 'em around easily. Balls come in a variety of weights, one suitable for everyone. Sometimes, they have a kooky name etched in them like "Rocko" or "Wilma."

What to Do with All Those Bowling Balls

Go bowling. It's one of the few sports where you can eat, smoke, and drink alcoholic beverages while playing the game. You also spend most of the time sitting down. If you plan to play, pick a ball that's the right weight and check the finger holes for comfort. Fifty cents spent on a buff job at the bowling alley will give your ball a new shine. Don't forget to thrift a pair of bowling shoes. You make back the cost of the thrifted shoes in just one or two bowling-shoe rentals. Not that good a bowler? Nobody will know after you thrift a few bowling trophies. (Put 'em on a high shelf where nobody can read the names.) And look in the jewelry case for tiny 200-point and 300-point game pins.

AROUND THE GARDEN

- Thrift a colorful selection of cheap bowling balls and toss them out in your backyard. They add color, you can shift 'em around (never the same pattern twice!), and nobody will ever steal them. They will withstand any weather, and during the winter, they are a very handy gauge to see how much snow fell (as in, "Uh oh, the bowling balls disappeared again . . . ").

Easy-to-do yard art
PHOTO BY AUTHOR

- Fill the finger holes with dirt and see if you can get something to grow out of it. It's like a giant Chia pet.
- Use them to edge a flower bed or tree in your garden. They look best if half-buried.

AROUND THE HOUSE

- A bowling ball still in its bag makes a nice doorstop. I love those old plaid bowling-ball bags.
- Keep by the front door as a defense against traveling salesmen and evangelists. Imagine their surprise when you come to the door with your fingers deep in a bowling ball. If that doesn't unnerve them enough that they leave, fake out like you're gonna throw it. If necessary, throw it.
- Use several as a furniture base. I've seen bowling balls used to support low beds, end tables, coffee tables, and chairs. Ask at the hardware store what kind of super glue you need.

AROUND THE OFFICE

- Keep a bowling ball in your cubicle for no apparent reason.

EXERCISE EQUIPMENT—THE BANE OF THE THRIFT-SHOP FLOOR!

If you ever needed proof that home exercise equipment doesn't work (either because the product is crappy or the user didn't keep the regime up), look no further than the nearest thrift. They're getting *clogged* with discarded exercise equipment and it's only going to get worse!

The 1980s and 1990s fitness boom spewed out an unbelievable amount of exercise equipment. People really tumbled (and still do) for this stuff. Everybody is convinced that being fit is a good idea, and toward that goal, it's super easy to follow the first instruction— buy some specialized piece of exercise equipment. Unfortunately, that's about as far as most people get. The item is purchased, it's sporadically or never used, and then it gets dumped at the thrifts. As much as I don't like exercise, I feel benevolent toward those people who do end up using the equipment, if for no other reason than that it's still in their house and not getting in my way at the thrift store.

An alarming amount of the latest exercise equipment is huge— exercycles, ski-track thingies, weight benches, rowing machines, Soloflex (and its imitators), and electric steps. These gigantitron muscle stretchers make hang-it-on-the-wall exercise doodads like the Thighmaster or Gutbuster look positively benign. I see thrifts putting out obviously broken pieces of exercise equipment. They wouldn't display a broken fridge or table with three legs, but they'll take up good floor space with a Soloflex knock-off with snapped cables. Because of the continued popularity of fitness and exercise (at least as a concept), the thrifts feel justified in dragging out all this crap and giving it prime frontage on the floor! Thrift floor

---

EXERCISE EQUIPMENT THAT MIGHT BE FUN THAT YOU HARDLY EVER SEE

- **Giant trampolines**

- **Scooters that you push with one foot**

- **Steam tanks**

- **Big rubber-band-around-the-belly mixers**
  While resting once on a thrift-shop couch, I stared agape as three very overweight people took turns "riding" a vibrating rubber-band machine. I had a rear view and I guarantee this machine really shakes up the flesh. As she stepped away, one woman declared, "I feel pounds lighter already." The other declared it was a good buy at $39. The third was not completely impressed. "It makes you itch to vibrate yourself."

space could be better occupied by something truly useful, like dinette furniture.

Even if the thrifts *do* sell this stuff, we're not escaping the cycle. Just like in the retail world, the majority of people who purchase a piece of home exercise equipment are probably gonna use it rarely or never and then *return* it to the thrift! It's gone, it's back, it's gone, it's back. This is a very real problem for the future, especially when you factor in the cost. Shoppers are less likely to make an impulsive buy on a $1,500 ski-track thing new if they're not sure they're gonna use it, but for $20 at the thrift, those *less* inclined to use it will be encouraged to take a chance. This creates the illusion for the thrift-store owners that this stuff *does sell* when all that is really happening is someone is taking it for a brief home visit before dumping it back at the thrift.

CB RADIO CRAZE OF '76

CB (Citizens' Band) has been available as a technology since 1947. Legend has it that when the gas and oil crises of the early 1970s dropped the speed limit to double nickels, truckers jumped on CB radio as a means of avoiding Smokey Bears. (Adding *any* communication to a boring, solitary job could only have caught on.) The legend continues that when truckers were televised staging organized protests against speed limits and fuel hikes—all coordinated by CB radio, complete with colorful language and outlaw names ("handles"), well, America just fell in love with those renegade gear-jammers and that crazy CB talk.

Whatever the true origins—and observers of popular culture know that fads can materialize out of thin air—25 million CBs were sold in 1976. People rushed to acquire radio sets, handles, a jargon dictionary, and get on the air. Many mobile CB-ers and outlaw wannabes were undoubtedly interested in avoiding Smokey Bear, but were sold on other "safety" features such as weather and road conditions info and emergency use. (Ask somebody today why they got a mobile phone/beeper and you'll hear the same spiel.) Of course, do not underestimate the attraction of "being on the air," surreptitiously listening to other people, communicating behind a screen of anonymity with a colorful new "CB personality," and plain ole shootin' the bull. With a CB you weren't alone, but a "good buddy" of everybody out there in that great egalitarian CB-land. (Ask somebody today why they just got on-line and take note of similarities.)

But it wasn't just radar-evaders and lonely traveling salesmen caught up in The Craze. Big East Coast educated urban-dwelling media declared: "It might well have a cultural and social impact on American life almost as profound as the last electronic communications gadget to sweep the country—television."[2] CB manufacturers were openly weeping with joy. Detroit began to factory-install CBs. (Chrysler predicted that 80 percent of cars would be CB-equipped by 1979.)[3] But just one month into 1977, CB manufacturers reported sales drops of 30 to 40 percent. Ten-four, good buddies, The Craze was over.

But while it lasted, America was hit hard. CB was a cultural phenomenon *so significant* that it generated movies, songs, phony CB performers, pranks, jokes, urban legends, TV shows, and consumer goods, and added dozens of words to the American lexicon. Name another modern fad whose white heat burned so brightly and for such a short time—yet whose influence was felt coast to coast (the old, the young, and the middle-aged, men, women, and children, the First Lady of the United States), elevated an entire subclass of yabbering truckers to hero status and left behind so much cultural debris.

EYEBALLING THE DEBRIS

What *wasn't* there? There were glasses and mugs covered with CB lingo, patches to sew on your jacket, T-shirts, belt buckles to tell the world you had your ears on, bedspreads and sheets for slumber in CB-land, and games to play (Breaker 19—The CB Truckers' Game, and Breaker, Breaker, Good Buddy.) Still need more? How 'bout records, 8-tracks, books, ashtrays, cologne, and toy CB and truckin' sets. There's still loads of it out there in the thrifts!

And pick yourself up a CB while you're out. They're collecting dust at the thrifts, too. Look for the portable kind that plugs into the cigarette lighter—and an accompanying antenna's a good idea too. And useful! What do you want a cellular phone for anyway? Breaker 9 gets you a Smokey if you need one—and the airtime's free! Most people think the CB Craze has gone permanently 10–7. CB-land *is* a quiet place these days—just some truckers spottin' Bear—but you gotta be careful with national fads, they can come back in a flash. I see no reason to be unprepared when it's so easy to stockpile now.

CB Movies: CB and the co-opting of truck culture was such a huge cultural paradigm that only some of America's most esteemed film directors dared to address it: Steven Spielberg (*Duel*), Jonathan Demme (*Handle with Care/Citizens' Band*), Paul Bartel (*Cannonball*), Sam Peckinpah (*Convoy*), and famed First Amendment envelope-pushers, the Mitchell brothers (*CB Mamas—XXX*). But break for a reality check—most of these movies sucked. A few are redeemable if you're drinkin' enough beer, but there can be *no* denying their critical berth in CB lore. The most interesting of them is probably *Handle with Care,* which actually addresses The Craze itself. Like all traditional comedies, it ends with the requisite marriage—marriage via CB, of course.

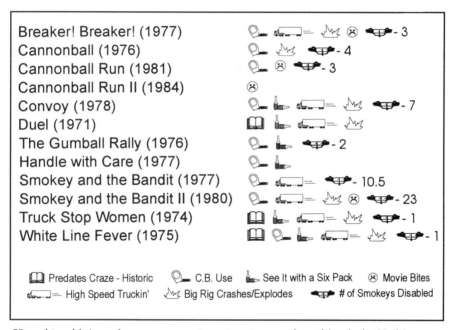

CB and truckin' movies you can see to get up to speed on this whole CB thing

Books: There were plenty of books during The Craze to get you rollin'. Most contain *pages and pages* on the tedious process of installation ("Your transceiver's ground [negative] lead should . . . ") and nearly all (even the joke books) reproduce the FCC Rules and Regulations. Here's a look at some representative CB books to search out in thrifts—for pleasure, for learning, and for ministering.

- *CB Jokes*—"Why do you call a car that's always being repaired a 'CB car'? Because it's always going . . . breaker . . . breaker . . . breaker. . . ."[4] I got a million of 'em!

- *How to Hear and Speak CB in a Short-Short* from the Whacky World of Whiskerman—a rodent dressed like a pimp and his buddies Mystery Man and Capt. Beaver (!) provide CB enlightenment in a narrative form. Many other CB jargon dictionaries are also available.
- *CB For Christians: How to Minister and Witness with CB*—How to witness on the CB! Share your faith over the squawk box! Stranded motorists are often mentally frazzled and can do little to resist a Good Buddy spreading the Good Word. "Make the modulation more meaningful." This book tells you how to engage in the usual CB banter and small talk and then how to move toward a meaningful witness. It even gives examples of snappy Christian sign-ons and sign-offs: "May the Good Lord take a likin' to ya, the Jubilee Kid southbound and down." That's a big 10–4![5]

CB Music: There was already a tradition of truck-drivin' songs in country music when the CB Craze hit, so it was natural that C&W artists would step up with CB tunes. But, as history would have it, the two most popular CB tunes of 1976 came out of a much older tradition: advertising.

- "Convoy" by C.W. McCall (Real Name: Bill Fries; Real Occupation: ad agency art director): "Convoy" rocketed to #1 in December 1975, sold 7 million copies, and provided the narrative for a ninety-minute film. Undoubtedly *key* in firing up The Craze of 1976. "Convoy" is a tight narrative of a lot of little guys takin' on the law. The rhyming and cadence is superior to other CB songs and even though it is totally phony, it inspires an air of spirited, successful rebellion. Yeeehaw! Runnin' road blocks!
- "The White Knight" by Cledus Maggard and His Citizen's Band (Real Name: Jay Huguely; Real Occupation: actor): An ad company president thought that the CB Craze had cash potential if somebody wrote some fun songs about it. He put Huguely on the job even though Huguely had *never* heard a CB transmission in his life. Armed with a CB and a jargon dictionary, he spent a day on the highway and churned out a whole album of densely worded CB songs. "The White Knight" peaked at #19 on the charts.
- "Teddy Bear" by Red Sovine: Sovine was a veteran of the truck-drivin'-song school. "Teddy Bear" was about a lonely little crippled boy who used his dad's CB (his trucker pa was killed in a wreck trying to get home in a bad snowstorm) to tell truckers that all he wanted was to ride again in a truck like his daddy's and. . . Oh, this is too sad. . .

- Radio Shack commissioned musicians to write songs specifically about CBs for their compilation *All Ears*. (By sheer coincidence, their line of CBs were photographed on the back cover. One tune even suggested going out to Radio Shack and picking up a CB.) The most execrable of these tunes is the Chipmunks-like "Hello Shirley, This is Squirrely"—two rodents modulatin' in speeded-up voices. Not one track on this record sounds remotely "authentic."

While most truck-drivin' songs hold some charm (they sound especially good when you're drivin'), most of the "funny" CB songs just aren't anymore, if they were at all. Without question, the thrift bins are holding this vinyl. Keep your eyes peeled for "truck" compilations—the post-1976 sets contain CB songs. Also, look for CB instructional records. And don't overlook those 8-tracks! You'll soon be rollin' down that long, lonesome highway with the best of them!

SUPERMARKET OF ART

Amateur art, more than anything else donated to the thrifts, really makes you sit and ponder. Who painted this? Why did they choose this medium? Was the subject matter assigned (like for a painting class)? Was it a random image or were they really motivated to paint two stallions fighting? How come such a personal thing (whether the artist kept it for themselves or gave it as a gift) was ditched at the thrifts? The charm of amateur art is in finding the odd piece that truly reflects someone's personal vision and is not just a rehash of established art motifs like landscapes or flowers in a vase. The dog dressed as a clown, the dripping world suspended from a noose, the floating arm (disem-bodied images seem more common in thrift art than you'd think they ought to be)—these are the kinds of unique sub-jects that will keep you and your guests speculating for years.

Thrift oil portrait by M. Dolores PHOTO BY AUTHOR

I am rarely intrigued by nor do I pur-chase "professional" paintings or draw-ings. They're deadly dull—the same old tired snowy river scenes, waves crashing against the rocks, or abstract splatter-ings. And most of the "real" art that goes to the thrifts shows up in the form

---

PHOTOS OF SOMEBODY ELSE'S LIFE

Ilove found photographs, especially of people. It's an appreciation I learned from my mother. She once lined our hallway with a couple dozen thrifted old framed portrait photographs. Friends would come to visit and say, "Is that your grandfather?" and I would reply, "No, I have no idea who that is." Insert big blank stare. But I remain fascinated by found photos. I can spend hours staring at them and poring over all the details, trying to guess who the person was, why the photo was taken, or what might have happened later. Some photos are so downright odd they defy speculation. (I have one of an old guy sitting atop a ladder in the middle of a river. It's anyone's guess what's going on.) Some thrifts try to charge a lot if the photo looks particularly old (1950 seems about the cut-off point). Don't pay high prices. In one weird way, old photos (especially aesthetically uninteresting head shots) are valueless. Their real value is in sentiment, but somebody relinquished that when they gave the photo to the thrift. Simply being old isn't reason enough to mark up a photo of a bride and groom. There's *no* shortage of personal photographs on Earth.

---

of a cheap reproduction, usually framed but rarely with glass. With amateur art, you can take home the original.

Why not pick a theme or motif and thrift all available art that meets it? Imagine a wall filled with two dozen different-sized depictions of boats in all media (oils, watercolor, string art, paint-by-number, photography, etc.). The more specialized your requirements, the more stunning your display can look. I met someone who was collecting *just* clowns on black velvet—one is scary, but a wall full is a new level of hell.

Natural Art

There's a subcategory of amateur art that involves the use of "natural" products artfully arranged. Macramé is the most popular one. Turning a ball of twine into an elaborately knotted pot holder is *some* kind of artistic gift. Macramé art also includes those odd rope and twine wall hangings. Most come in one of two designs: the abstract mass, which resembles a doormat hung on its side, or the

TIP Can't play an instrument? Take a look at those stacks of old sheet music anyway. Some have fabulous covers—lots of dreamy moonlight scenes suitable for framing. Oddly, musicians were in the habit of signing their name across the front of sheet music. Hopefully they did it in a not-too-obtrusive fashion.

Craft Sets: Don't have time to learn an arty craft? Pick one up in a box! Unused craft sets—often given as gifts—clutter up the thrifts. Your artistic genius is just pennies away. There's sand painting, paint-by-numbers, fake fur flowers, string-and-nail art, and bead kits. If you're more adventurous, wander over to the book section and pick up a booklet on creating crafts from tissue paper, aluminum foil, macaroni, string, or assorted refuse like paper-towel rolls and juice cans. Alas, if you find the coveted pop-top craft book, all you can do is dream of art that may have been.

The thrift perennial—
knotted-owl-on-a-stick
PHOTO BY AUTHOR

owl. It's *always* owls—I never see any other wildlife represented! To maximize naturalness, these works of art should be hanging from a real-life stick or, ideally, a piece of driftwood.

But the use of natural media hardly stops at string! There's clever mosaics made with beans, rice, dyed rice, pasta, twigs, and sand. (By "sand", I mean *real* sand, not that fake colored stuff you find in sand-painting kits.) I have a quite marvelous five-color map of the United States executed in colored rice. Art doesn't have to be flat. Chunky 3-D bits of nature like pine cones, seashells, driftwood, rocks, pebbles, and cypress knees have all been turned into adorable sculpture—sometimes abstract, sometimes cute like a frog made from pebbles. Though technically trash or household sculpture, Popsicle-stick and toothpick art also has a certain natural charm.

ON BEYOND THRIFTING PROFILE NO. 4

Who: Jim Shaw, Los Angeles artist.
Thrifting Origins: Jim Shaw is an L.A. artist who has been collecting thrift store paintings since the mid-1970s. More recently, he has been exhibiting them in galleries and other art spaces and many of the paintings from the exhibit were compiled in a book, Thrift Store Paintings. His collection currently holds over 150 paintings. When not on exhibit, they're piled up around his house.

• • •

Shaw started collecting the paintings in earnest as an adjunct to his collection of lurid paperback covers. Paperbacks were going up in price after a paperback price guide was published with inflated values. "I thought, well these could never go up in value since they are one-of-a-kind items." The cheapest painting was free from the trash; the most expensive was a set of seven for $300. It would be impossible to buy all amateur paintings found in thrift stores. Shaw tends to buy only the paintings that are weird or perverse. "The paintings have all sorts of qualities I admire; though I do laugh at some of them, I could never paint like any of them. I am too well trained. I fantasize they were made for some 'pure' reason, but who really knows."

Just what is this naked man doing? Is it even a man at all? From the thrift art collection of Matthew Veltkamp
PHOTO BY AUTHOR

In the reviews of his art show and book, critics have attributed many motivations to Shaw and the purpose of his collection (satire, mockery, art slumming, "real" American art, comment on "high art," the "latent meaning of junk"), but he says he prefers to let the audience draw their own conclusions. The paintings are exhibited with only the artist's name (if known) and a descriptive title that Shaw gives them ("Man Holds Balloon Out to Child").

He hasn't attempted to contact the original artists, but he doesn't avoid them if they do contact him. "In Hawaii I met the woman who painted 'Woman in Barrel with Yellow Roses, Typewriter and Chair on Boxes,' and she said that she'd painted it in Northridge, California, in the early 1960s and given it to her sister-in-law after her husband convinced her to give up painting. It made its way to the Pasadena City College swap meet where I paid $15 to $25 for it. I gave it back to her in Honolulu, where her sister-in-law was about to arrive for a visit and she was going to suggest they go see this interesting show of thrift-store paintings."

Shaw has some basic advice for people who might want to start their own thrift-store art collections. "Buy what you like and don't pay very much money." He is aware that his own well-publicized project has probably contributed to the current interest in thrift-store paintings and price increases. "Although there is now a 'market' for 'thrift-store paintings,' if nobody buys the paintings for high prices, the prices will come down to reasonable levels. If my funds were limitless, the $45-to-$250 asking prices I encountered at the PCC swap meet recently might have tempted me and I would have

---

FOOD AND FRAMES DON'T MIX

People sometimes decorate frames themselves, especially those desktop frames. They may glue rhinestones on or appliqué flowers. The weirdest decorated frame I ever saw was a rather ordinary 5-by-7-inch frame completely lined with sixty-two colored Milkbone dog biscuits!

---

been part of the inflationary demand. When I first decided to do the show (at the Brand Library Art Gallery in Glendale, which evolved into the book), I felt responsible to have the best show possible and I was working and earning enough money to pay a bit more. My limit crept up from $10 to $25—but now that I'm broke, it can stay low.

"I was once offered $100,000 for the whole collection, but I'd already told too many people I'd never sell them, so I had to say no. If the collector had offered $1,000,000, I don't know if I'd have had as much honor." He also told *USA Today* that to sell them would make him someone who was speculating on someone else's art.[1] "I'd like to donate them to a proper sort of institution that could show them publicly since they don't do anyone any good in my basement.

"I'm still finding them in thrift stores. There's always some perverse quality of superiority to any painting (or shirt or LP, etc.) found in a thrift store, compared to the greatest item bought at an antique swap meet or a Melrose Avenue resale boutique. When you've got more money than time, these institutions are useful, but if there's anything about going back to poverty that isn't depressing, it's that shopping in thrift stores has never lost its appeal to me, whether I did so out of necessity or curiosity."

• • •

Every Home a Museum: A Guide to Buying Paint-By-Numbers Art

BY CANDI STRECKER

A paint-by-numbers painting sounds like the very definition of "foolproof." The manufacturers chose the colors, printed out the cardboard "canvas," and laid out the numbered zones where each shade would go. They pretty well took care of all the ways that a kitchen-table artist could go wrong. Right?

Hardly. In fact, there are so many ways of going wrong that, for every paint-by-numbers (or PBN) masterpiece I buy, I pass up twenty or thirty ineptly done ones. Two major flaws occur over and over again. One is the failure to make the areas of color meet. Many painters, probably skittish or compulsive types who took the notion of "staying within the lines" literally, left the pale-blue printed guidelines showing as thin channels between the zones of paint. Another chronic problem is not mixing the paint properly, so that some brushfuls had too much thinner and not enough pigment. This semitransparent mix would let the numbers and lines show through. My rule of thumb is to pass up any PBN with either of these flaws. (But I will buy a half-finished PBN; they're interesting to my eye, plus they suggest a painter who *wised up* halfway through the process.)

The main thing to keep in mind is that there are plenty of PBNs out there, so there's no reason to buy one unless it's competently done and totally cool. And by collecting something this cheap and plentiful, you can quickly take advantage of the increased impact of displaying them *en masse*. Here are a few more points to consider when you shop.

Price: Fifty cents is nice; I seldom go over two or three bucks apiece, framed. Now that they're becoming ironic-hip collectibles, I've seen PBNs priced at around fifty *bucks* in big-city hipster antique shops, though the thrift stores in the same big cities still sell them for pocket change. Just keep in mind that PBNs have no worth whatsoever to anyone but the person who painted 'em; avoid giving the folks at the thrift shops and flea markets the notion that these are future collectibles, folk art, or real art. You may be buying the painting as all those things, but don't let your dollars give PBNs a hyperinflated marketplace value.

Frames: You'd be surprised how many proud *artistes* sent their finished PBNs out to be expensively framed. I don't bother with unframed ones, unless they're outstanding in some other way.

Themes: You may want to add impact to your PBN display by specializing. Common themes you can build a collection around include landscapes, animals, religious motifs, floral designs, big-eyed kids and animals, exotica (world travel scenes), and the ever-popular happy-sad clowns.

Size: Either extreme in size is cool. Big paintings imply herculean effort and will cover all but the largest holes in your walls. But I like smalls best. Because smalls usually came in kits for children and beginners, they're often less detailed, and poorly executed to boot. So smalls with complexity and eye appeal are rare finds.

Sets: Be aware that PBN kits often contained pairs of related images (two kittens, two jungle beasts, two Paris street scenes) or one big image plus two related smalls. One half of a pair, alone, may look forlorn; then again, you may like that effect.

And of course, some paint-by-numbers paintings are just cooler than others. It can be a mysterious quality inherent in the way the work was designed, with extra-ziggy shapes or especially intriguing colors. Or it may be a touch added by the painter: I have an Alice-In-Wonderland scene (a signed "Edna Kalin") in which Alice's eyes have a disturbing Lolita leer. My husband, who designs computer games, cherishes a small PBN head of a skeleton with a pirate hat and eyepatch: "He's a software pirate!" You're sure to find PBNs that speak to you, if you trust your instincts and shop with both your eyes and your heart open.

Suitable for Framing

Frames alone are cheap. Paintings alone are cheap. Smart shoppers buy separately and put the two together later. Sometimes bad art comes in a great frame. Keep the frame and redonate the art. Could be somebody else's taste. If you're not particularly clever with framing or you don't want to invest the time and money, hold out for frames that have glass. (The missing piece of cardboard backing, hook, or string are easy to add yourself.) An odd-sized frame without glass will probably necessitate a purchase of specially cut glass. Occasionally, the frames alone are so ornate and interesting looking, you can just hang them on the wall empty.

BIG EYE PAINTINGS

I am not generally susceptible to "sad and cute"—a dog leashed to a lamppost does not move me. But, I got some kinda jones for those Big Eye paintings. The thrifts have been cluttered up with these paintings for years, and for the most part, I ignored them. They were just another piece of omnipresent 1960s/1970s tacky schlock that didn't appeal to me. Then one day in Goodwill, I saw this set of four paintings—two girls, two boys—in mid-'60s rock 'n' roll dancing poses. I was transfixed. The incongruity of the rock 'n' roll setting (which is all about frantic energy even for fans) and these zombie-like children frozen in mid-frug staring with complete vapidity at me was jarring. Who are they supposed to be?! Nico? What were they drugged out on anyhow? I was hooked, and my buying spree had begun.

The common perception is that these Big Eye paintings were so very very popular because they are "awwwwww" cute and adults are suckers for cute kids, dogs, and cats. Maybe, but I don't think they're cute at all. I think they're downright weird, but I can't stop looking at them. The kids and animals seem like they've been abused. They stare out at you the way those caged lab monkeys do—"Please take the spike out of my head." How are we suppose to "help" these kids and animals? At least maybe you could track down the monkey and turn the electrodes off, but these kids remain trapped in this two-dimensional hell, their eyes forever silently pleading.

The Eve go-go kids that started my obsession
PHOTO BY VANESSA DOMICO

The Big Eye Boom

We have Walter and Margaret Keane to thank for popularizing the genre of Big Eye paintings. Like all great success stories, theirs is clouded by myth, conflicting stories, and lawsuits. The saga of the Keanes is worth an entire book in itself, but briefly here's what happened.

In the early 1960s, the Keanes's Big Eye paintings go boom! The Keanes were not suffering artists in a garret, and Walter especially was a brilliant marketer and media manipulator. The Keanes were soon riding a huge wave of hype about their paintings of Big Eye waifs. Original paintings, reproduction prints, postcards, dolls, and greeting cards flew out the door while Walter blathered on to the public about their work. He related that while traveling through Europe after World War II, he had been inspired by real-life waifs, the war orphans. He felt obligated to recapture their pathos through art. He told *Life* magazine in 1965, "In their eyes lurk all of mankind's questions and answers...I want my paintings to clobber you in the heart and make you yell "DO SOMETHING!"[2] (Math types will note that the introduction of the paintings to the world occurs nearly two decades after the prime war-orphan viewing time.) "Real" art people naturally dismissed the Big Eye paintings as being sentimental crap. An exception was another art-guy-cum-media-manipulator, Andy Warhol, who said of the Keanes's work, "It has to be good. If it were bad, so many people wouldn't like it."[3]

What was it about the paintings that touched people? The paintings were terrifically popular (even big celebrities like Jerry Lewis, Liberace, and Joan Crawford commissioned their portraits to be done à la Keane). One unnamed collector surmised that people bought the Big Eye paintings "because they feel guilty about not having foster children. By buying the pictures, . . . they can share their plight without being depressed."[4] Well, that's one interpretation, though there's no hard evidence to show that millions of people felt guilty about not taking in foster kids. Other analysts claimed that the lure was more primal—that it was the large eyes themselves and that as humans we are conditioned from birth to respond to eyes. Interesting, but I'd have to go with the art-world critique. The paintings *were* sentimental crap, but nobody ever went broke fobbing off sentimental crap on the American public.

The future seemed rosy for the Keanes. They sat in their shared studio—Walter turning out round-eyed paintings, Margaret working on the more detailed almond-eyed portraits. But an ugly divorce soon shattered the happy myth. Margaret went public and claimed to have done *all* the paintings herself. Walter cried foul and declared that he had been the one who had taught the "untalented" Margaret to paint. Margaret organized a public paint-off in San Francisco's Union Square in the fall of 1970. She quickly executed a "Keane painting" for spectators and the press. Walter was unable to attend. An eight-year court battle over the true origin of the Big Eye

---

LOOKING IN AT BIG EYE HQ

Recently, I visited Margaret's Keane Eyes Gallery in San Francisco. It feels just like a small art gallery—there's no hint of camp or irony about it at all. I feared the salesman could see right through me and know that my intent was not to admire Margaret Keane, the artist, but to snicker at some Big Eyes up close. I already had a houseful of cheap to very cheap Keane reprints, and no matter how many times you read "Art in the Age of Mechanical Reproduction," nothing prepares you for coming face-to-face with a *real* copy of some cheap print you have propped up by the radiator. Very unnerving. (Upon closer inspection, the painting in question turned out to be *not* the original but a "repligraph"—some sort of oil-paint transfer process. *Caveat emptor.*) This place was delightfully unaware of its own weirdness. Displayed in the front window was a painting I almost could have spent $800 on. A tiny gilt-framed image, the painting itself was no more than 3 by 4 inches, and it was a close-up of a single sad eye! I reeled at the brilliance! The entire Keane oeuvre had been distilled down to its very essence, the sad eye.

paintings began in 1982. Suits and countersuits flew—including another paint-off, this time inside a courtroom. Margaret took fifty-three minutes to whip off a Big Eye; Walter claimed a sore arm prevented him from painting. The court awarded in her favor. Walter continues to claim ownership of the Big Eyes, but it's to little avail. The revelation that Margaret did all the painting was well publicized and is now generally accepted. And perhaps most importantly, Margaret still paints and sells Big Eye portraits (albeit happier looking), while Walter grouses and nurses his shoulder injury that *still* prevents him from painting.

Who Were the Ersatz Big Eye Painters?

No stranger to hyperbole, in 1965 Walter Keane claimed there were "around 187" Big Eye painters at work.[5] It's a marvelous number, "187"—so precise, one wonders how he came by it. Nonetheless, there were plenty of Keane imitators frantically at work filling the dime stores with cheap reprints glued to pressboard ready to hang on the wall. Unlike the Keanes, these artists had no PR machinery in place, and there's little or no information to be found on them. (Tracking information down is further complicated by the imitators' frequent use of near-generic names: "Gig," "Lee," "Eve," "Maio," and "Goji.") Still, a little study quickly reveals that, while perhaps inspired by the Keanes's Big Eyes and emboldened by their success, the "imitators" are not without their own style.

Not surprisingly, this Gig painting is titled "Pity Kitty." PHOTO BY VANESSA DOMICO

My personal favorite is Gig, who turned his (or her) brush exclusively to portraits of "waif" cats and dogs. Scrawny animals with enormous eyes (the biggest eyes of the entire Big Eye school) staring out from oversized heads, these pitiful creatures look like some genetic experiment gone awry. But the artist has not meant for us to find pity in their misshapen heads. Gig kindly provides details within the paintings that guide our hearts—is the puppy escaping that burnt-out beachhouse in the background? What about this kitty living atop a trash can in a seedy neighborhood where "rooms" are for rent? And look, this puppy's leash has come undone! Where oh where could his owner be? It's sooooo saaaaad.

Then there's Eve, who gave us the saucer-eyed zombie go-go chil-

Lee's works have the highest "eye density"—here's ten huge sad eyes imploring you to care.

PHOTO BY VANESSA DOMICO

dren that first entranced me. Unlike most of the other paintings, these "waifs" are well-dressed—no tatters, no bare feet—but the contrast between their perfect little Beatles suits and their huge dead eyes is all the more heart-wrenching. Not so with Lee's paintings, which appear to be a blatant rip-off of the Keanes's kids *and* Gig's cats. Barefoot round-eyed children in torn clothing huddle in the rain clinging to their gigantic-eyed cats. And there are so many others (184 more if we are to believe Walter Keane)—Eden and Goji, who gave us pitiful harlequins; França, who managed the impossible by giving the round eyes a hooded effect; the "Hecho en Mexico" fluorescent waifs on black velvet; and still more unsigned masterpieces whose origins are lost to us.

Perhaps to the untrained eye, these paintings all do look remarkably similar, but I now know better. Having put up dozens of Big Eye Masters side by side, the differences are starkly visible and only add to the appreciation I feel for each Master. When I moved to a house with an extremely long and narrow hallway, I decided to round up all my Big Eye paintings and hang them there. It would be floor-to-ceiling misery—a Hallway of Sorrow. I am pleased to report that the effect is stunning—no matter how you twist and turn you cannot escape Big Eye upon Big Eye—a 360-degree panorama of sadness. And incidentally, visitors cannot escape this journey into the deepest Pit of the Big Eye—this is the hallway to the bathroom! I've had guests run sobbing from the house wailing, "I just wish I could *help* them somehow!" Well, that's not true, but I'm hoping for it.

There's been a recent wave of re-affection for Big Eye art, especially in the ironic use of the Big Eye imagery. The Big Eyes have been incorporated into hipster irony shorthand. They've been used as set dressing on MTV and in sitcoms. The cover art of the 1994 alterna-bands-do-the-Carpenters *If I Were A Carpenter* CD featured a stylized illustration of Richard and Karen clearly inspired by the paintings of Big Eye Master, Eve. They're insta-cheese, immediately recognizable like lava lamps or Elvis-on-black-velvet.

Do *not* pay a lot for these paintings. I've heard horror stories of ridiculous prices charged for copy #12,456,236 of a Keane-on-cardboard. There were millions and millions of these cheap prints. And if you're really a fan of these paintings, just wait till the current fad for them passes and all the suckers who paid bucks for the "collectible" will tire of them and ditch them back in the thrift. It takes a strong person to keep these paintings on your wall for more than an evening's amusement. Remember, they'll break your heart every time you pass them.

"I Love You This Much"

Mired one day in my Hallway of Sorrow, I had a brilliant inspiration. Why not construct an antidote to the pain so that when you left the Hallway, you'd be embraced with comfort and love? And what better item to convey this warmth and inclusion but with those thrift store perennials—the little statuette of the guy with beseeching eyes and arms flung open that says "I Love You This Much"? I began my quest that weekend and was surprised and delighted to pick up half a dozen *different* "I Love You This Much" figures. So far I have found seventeen unique ones all meeting the criteria of outstretched arms, moist eyes, and the proper phrase. (I made one exception for "This is How Much I Love You.") All was fine until I realized that, in my frantic quest for happiness, I had overlooked a heart-breaking point. *Nothing* could be sadder than a statuette that says "I Love You This Much" that the recipient had later dumped at the thrift store!

Most of the little plastic figurines-with-a-message in thrifts were made by the Russ Berrie Co. They're so omnipresent in thrifts, the temptation is to collect them all, from "CB-ers Make Better Lovers" to "World's Greatest Golfer." (They're *so* conveniently numbered and dated on the back.) The current card-shop incarnation of these impulse gifts-with-a-message are those cloying Precious Moments. At first glance, they are similar—super-cute children in pale pastels with an assortment of *bon mots* for every occasion. Closer inspection reveals some major differences! Average cost seems to be about $30! There are no guffawing-type jokes like "Lay Down, I Think I Love You." In fact, many of them have a religious slant. The Precious Moments small boy with requisite outstretched arms and upturned eyes did not say "I Love You This Much," but "Hallelujah for the Cross"! I suppose these sickly-sweet little darlings (they make Hummels look like grunge kids) will all go to the thrift one day, but I bet they go behind the counter.

DRESSING UP YOUR WINDOWS

Shades and Blinds

It's not easy to test the "spring" on a shade in a thrift, but remember, a broken spring may be why a perfectly good-looking shade was ditched. If you think you'll never raise the shade at home, then don't worry about it. Also common in the thrifts are roll-up matchstick shades and miniblinds. Any window treatment that rolls up on a pulley system is apt to be a tangled mess. Many go to the thrifts because the roll-up setup got broken; others get snarled in transit or while lying around the thrift floor. Not impossible to repair yourself, but a tedious project. Miniblinds are prone to more tangling problems (besides the pull-up cord, there are also cords that run through the blinds) and mechanical failures. Often donated miniblinds are just tossed on the store floor, so the slats get all trampled on and bent out of shape.

✳TIP✳ **Traveling with a tape measure while thrift-decorating is a smart idea. Before you leave home, take measurements of window size, picture dimensions, available wall space, or whatever it is you're trying to augment by thrifting.**

Curtains

Your easiest window treatment (besides just tacking a sheet up) is curtains. Most windows already have curtain rods in place (or they are simple to install). If the place you're living in isn't your own, curtains are the perfect solution. Easy to put up and take down, they don't harm anything and they let you cover up existing ugly shades or blinds you can't take down. In the case of existing hideous curtains, simply remove ugly ones. Store in box. Put up your cool ones. When it comes time to move, reverse the process. Window areas can be big. Don't tolerate gigantic swatches of other people's bad taste.

If you're lucky, you might find curtains you like all ready to hang up—either they're seamed along the top to insert a curtain rod, have rings sewn on, or are pleated to hold curtain hooks. (Curtain hooks usually live in those hanging plastic bags in thrifts.) You may find just fabric. The easiest way to turn raw fabric into a curtain is simply to fold over a few inches along the top and sew along the edge of the fabric. Leave the sides open—this is where you'll slip the curtain rod in. You can sew this by machine, by hand, or even staple it if you're

TIP I always check the rolls of wallpaper in the thrifts. I haven't found anything yet that meets my tastes (I'm holding out for some leftover fabulous wallpaper from the 1940s or 1950s), but some of it might be attractive to you. Chances are slim that you'll ever find enough of one pattern to do a whole room, but you can cover some shelves or an odd bit of hallway. If it's the old paper type of wallpaper, you can always cut it up for wrapping paper, stationery, and envelopes.

in a hurry. Hopefully, the top of the curtain will be out of sight anyway. The bottom edge of the fabric should also be folded over and secured so it doesn't unravel or look scraggly. Sew or improvise with duct tape.

Wall mirrors are pretty common in thrifts. Look for good-quality heavy ones, without lots of discolorations in the silver. If the mirror isn't framed, make sure the edges are finished. Some cheap frameless mirrors have sharp edges that can cut. Don't buy a plastic mirror—they're worthless and shabby-looking. Some people hate mirrors and won't have one around anywhere; others adore mirrors. No vain person should be without at least one mirror in each room so you can check your bad self wherever you are. Mirrors, used cleverly, can open up small rooms and they bounce light around nicely. A wall of differently framed, shaped, and sized mirrors is quite an eyecatcher.

Whatnot shelves and shadowboxes are perfect for double-duty decorating. They look swell by themselves and provide an attractive setting for some of your most prized tchotchkes. These small shelves have a tendency to turn up at thrifts in the most awful colors. I think people paint them to match their walls. Rejuvenate them by slapping on a little preferred paint of your own.
PHOTO BY JIM BRENNAN

LET THERE BE LIGHT

Everybody needs light, and lamps are nearly always a good buy at thrifts. I've purchased over fifty lamps in the past few years, and they all worked once I put a lightbulb in them. They weren't all perfect, but whatever mysterious process makes lightbulbs light up seems to function.

Thrift-lamp problems are listed here in order of increasing complexity:

1. They're really ugly. True, most are, but they work. Better to thrift a single gruesome lamp than to curse all darkness. At a couple of bucks, you can swap it out later.

2. The shade is missing, wrong, or ugly. Don't fall into the trap of perfect lamp–perfect shade ready-to-buy combo. Buy good lamp bases and great lampshades when you see them. An attractive lampshade in decent shape is the rarer commodity. Once you have several of both, mix and match them. Swapping around lamps and their shades is quick and dirty redecorating. You're apt to have more imagination than the lamp manufacturer ever did.

If your finances or patience are low while searching out the right shade for your lamp, measure how big a shade you need and have a tape measure or an appropriately sized bit of string on you when you thrift. Also note which kind of shade you need—does it fit over the lightbulb? Hang on a frame?

The next two problems are easily fixed but require a bit of handymanism. Both call for a short and inexpensive trip to the hardware store. Replace the broken or missing part and the lamp works like new. Lamp workings are blessedly standard.

3. The socket is missing, bent, or broken. The on/off switch is broken or missing. These are easily replaced by a single unit socket/switch component.

4. The electrical cord is badly frayed, missing, or has an ancient and incompatible plug on it. Replace the cord.

The range and variety of lighting for sale in thrifts may surprise you. And make sure you search out the whole store. Pole lamps, for instance, are often stored in some stray corner and not with the table lamps.

Table Lamp: Couples will want to thrift the matching set of bedside lamps—one for each side. A variation of the table lamp is the Desk Lamp, which has an angled shade designed to cast the light down. (This Desk Lamp should not be confused with the Student Desk Lamp. Those bolt to the wall or desk edge, and the light source is at the end of a flexible and extendible arm.) The most

✳TIP✳ **Check the whole lamp for lightbulb sockets. Some bedside lamps will take another lightbulb within the base (functions as decoration or nightlight), and I've seen floor lamps with a socket underneath the base. Once home, it's also a good idea to test all your new lamps with a three-way bulb to see if they're wired for three wattages.**

common lamp in the thrifts is the "American Lamp"—the one with the eagle base and colonial-pattern shade. They're pretty unattractive, but what if you had ten or twelve in one room?

The thrift store is also where you happen upon the homemade lamp. Often it's only the base of the lamp that is unique—the socket, wiring, and shade are all standard. Some people are not content with a store-bought lamp and build their own using spare material or some object of sentimental value. I have seen lamp bases made from the bowling pins (both plastic and wooden), bowling balls, bottles, beer and soda cans, military shells, seashells, driftwood, and a badly cut chunk o' wood.

Floor Lamp: A very basic design—flat base, three- to five-foot pole, and a lamp at the top. Some require shades, but the common brass and fake brass ones have built-in shades. The design of the floor lamp is so basic that any old cheap and boring one can be spruced up with just the right kicky shade.

An odd variation of the Floor Lamp is the Pole Lamp that has three or four shaded lights along an extendible or sectioned spring-loaded pole. These were terrifically popular in the 1950s and 1960s, and they really do favor a low-ceilinged ranch house! The poles only extend out about eight to ten feet. If you're desperate to use them in your fourteen-foot-ceiling home, you can prop them up in a corner, but they get horribly dwarfed. (I've often thought they could be salvaged by mounting them diagonally along a big wall, but I haven't tested this theory yet.) The big advantage of the pole lamp is that you can erect it anywhere in the room, though you should keep it out of traffic areas.

Hanging Lamps: include those kooky fiberglass balls, floating disc-shaped lamps, and chandeliers. They look swell, but these lights are trickier to place in your home.

Decorative lamps aren't designed to illuminate an area but to be enjoyed as *objets*. They include funny bar lamps, various op art lights of the 1960s and 1970s (like the fiber optic flowers), mood lighting (a lightbulb concealed in a fiberglass box that just gives off a weird glow), lava lamps, and TV-top lamps. As if looking at the TV wasn't enough of an attraction, a TV-top lamp is usually a piece of pottery that takes a tiny bulb in back. They also make a decent, albeit big, nightlight.)

Drama-themed TV-top lamp
PHOTO BY VANESSA DOMICO

Thrifts are often a good source for industrial lighting—giant hulking metal lights and light racks. This stuff is expensive new, but a steal at thrifts where it's considered ugly. Clever thrifters can integrate this stuff nicely into their homes, especially if they're going for a high-tech look. Avoid poorly made fake industrial lighting sold throughout the 1970s and 1980s to those in pursuit of the high-tech look. The real stuff tends to be pretty sturdy. Also in the discarded metal bin, you might find old fixtures that hold the small fluorescent lamps you see in old bathrooms. These take a little more work to replace, but everybody needs a hobby. Ditto with other wall-mounted lamps, but if you can thrift a good Do-It-Yourself book, you'll be ahead of the game.

Glass fixtures: Keep an eye out for glass shade fixtures. They're cheap and easy to find. Check your home light to see which sort of fixture it needs—the flat dish sort that are suspended beneath a ceiling light or the bulb kind that completely encase the lightbulb.

Once you get a few good light sources home, use your imagination to place them. No reason you can't suspend a fiberglass ball lamp over your work desk. And don't forget those emergency light sources—battery-operated camp lights, flashlights, and candles.

The Big Lamp Party

I am indebted to Matthew Tinkcom in D.C. for providing this hilarious idea.

We are all familiar with those gigantic lamps that take up so much space in thrifts—you know the ones with a base as big as a small economy car and a shade of equal proportions. Propose a party. Tell all your thrifting friends that admittance to the party requires bringing the *biggest* lamp they can find.

There will be much excitement, squealing, and groaning as each new humongous lamp makes its debut. Establish a quantitative measurement system—tally up the width and height of both base and shade. Here's the kicker: the person who brought the *smallest* of the huge lamps has to take all the lamps home!

18 Patio and Pool

THE BARBECUE

Well, you made it! You've got the house, the backyard, the social connections, the free time, and the spare cash. What to do? Have a barbecue! The backyard social event, known to us all as the BBQ, was another gift of the 1950s. Previously only hobos cooked outside. But a BBQ meant status—it meant you had the attractive yard space, a set of specific outdoor cooking tools, and the time to noodle on all-afternoon burger flipping.

The BBQ concept was such a hit that soon the ultimate BBQ required far more than just a grill and some big forks. The marketplace was filled with ancillary items necessary to the Big BBQ experience. You needed the right furniture, dishware, glassware, serving and cooking implements, and special clothing. BBQ became a hobby, even a lifestyle, if you could believe *Sunset* magazine. ("The Magazine of Western Living" was a veritable BBQ bible.)

TOOLS NEEDED FOR FIRE ENGINEERING

I did thrift my BBQ—a splendiferous chartreuse hooded contraption from the 1970s. Low on looks, but a backyard bargain at $7. A buddy gleefully reported a thrift sighting of a Ball-B-Q, a completely round BBQ on a stand. Long before you decide which kind of barbecue to get—tabletop, portable, gas grill, electric grill, hibachi, or brazier—you can stock up on the equipment. Dig around the thrift and

Any crazy pattern is appropriate for BBQing, but this shirt is the yummiest.
PHOTO BY VANESSA DOMICO

search out extra-long cooking implements (long-handled fork, knife, tongs, and basting brush), a giant serving tray (a BBQ motif is swell), meat-markers (small spiked signs or cow heads that say "well done" and "rare"), an appropriate tablecloth, mitts, skewers, spiked potato-bakers, and a long-handled salt-and-pepper shaker. When in doubt, remember all trappings are big—dare I say it—*man-sized*.

The BBQ apron may be your most important accessory. It's like the king's crown—to wear it is to rule! Today's BBQ aprons don't have the same *joie de vivre*. Too often they are red-and-white checked and rely on a stupid slogan for laughs like "Kiss the Cook." BBQ was taken seriously in the '50s and '60s but it was not without humor. The older aprons usually had some cartoon drawings of the BBQ chef at work, BBQ tools, or BBQ scenes. Some BBQ aprons turn up in great shape—probably given as gifts and never worn. Others show war damage like stains, tears, and burns. No biggie, you'll get it dirty yourself probably. And fun fashion aside, it's a smart garment to have on hand. It's another layer of cloth between you and the flaming coals and spitting meat.

OUTDOOR SEATING AVAILABLE

When I rule the world, ownership of white molded-resin chairs will be strictly prohibited. I will continue to fund NASA but for the exclusive purpose of blasting shuttles full of resin chairs deep into space where hopefully they will orbit in perpetuity around Pluto. Resin chairs are cheap cheap cheap and look it. Other sins include: cracking, making your butt sweat, blowing around in the wind, and just not being very comfortable. They also don't move. Good patio furniture should move—either rock,

A common BBQ apron motif is the self-referential drawing of the aproned BBQ chef who is wearing the *same* apron and so on into infinity.
PHOTO BY VANESSA DOMICO

PASSING DOWN THE MANLY ART

"A boy is almost certain to find some barbecuing experience useful later in life—especially if he lives in the West. And this is one art of cookery that his father may be best equipped to teach him." (From *Teaching Your Son to Be a Teen-age Barbecue Chef.*)[1] The BBQ was the outdoor equivalent of the Manly Den—it was the man's domain. Women could participate—maybe make a relish or two, wash dishes, mind children—but the true BBQ engineer took his host duties very seriously. He planned menus, prepared side dishes and the main meat, mixed drinks, created fire, and even cleaned the grill himself! (It still remains one of the great mysteries of our culture why men can turn out four-course meals over a flaming split barrel but are reduced to helpless pudding in front of the automatic electric kitchen range.)

---

glide, or bounce. Think soothing. I implore you not to bother with the resin chairs. There's plenty of other good outdoor furniture available in the thrifts.

- Pressed-steel springer chairs with tubular legs that bounce slightly are very common in porch-settin' parts of the country. These steel chairs are surprisingly comfortable, but you can always augment them with a pillow. They do rust if left outside, but it takes decades for them to become unusable. A little rust is part of the charm. Better they should rust away and return to the earth, unlike those resin chairs that probably have a half-life of two million years.

- Aluminum chairs hold up better in the weather—though they can really travel some distance in a strong wind! They are fairly light, but this can be a plus if you need to move the chair around a lot. Inspect the cross-straps on webbed chairs—when they go, they're a pain to fix.

- There's a wide range of wooden outdoor furniture—picnic tables, benches, sand chairs, and Adirondacks chairs. I find wood to be less comfy than metal, but that's where those 50 cent pillows are so useful. Wicker or rattan furniture shows up less frequently. Don't worry if the pillows are missing or ugly. They can be replaced or recovered. Wooden furniture will last longer if you don't leave it out in the rain.

- Sometimes, it's the odd-shaped chairs that are the comfiest. Basket chairs are great for outdoor sitting (they look something like half a squeezed orange and have a straw or plastic weave attached to a metal frame). Butterfly chairs, director's chairs, camp stools, and those folding canvas-and-frame beach slings are all swell out on the deck, and they fold up nicely for carrying and storage.

PATIOWARE

You can use your regular dishes and glassware outside, but why risk the breakage? And remember, glass is dangerous around the pool! There's a special class of outdoor eating and drinking materials called "patioware" or "picnicware" (real words, I swear!). Melmac plates will do in a pinch, but look for lightweight and specially molded plates for outside. They're often sectioned like cafeteria plates and come in lots of bright colors.

Disregard today's cheap plastic cups and mugs and look for older plasticware from the 1950s and 1960s. There's lots of Thermo-Serv at the thrifts. These glasses, mugs, and pitchers are made from a double layer of plastic—the top layer is clear and there is often a piece of illustrated paper behind it. The base plastic is usually black, but you'll find other colors too. A very popular outdoor drinking set was similar to Thermo-Serv and had a bit of woven grass suspended inside and pastel rims. Look out for the tumblers, the mugs, the pitcher, and the ice bucket. Pick up them singly and soon you'll have a set worthy of your best homemade lemonade. Another common patio set was Raffiaware—these are opaque white or beige ribbed-plastic glasses and bowls with a ring of color around the top.

PHOTO BY VANESSA DOMICO

Many more casual housewares were made from aluminum. Aluminum housewares were a popular gift in the 1950s, especially hammered aluminum—glasses, trays, cake plates, bowls, coasters—with pounded-on images of flowers, trees, deer, birds, fruit, and abstract designs. Older aluminum pieces are thick and sturdy, not flimsy like an aluminum foil roaster pan or those ashtrays you can bend in half with one hand. Obviously the metal will dent again if you hit it or drop it hard enough. But the advantage is that a well-hammered piece is already covered in bumps and ridges and probably wouldn't show your new dent. Hammered and colored aluminum, still common in many thrifts, is entering the collectibles zone, so be wary of high prices.

✳TIP✳ Always dry aluminum tumblers separately—don't stack them! They will stick together forever. If you have the room, it's best to even store them separately.

CARING FOR PLANTS

I'd like to commend the Village Discount Outlet chain of thrifts in the Midwest for actually putting plants into the planters they sell! Sure, they're just cheap little coleus plants, but why not? (This spot o' green almost makes up for the gut-clenching odor from their hot dog and nacho stands.) While you can put plants in anything, a plant is always happier in a pot that has a built-in saucer bottom, cut so there can be water drainage. Most plastic planters are pretty cheap-looking, so hold out for the ceramic ones. Thrifts will often mark down ceramic planters with chips. The chip hardly matters to your plant, and you can simply turn the chipped side away from view.

During the 1970s, the ultimate way to display your plants was to suspend the pots in elaborate macramé hangers. What possessed thousands of men and women to spend hours knotting rough cord till their fingers bled? There was the attraction of doing a handicraft yourself. It must have been quite a sense of accomplishment when you'd done the last of 6,000 knots. Macramé had an authentic "rough" look that was popular in some '70s homes. And let's not forget the plants. Plants were given primary status in the '70s. They had feelings; you were meant to talk to them and carefully tend to their specific needs. A big fuzzy knotted mass of jute is a much more natural environment for your sensitive plant to hang in. No shortage of macramé hangers in the thrifts. Besides your traditional string macramé, you'll also find plant hangers made from beads, shells, drapery cord, and synthetic rope.

Maybe you'll be inspired to whip up your own plant hanger? Then grab one of the zillions of leftover macramé instructional books. I was flipping through some thrifted macramé guides wondering why on earth macramé had been so popular when I stumbled across a possible answer: "A friend taught me three basic knots and I just went berserk."[2] I guess it's kind of like drugs—a "friend" gives you a little taste and soon you're out of your mind, knotting up six-foot-long plant holders. The books all say easy and fun—but after looking at some of the schematics, I think it'd be faster to build a rocket ship from scratch.

Tiki Party Tonight!

Tiki Tacky: The idea of a tiki party is not so much to re-create the authentic atmosphere and culture of the Pacific Islands— but rather to re-create the *re-creation* of that culture.

Post–World War II America saw a distillation, homogenization, and outright misrepresentation of Pacific Island culture, motifs, customs, and trappings into numerous silly pieces of Polynesian schlock—the bright green tiki-shaped mug, the South Seas paint-by-number, and the Hawaiian fabric swimming trunks. "Authentic" Polynesian cuisine and libations stretched from the suburbs of Boston to the back patios of Glendale. We'll leave the cultural outrage for another time (deserved as it might be)—we're here to have a party—and trapped as we are in our generational ironic distance, we wanna have the party with the greatest overkill of pop culture items.

Indoor or outdoor, intimate or free-for-all, summer or winter—the raw materials you need for your tiki party are just blocks away at your thrift. Plan ahead. If you need more direction or are interested in period Polynesian party planning, get yourself to the thrift book section. Numerous books were published in the 1940s, 1950s, and 1960s that outlined how to throw a tiki party, packed with decorating tips, craft projects, food and drink recipes. Also generally themed hostess books and Home Economics texts (the Polynesian Prom was popular) from that time often included sections on tiki party throwing.

Decorations: Whether you're holding your party inside or out, you'll want to hide or disguise as much of your Mainland look as possible.

Inside: Cover the walls with split bamboo or matchstick shades—easily thrifted and easily hung up. Any tropical scene artwork should be brought to the forefront. Cover the floors with straw beach mats. Make use of any tropical (Hawaiian, tapa, souvenir tablecloths) fabric that comes your way—drape over furniture, pin to wall, use as tablecloth. Now is the time to show off any bamboo, wicker, or rattan furniture you might have. Scatter excess Hawaiian shirts, record album covers, or coconut souvenirs about. Subdued lighting is important—put candles in tiki holders or monkey pod bowls (line these with aluminum foil and keep an eye on 'em). Cover lampshades with souvenir scarves. Backyard-style strings of colored party lights bring an outside feel to an indoor party.

Outside: Cover any inappropriate fencing or walls with the above suggested coverings. Hang record albums, shirts, giant Polynesian forks and spoons from trees. Those straw beach mats will make the driveway seem more exotic. String party lights or use colored light-bulbs. Maybe you'll be lucky enough to thrift one of those flaming torches!

Cover the table with fabric, an appropriately themed tablecloth, or one of the above-mentioned shades or straw mats. Scatter plastic flowers, shells, or seed necklaces. A cheap and easy way to get loads of shells is to thrift a hanging macramé-style plant holder made from small cowrie shells. A few snips and you've got hundreds of shells to decorate with. Lay out books with good tropical covers or themes and give them away later as door prizes.

Music: There's an enormous selection of music—the trendy exotics (Denny, Lyman, Baxter), Hawaiian guitars, atmospheric noises (bird calls, waves crashing), Hawaiian muzak, or the vocal styling of Mr. Don Ho—in thrift stores. The choice is yours. You only need a couple of records to put together a tape. I suggest premade tapes that can be played from a *hidden* tape player so that the music seems to waft quietly from the air. Even if you can only find really bad Hawaiian music, lowering the volume will add to the atmosphere and keep your guests from really hearing the tortured tunes.

PHOTO BY VANESSA DOMICO

Refreshments: Whether or not you choose to serve alcoholic beverages (those old Home Ec books will give you those under-21 punch recipes), the tiki mug is the vehicle of choice. (Should you not be able to provide enough mugs for your guests, suggest they bring their own.) If you're hosting a huge party (or perhaps you don't want to circulate all your mugs)—thrift lesser-quality tiki drinkware like those frosted glass tiki mugs from Disneyland or bad souvenir glasses from Hawaii.

A bamboo-covered (real or faux) or pineapple-shaped ice bucket is a nice addition to the bar area. So are swizzle sticks. While you could cheat and purchase little umbrellas in a real store, keep your eye on those plastic bags of crap they hang in weird places in thrifts. They often contain things like swizzle sticks (maybe even ones from tiki bars!) and party items. Keep an eye out for souvenir ashtrays too that can be used for snacks or decorations at no-smoking affairs.

Polynesian Platter: Serve whatever you like. Garnish with pineapple. There are lots of those monkey-pod wooden bowls in the thrifts and many are conveniently shaped like pineapples. Perfect for snacks. Look for souvenir trays and plates from Hawaii as well as silverware with bamboo handles or a bamboo motif.

Aloha Wear: The Hawaiian shirt is the obvious fashion choice here. Suggest (or demand) that everyone wear one. Have some extra

---

AFTER THE PARTY

You went and spent six months and $40 buying up stuff for your Tiki
Party—the fab party you had *last* night—so *now* what do you do with
all the South Seas crap? The answer is deceptively simple: use all the stuff
for *what it was intended to be!* Hang the bamboo shades in your window,
drink any beverage from your tiki mug, set the table with the Hawaiian
island tablecloth (everyday use of the Giant Fork and Spoon is not recommended, however), wear the Hawaiian shirt on work casual days, take the
straw mat to the beach, and read *Kon-Tiki.*

---

shirts on hand for errant guests. Quality varies, but you'll find a
wide array of cotton and polyester shirts in many agreeable and dis-
agreeable patterns. Old rayon Hawaiian shirts are highly prized and
scarce but not impossible to find. (Myself, I'm partial to cotton, and
I insist on a "Made in Hawaii" label.) Don't overlook those batik
prints and guayabara shirts (see-through front-ribbed shirts that
Ferdinand Marcos used to wear). All very tropical. Ladies might
consider a tropical patterned muumuu. You'll be in-theme and marvelously comfortable. Other clothing accessories: Panama hats;
Hawaii souvenir scarves; tropically patterned shorts, skirts, dresses,
and beachwear; leis; grass skirts; sarongs for men (wrap tropical
fabric around your waist like a towel); wooden, seed, or shell necklaces; and bare feet. Aloha!

SWIMSUITS A GO-GO!—THRIFTING FOR OLD SWIMSUITS

Some old swimsuits for men and women are adorable, and maybe
you'd like to create some sort of Lana Turner/Steve Reeves sensa-
tion around the pool in a kicky vintage suit? By all means, but read
on—there's information you should know about buying and especially wearing an old suit. If you just want to buy them for historical reasons or decoration, then some of the distinctions (like see-
through-ness) won't matter.

Most of my male friends complain that they are disadvantaged
shopping for cool old clothes (or even any clothes) in thrifts. They
say there is simply more women's clothing—and a better range of it,
too. Well, gentlemen, here's your chance to get even. Based on a
purely anecdotal study, it appears that there are far more men's vintage beach togs in the thrifts—and what's more, it's in better shape,
and because of the more sensible fit of men's swimwear (S, M, L),
it's more apt to fit!

Throughout their lives, women *do* own more swimsuits than men. Many women seem to have at least one new suit a season (and we all know those chicks with a suit for each day of the week), whereas guys seem to wear the same pair of blue trunks year after year after year. So it makes sense that the women's swimwear rack at the thrift is larger than the men's—and it is—but why do men's vintage suits turn up more frequently than women's?

The modern women's suit has been designed to cling to the female form and hence has been constructed from "cling and stretch" fabrics. Obviously any garment designed to be worn while stretched to its maximum width, and so worn, is going to eventually lose its elasticity and become an ill-fitting, shapeless rag.

Alternately, men's boxer-style suits are usually made of sturdy all-cotton or rayon, with a reinforced elastic waistband and waist tie. Barring falling into the beach BBQ, they've got a good life span. If you like the pattern and they fit you around the waist, they're yours. The exception is the "ball-catcher" or whatever that thin white-mesh sewn-in-panty in men's swim trunks is called. Check your older suit carefully here. This bit of the garment can be missing, torn from the main seam, or stretched out enough to no longer be effective. If the interior lining is missing or in poor shape and the outer fabric is a thin light color, you may want to refrain from getting this particular suit wet. Your own personal level of modesty will set the standard.

The other style of vintage men's swimsuit is the form-fitting swim trunks. Since these are made to cling, they are vulnerable to getting stretched out over time and losing their elasticity. This can cause embarrassing gaps where the suit meets the thigh and you may find that the waistband won't hold and slips south.

Some older women's suits from the 1940s, 1950s, and 1960s will still fit fairly well despite a lack of elasticity because of other supporting devices built into the suit. Built-in bras and girdles, wire, foam, heavy interfacing, and plastic rods (alone or in combination) are not unusual to find in suits of these times. A suit that is so reinforced that elasticity no longer matters will generally hold a "full rounded shape" even while on a hanger. A suit that *zippers* shut will probably still fit snugly.

PHOTOS BY AUTHOR

Even never-worn vintage swimsuits are not immune from elasticity problems. The rubber and various synthetic fibers that provide for stretch can deteriorate over time just sitting on a shelf. Give the suit a good tug—if there's no "give" or it "gives" once and collapses (sometimes you can even *hear* the old latex breaking apart!), that suit is not gonna be your second skin.

Comfort is a different issue. If you are planning to wear a vintage suit, you must determine just how much discomfort you are willing to endure for the look you hope to achieve.

Fabric: The fabric of older suits is much much thicker and rougher than today's slimy smooth suits. Suits were made from wool, cotton, silk, rayon (or blends), and then intertwined with rubber, lastex, latex, or other synthetic elastic material. When the elastic fibers break down, the fabric gets particularly scratchy. I had a 1960s suit that was so scratchy that within five minutes of putting it on I had torn it off and pitched it in the trash. Thicker fabric will also be warmer in hot weather. Once wet, the suit may take hours to dry.

Reinforcing: Ladies, either you have worn a suit that's completely reinforced with wires and whatnot or you haven't. Suffice it to say, even if the suit fits you like a glove, you'll find the reinforcing might pinch, chafe, poke, bind, and hurt even more once wet. You may find yourself physically restrained enough that swimming is difficult or uncomfortable. On the upside, your soggy body will be rearranged into an attractive shape.

Styling: Remember, it was a more modest time. The older suits will cover nearly all your torso—including much of your back, upper chest area, and upper thighs. Again, this may reduce your physical comfort level and be more confining while moving about.

If you're gonna wear an old suit, girls *and* guys, test it out at home or wear it in a small backyard setting first. I've worn cute old suits and then been stuck in them all day, suffering. A pretest will give you an opportunity to check out the comfort level, how it looks and how it feels—*both dry and wet*. Older swimsuits have their quirks, and you might be very glad you tested them in the privacy of your bathtub.

Beach Towels: The best towels going in the thrift are the big beach towels, and shoppers often overlook them. You can get a plain beach towel, but I much prefer the kooky ones. The market for most beach towels is kids and teens, so the graphics are bold, bright, and fun. Like T-shirts, many come with slogans and trendy illustrations so you can pick to suit your tastes—favorite beer, cool vacation spot, funniest cartoon character, etc. Lots of leftover fads and celebrities—I have two disco towels, a bunch of Dukes of Hazard, a Wacky Packages towel, a couple of 1960s "with-it" towels, and my fave "naughty" free-love towel: Uncle Sam Says Don't Forget to Take Your Pill Today! Plenty of other great moments in history are well represented in the beach towel section—California Raisins, professional sports teams, Transformers, stock-car racing, and Ninja Turtles.

Extra-large bath towels are not that common at thrifts, so consider using a beach towel in your bathroom. Sadly, many beach towels are cheaply made and paper-thin. Persevere till you find a big fluffy one.

19 Thrifting for Pets

Oh, you say, I *never* see animals at the thrift stores! Well, dig this. What if I told you there was a place (usually in a grubby neighborhood) where you could pick out a dog, cat, or some other animal that had been devalued and discarded by its previous owner? And these "used" but perfectly functional animals were available for a few bucks, with the money being returned to the charitable organization that provided it? When you entered this place you had no idea what might be "in stock," but you were psyched to come away with a purchase anyhow? What if there was the tantalizing possibility that for almost no money you might acquire an unrecognized animal of value, like one of those cats that sells for $300 "new"? Do the words "Fresh Stock Daily" sound familiar? Does this sound like thrifting? I've thought about it a hundred ways and it seems irrefutable that animal shelters are simply thrift stores that specialize in pets. I urge you to patronize them.

SWELL STUFF FOR FLUFFY—PRACTICALLY FREE!

Like every other member of your family, your pet can be provided for cheaply and creatively from the thrifts. Old blankets, quilts, coats, and sweaters make cozy bedding. When bedding becomes too disgusting with hair and drool, simply discard and thrift another $2 blanket. For those smaller creatures, there's plenty of baskets out there—and who doesn't just *adore* the sight of a Chihuahua in a little basket? Any old pillow can go in the basket.

Toys: A dog doesn't recognize a plastic bone with a smiley face on it as being a toy. It'll play with anything. Ditto for cats. Anything that rolls is good. A bag of used tennis balls will keep a dog happy for months. Or how about those el cheapo bags of torn-up stuffed animals? Dole 'em out to Rover one at a time. Yummy. (Cut off the plastic eyes first.) I once thrifted an old mink stole—the kind made of whole minks with heads, feet, and tails. I separated the minks and gave 'em to the cat to play with. A big hit. Very *Wild Kingdom* watching the cat drag a dead flat mink around.

Bowls: Don't give your pet one of those horribly ugly plastic feeding bowls they sell at pet stores. There's thousands of cool bowls out there—all just as functional. When dealing with a hungry animal, the bowl's stability counts. The heavier the better, so diner china, Pyrex, or metal mixing bowls (for that high-tech look) are good choices. Remember, the pet only sees the food. You're the one who has to look at the bowl, so pick out a nice one. When I go away on vacation, the cats eat from a reserve of food in a giant Fiestaware mixing bowl. This *horrifies* fussy collectible-types, but hey, it's a bowl! What are the cats gonna do—eat it?

People can get obsessive about "thinking for" their pets, but remember the obvious: However cute and clever you think they might be, their brains are much, much smaller than ours. They have *no idea* if something is "used" or didn't come from the pet super-store. If you buy Fluffy a new bowl that says "cat" on it, you're the only one who can read it, and do you really need to be reminded?

Other pet items—both intended for pet use and not—turn up in thrifts. Dog- and cat-carrying cases are quite common. (I once followed a woman all around a store hoping she'd put back this beautiful old wicker cat-carrying case. She did not, and I've never seen another like it.) "Housing" is available—Habitrails for hamsters, birdcages, rodent cages, and aquariums (good for fish, lizards, tarantulas, small turtles, newts, rodents, etc.). Don't pay too much for an aquarium. Somebody might have given it away because it leaked, but it's more likely that they got bored with whatever used to live inside it. A good hearty scrub with some disinfectant (then rinse thoroughly!) will make any living quarters fresh and clean for your pet.

This cat is just as unhappy in a used carrying case as in a brand-new expensive one.
PHOTO BY VANESSA DOMICO

PET BOOKS

Don't forget the book racks. Pick up a book about the care and feeding of your pet. Or look out for those gift books for hyper-pet people. There are people out there who appreciate books like *Does Your Cat Have ESP?* or *Famous Dogs in History*.

And speaking of fish . . . If you think a cat's brain is small, you should see a fish brain. No need to buy those silly little castles they sell in pet stores that are supposed to provide the fish with diversion and under-the-sea verisimilitude. Those aquarium *objets* turn up in thrifts—but even easier, anything waterproof can go into the fish tank! Use your imagination—how about one of those "World's Greatest Fisherman" statuettes? Mismatched salt and pepper shakers? A cup and saucer? Just clean the object well and stick it in the tank. The fish will love you for it.

Notes

CHAPTER 2

1. Fritz, Michael, "Collectibles Are Not Forever," *Forbes* (August 8, 1988), p. 100.

2. Scott Bruce quoted in Fritz, "Collectibles Are Not Forever," p. 101.

3. Robert Williams quoted in "Bucks From the Bicentennial," *Time* (September 29, 1975), p. 73.

4. Lendler, Ernest, "The Great American Bicentennial Sale," *New Times* (November 28, 1975), p. 41.

CHAPTER 4

1. Kendall, Helen and W. E. Coughlin, "Five New Miracle Fibers," *Good Housekeeping* (September 1951), p. 197.

2. Diane Cantua, Textile Instructor, Fashion Institute of Design and Merchandising, quoted in *Museum of Modern Mythology Newsletter* (vol. 4, no. 3/4, fall/winter 1987/88, San Francisco, CA), p. 5.

3. Diana Vreeland quoted in *Cheap Chic: Hundreds of Money Saving Hints to Create Your Own Great Look* by Caterine Milinaire and Carol Troy (Harmony Books, New York, 1975), p. 56.

4. Wolfe, Tom, "The Me Decade and the Third Great Awakening," *Mauve Gloves & Madmen, Clutter & Vine and Other Stories* (Farrar, Straus & Giroux, New York, 1976), p. 130.

5. Jeff Errick quoted in *Museum of Modern Mythology Newsletter* (vol. 4, no. 3/4, fall/winter 1987/88, San Francisco, CA), p. 4.

6. Ellen Sweeney quoted in "The Fabric of Our Lives? Polyester Makes a Comeback," by Peter Callahan, *OMNI* (August 1993), p. 20.

7. Liebowitz, Fran, "Clothes with Pictures and/or Writing on Them: Yes—Another Complaint," *Metropolitan Life* (E. P. Dutton, New York, 1978), p. 122.

8. Gaines, Stephen, *Simply Halston* (G. P. Putnam's Sons, New York, 1991), p. 237.

9. Bud Johns quoted in "Derriere Cri" by Subrata N. Chakravarty, *Forbes* (October 27, 1980), p. 50.

10. Halston quoted in *Obsession: The Lives and Times of Calvin Klein* by Steven S. Gaines (Carol Publishing Group, New York, 1994), p. 215.

11. Keenan, Joe, "It's All in the Jeans," *Vogue* (August 1992), p. 297.

12. Paul Guez quoted in "Dungaree Dupe" by Dan Dorfman, *Esquire* (January 1, 1979), p. 12.

13. Calvin Klein quoted in "The Snooty Dame at the Block Party" by Gerri Hirshey, *The New York Times Magazine* (October 24, 1993), p. 142.

14. Calvin Klein quoted in *Obsession: The Lives and Times of Calvin Klein* by Steven S. Gaines (Carol Publishing Group, New York, 1994), p. 266.

15. Calvin Klein quoted in Gaines, *Obsession*, p. 274.

16. Howard Goldstein quoted in "Designer Jeans Bottom Out" by Bernice Kanner, *New York* (May 1982), p. 25.

17. Duka, John, "The Top Ten Designer Jeans," *New York* (July 23, 1979), p. 55.

Chapter 6

1. Johnson, Joyce, *Minor Characters* (Picador, London, 1983), p. 34.

2. Johnson, *Minor Characters*, p. 192.

3. Lipton, Lawrence, *The Holy Barbarians* (Julian Messner, Inc., New York, 1959), pp. 149–50.

4. Lipton, *The Holy Barbarians*, p. 155.

5. Selvin, Joel, *Summer of Love: The Inside Story of LSD, Rock 'n' Roll, Free Love and High Times in the Wild West* (Plume/Penguin Books, New York, 1994), p. 5.

6. Jerry Hopkins quoted in *I'm with the Band: Confessions of a Groupie* by Pamela Des Barres (Jove Books, New York, 1987), p. 156.

7. "Secondhand Chic," *Time* (January 13, 1975), p. 52.

8. Milinaire, Caterine and Carol Troy, *Cheap Chic: Hundreds of Money Saving Hints to Create Your Own Great Look* (Harmony Books, New York, 1975), p. 9.

9. Milinaire and Troy, *Cheap Chic*, p. 86.

10. Ruth Morley quoted in "'Annie Hall' Appeal: Whimsy, Keaton Fun" by Alexandra Anderson, *Vogue* (August 1978), p. 178.

11. Malcolm McLaren quoted in "McRock: Pop as a Commodity" by Mary Harron, *Facing the Music*, edited by Simon Frith (Pantheon, New York, 1988), p. 198.

12. James Laver quoted in *Taste: The Secret Meaning of Things* by Stephen Bayley (Pantheon Books, New York, 1991), p. xiv.

Chapter 7

1. French, Marilyn, *The Women's Room* (Jove Publications, New York, 1977), p. 349.

2. Richardson, Harry, "Every Man Needs a Corner of His Own," *Better Homes and Gardens* (May 1949), p. 55.

Chapter 9

1. Outstanding Men Cooks, *Men Cooking* (Lane Book Company, Menlo Park, CA, 1963), p. 9.

2. Mondale, Joan, *The Mondale Family Cookbook* (Mondale for

President Committee, Inc., Washington D.C., 1984), p. 100.

3. Truax, Carol, *Liberace Cooks!* (Doubleday, New York, 1970), p. 108.

4. *Put Some Kraut in Your Life*, The National Kraut Packers Association, 108½ East Main Street, St. Charles, IL 60174, p. 27.

5. Mazel, Judy, *The Beverly Hills Diet* (Macmillan Publishing Co., Inc., New York, 1981), p. 124.

6. "Fondue Pots: Playing with Fire?," *Consumer Reports* (March 1972), p. 141.

CHAPTER 11

1. Blochman, Lawrence, *Here's How!—A Round-the-World Bar Guide* (New American Library, New York, 1957), p. viii.

2. Blochman, *Here's How!*, p. 66.

CHAPTER 12

1. Pollak, Richard, "Romance Slaves of Harlequin," *Nation* (March 16, 1992), p. 336.

2. Ibid., p. 334.

3. Radway, Janice A., *Reading the Romance: Women, Patriarchy and Popular Literature* (University of North Carolina Press, Chapel Hill, NC, 1984), pp. 59–60.

4. Pollak, "Romance Slaves of Harlequin," p. 336.

CHAPTER 15

1. Charley Lang quoted in "The Decorations All Go Together in Charley Lang's House of Puzzles" *People Weekly* (November 28, 1988), p. 117.

2. Reilley, Ottilie H., *Canasta: The Argentine Rummy Game* (Ives Washburn, Inc., New York, 1949), p. 63.

CHAPTER 16

1. Borden, Fred, *Bowling: Knowledge Is the Key* (Bowling Concepts Inc., Akron, Ohio, 1987), p. 78.

2. Harwood, Michael, "America with Its Ears On," *The New York Times Magazine* (April 25, 1976), p. 28.

3. Langway, Lynn, "Cashing In on C.B.," *Newsweek* (May 31, 1976), p. 64.

4. Arneson, D. J. and Tony Tallarico, *C.B. Jokes* (Charlton Press Inc., Derby, Conn., 1977), p. 15.

5. Overview of Beau Colle, *C.B. for Christians: How to Minister and Witness with C.B.* (Broadman Press, Nashville, TN, 1976), provided by Randy Reeves.

CHAPTER 17

1. Jim Shaw quoted in "An Art-Felt Collection of Abandoned Works" by Katy Kelly, *USA Today* (August 11, 1994), p. D8.

2. Walter Keane quoted in "The Man Who Paints Those Big Eyes" by Jane Howard, *Life* (August 27, 1965), p. 42.

3. Andy Warhol quoted in Howard, "The Man Who Paints Those Big Eyes," p. 42.

4. Quoted in Howard, "The Man Who Paints Those Big Eyes," p. 42.

5. Walter Keane quoted in Howard, "The Man Who Paints Those Big Eyes," p. 39.

CHAPTER 18

1. "Teaching Your Son to Be a Teen-age Barbecue Chef," *Sunset* (August 1959), p. 87.

2. Hodges, Betti and Joe O'Toole, *Macrame Boutique* (Craft Publications Inc., Stone Mountain, Georgia, 1976), p. 2.

Bibliography

GENERAL

Bayley, Stephen. *Taste: The Secret Meaning of Things.* New York: Pantheon Books, 1991.

The Berkeley Pop Culture Project. *The Whole Pop Catalog.* New York: Avon Books, 1991.

Brown, Curtis F. *Star-Spangled Kitsch: An Astounding and Tastelessly Illustrated Exploration of the Bawdy, Gaudy, Shoddy Mass-Art Culture in This Grand Land of Ours.* New York: Universe Books, 1975.

Carter, Mary Randolph. *American Junk.* New York: Viking Studio Books, 1994.

Corn, Joseph J. and Brian Horrigan. *Yesterday's Tomorrows.* New York: Summit Books, 1984.

Cornfield, Betty and Owen Edwards. *Quintessence: The Quality of Having It.* New York: Crown Publishers, Inc., 1983.

Edelstein, Andrew J. and Kevin McDonough. *The Seventies: From Hot Pants to Hot Tubs.* New York: Dutton, 1990.

Hine, Thomas. *Populuxe.* New York: Knopf, 1986.

Johnson, Richard A. *American Fads.* New York: Beech Tree Books, 1985.

Kennedy, Pagan. *Platforms: A Microwaved Cultural Chronicle of the 1970s.* New York: St. Martin's Press, 1994.

Marling, Karal Ann. *As Seen on TV: The Visual Culture of Everyday Life in the 1950s.* Cambridge, Mass.: Harvard University Press, 1994.

Massey, Anne. *Interior Design of the 20th Century.* New York: Thames and Hudson, 1990.

Panati, Charles. *Extraordinary Origins of Everyday Things.* New York: Perennial Library, 1987.

Stern, Jane and Michael Stern. *The Encyclopedia of Bad Taste.* New York: HarperPerennial, 1990.

———. *Jane and Michael Sterns' Encyclopedia of Pop Culture.* New York: HarperPerennial, 1992.

FASHION

Cunningham, Patricia A. and Susan Voso Lab, eds. *Dress and Popular Culture.* Bowling Green, Ky.: Bowling Green State University Popular Press, 1991.

Finlayson, Iain. *Denim: An American Legend.* New York: Fireside Books, 1990.

Gaines, Steven S. *Obsession: The Lives and Times of Calvin Klein.* New York: Carol Publishing Group, 1994.

———. *Simply Halston.* New York: G. P. Putnam's Sons, 1991.

Houck, Catherine. *The Fashion Encyclopedia.* New York: St. Martin's Press, 1982.

Johnson, Quendrith, ed. *Museum of Modern Mythology Newsletter,* vol. 4, no. 3/4, fall/winter 1987/88, San Francisco, Calif.

Leibowitz, Fran. *Metropolitan Life.* New York: E. P. Dutton, 1978.

Martin, Richard. *Splash!: A History of Swimwear.* New York: Rizzoli, 1990.

Melinkoff, Ellen. *What We Wore: An Offbeat Social History of Women's Clothing, 1950 to 1980.* New York: William Morrow and Company, Inc., 1984.

Molloy, John T. *Dress for Success.* New York: Warner Books, 1976.

———. *The Woman's Dress for Success Book.* New York: Warner Books, 1977.

Plutzik, Roberta. *Bargain Chic.* Secaucus, New Jersey: Lyle Stuart, Inc., 1985.

Steele, H. Thomas. *The Hawaiian Shirt.* New York: Abbeville Press, 1984.

Sudjic, Deyan. *Cult Heroes: How to Be Famous for More Than 15 Minutes.* New York: W. W. Norton and Company, 1989.

Wolfe, Tom, "The Me Decade and the Third Great Awakening," in *Mauve Gloves & Madmen, Clutter & Vine and Other Stories.* New York: Farrar, Straus & Giroux, 1976.

HISTORY OF THRIFT SHOPPERS

Des Barres, Pamela. *I'm with the Band: Confessions of a Groupie.* New York: Jove Books, 1987.

Frith, Simon, ed. *Facing the Music.* New York: Pantheon, 1988. (See in particular "McRock: Pop as a Commodity" by Mary Harron.)

Hebdige, Dick. *Subculture: The Meaning of Style.* New York: Metheun & Co., 1979.

Gold, Herbert. *Bohemia—Where Art, Angst, Love and Strong Coffee Meet.* New York: Simon & Schuster, 1993.

Johnson, Joyce. *Minor Characters.* London: Picador, 1983.

Kaplan, E. Ann. *Rocking Around the Clock: Music Television, Postmodernism and Consumer Culture.* New York: Routledge, 1987.

Lipton, Lawrence. *The Holy Barbarians.* New York: Julian Messner, Inc., 1959.

Lobenthal, Joel. *Radical Rags: Fashions of the Sixties.* New York: Abbeville Press, 1990.

Love, Harriet. *Guide to Vintage Chic.* New York: Holt, Rinehart and Winston, 1982.

McRobbie, Angela, ed. *Zoot Suits and Second-hand Dresses: An*

Anthology of Fashion and Music. Boston: Unwin Hyman, 1988. (See in particular "Second-hand Dresses and the Role of the Ragmarket" by Angela McRobbie.)

Milinaire, Caterine and Carol Troy. *Cheap Chic: Hundreds of Money Saving Hints to Create Your Own Great Look.* New York: Harmony Books, 1975.

Polhemus, Ted. *Street Style: From Sidewalk to Catwalk.* New York: Thames and Hudson, 1994.

Polhemus, Ted. *Style Surfing: What to Wear in the Third Millennium.* New York: Thames and Hudson, 1996.

Selvin, Joel. *Summer of Love: The Inside Story of LSD, Rock 'n' Roll, Free Love and High Times in the Wild West.* New York: Plume/Penguin Books, 1994.

Stern, Jane and Michael Stern. *Sixties People.* New York: Albert A. Knopf, 1990.

FURNITURE

Bosker, Gideon, Michelle Mancini, and John Gramstad. *Fabulous Fabrics of the 50s.* San Francisco: Chronicle Books, 1992.

Greene, Fayal. *The Couch Book.* New York: Hearst Books, 1993.

Schwartz, Marvin D. *Please Be Seated: The Evolution of the Chair 2000 B.C.–2000 A.D.* New York: The American Federation of Arts Exhibition Catalog, 1968.

Williams, Adele. *Thrift Shop Decorating.* New York: Arbor House, 1976.

KITCHEN, DINING ROOM, AND PATIO

Berland, Theodore. *Rating the Diets.* New York: Beekman House, 1983.

Bosker, Gideon. *Great Shakes: Salt and Peppers for All Tastes.* New York: Abbeville Press, 1986.

Deutsch, Ronald M. *The New Nuts Among the Berries: How Nutrition Nonsense Captured America.* Palo Alto, Calif.: Bull Publishing Company, 1977.

Di Noto, Andrea. *Art Plastic: Designed for Living.* New York: Abbeville Press, 1984.

Goldberg, Michael J. *Collectible Plastic Kitchenware and Dinnerware.* Atglen, Penn.: Schiffer Publishing Company, 1995.

Hodges, Betti and Joe O'Toole. *Macrame Boutique.* Stone Mountain, Ga.: Craft Publications Inc., 1976.

Klein, Maurice, ed. *The Celebrity Cookbook: Favorite Recipes from the Famous.* Encino, Calif.: Treasured Publications Inc., 1978.

Klever, Eva. *Fondues from Around the World.* Woodbury, N.Y.: Barron's, 1984.

Lifshey, Earl. *The Housewares Story.* Chicago: National Housewares Manufacturers Association, 1973.

Lindenberger, Jan. *Collecting Plastics: A Handbook and Price Guide.* Atglen, Penn.: Schiffer, 1991.

Mazel, Judy. *The Beverly Hills Diet.* New York: Macmillan Publishing Co., Inc., 1981.

Merriman, Beth. *The Fondue Cookbook.* New York: Grosset & Dunlap, 1969.

Mondale, Joan. *The Mondale Family Cookbook.* Washington, D.C.: Mondale for President Committee, Inc., 1984.

Outstanding Men Cooks, *Men Cooking.* Menlo Park, Calif.: Lane Book Company, 1963.

Rocknow, Hazel and Julius Rocknow. *Creative Home Decorating.* New York: H. S. Stuttman Company, 1953.

Sloan, Bob and Steven Guarnaccia. *A Stiff Drink and a Close Shave: The Lost Arts of Manliness.* San Francisco: Chronicle Books, 1995.

Stern, Jane and Michael Stern. *American Gourmet.* New York: HarperCollins Publishers, 1991.

Thaler, M. N. *It's Fun to Fondue.* New York: Centaur House Inc., 1962.

Truax, Carol. *Liberace Cooks!* New York: Doubleday, 1970.

BAR AREA

Bergeron, Victor. *Trader Vic's Bar Guide, Revised.* Garden City, N.Y.: Doubleday and Company, Inc., 1972.

Blochman, Lawrence. *Here's How!—A Round-the-World Bar Guide.* New York: New American Library, 1957.

Collier, Jim. *Cheers!* New York: Avon Books, 1960.

Collins, Philip. *Smokerama: Classic Tobacco Accoutrements.* San Francisco: Chronicle Books, 1992.

Duffy, Patrick Gavin. *The Official Mixer's Manual.* New York: Doubleday and Company, Inc., 1956.

Grimes, William. *Straight Up or On the Rocks: A Cultural History of American Drink.* New York: Simon & Schuster, 1993.

McMahon, Ed. *Ed McMahon's Barside Companion.* New York: Pocket Books, 1970.

LIBRARY

Bonn, Thomas L. *Undercover: An Illustrated History of American Mass Market Paperbacks.* New York: Penguin Books, 1982.

Radway, Janice A. *Reading the Romance: Women, Patriarchy and Popular Literature.* Chapel Hill, N.C.: University of North Carolina Press, 1984.

ENTERTAINMENT AREA

Goldman, Albert. *Sound Bites.* New York: Random House, 1992.

Hanson, Kitty. *Disco Fever: The Beat, People, Places, Styles, Deejays, Groups and The Latest Disco Steps.* New York: Signet Books, 1978.

Lanza, Joseph. *Elevator Music: A Surreal History of Muzak, Easy-Listening and Other Moodsong.* New York: St. Martin's Press, 1994.

Moore, Judy and Leslie Laurence. *Skating Craze*. Columbus, Ohio: School Book Fairs, Inc., 1980.

Vale, V. and Andrea Juno, eds. *Incredibly Strange Music Volume I*. San Francisco: Re/Search Publications, 1993.

————. *Incredibly Strange Music Volume II*. San Francisco: Re/Search Publications, 1994.

TOYS AND SPORTS

Borden, Fred. *Bowling: Knowledge is the Key*. Akron, Ohio: Bowling Concepts Inc., 1987.

Forslund, Ellen. *Bowling for Women*. New York: Ronald Press Co., 1964.

Kaye, Marvin. *The Story of Monopoly, Silly Putty, Bingo, Twister, Frisbee, Scrabble, Et Cetera*. New York: Stern and Day, 1973.

Kirchner, Paul. *Forgotten Fads and Fabulous Flops*. Los Angeles: General Publishing Group, 1995.

Reilley, Ottilie H. *Canasta: The Argentine Rummy Game*. New York: Ives Washburn, Inc., 1949.

Roth, Mark and Chuck Pezzano. *The Mark Roth Book of Bowling*. New York: The Rutledge Press, 1981.

Sabin, Francene and Louis Sabin. *The One, the Only, the Original Jigsaw Puzzle Book*. Chicago: Henry Regnery Company, 1977.

Scarpone, Desi. *Board Games*. Atglen, Penn.: Schiffer, 1995.

Steele, H. Thomas. *Bowl-O-Rama: The Visual Arts of Bowling*. New York: Abbeville Press, 1986.

Stern, Sydney Ladensohn and Ted Schoenhaus: *Toyland: The High-Stakes Game of the Toy Industry*. Chicago: Contemporary Books, 1990.

Tilley, Roger. *A History of Playing Cards*. New York: Clarkson N. Potter, Inc., 1973.

Williams, Anne D. *Jigsaw Puzzles: An Illustrated History and Price Guide*. Radnor, Penn.: Wallace-Homestead Book Company, 1990.

ART

Morton, Jim, ed. *Pop Void No. 1*. San Francisco: Pop Void Publications, 1987.

Parfrey, Adam. *Cult Rapture: The Revelations of the Apocalyptic Mind*. Portland, Oreg.: Feral House, 1995.

Shaw, Jim. *Thrift Store Paintings: Paintings Found in Thrift Stores*. Hollywood, Calif.: Heavy Industry Publications, 1990.

Shelby, Forrest. *Walter and Margaret Keane—They Give Shape to the Unseen*. Tomorrow's Masters Series. San Francisco: Johnson Meyers Publishers, 1962.

MISCELLANEOUS

How To Hear and Speak C.B. in a Short-Short. Kalamazoo, Mich.: Whacky World Productions, 1976.

Arneson, D. J. and Tony Tallarico. *C.B. Jokes*. Derby, Conn.: Charlton Press Inc., 1977.

Birnbach, Lisa, ed. *The Official Preppy Handbook*. New York: Workman Publishing, 1980.

Colle, Beau. *C.B. For Christians: How to Minister and Witness with C.B.* Nashville, Tenn.: Broadman Press, 1976.

Index

ABOUT THE CONTRIBUTORS

CANDI STRECKER is the author of the definitive and highly recommended 1970s study, *It's a Wonderful Lifestyle: A Seventies Flashback.* Parts 1 and 2 are available for $4.00 each from Candi Strecker, P.O. Box 515, Brisbane, CA 94004-0515.

JOHN MARR banged out issue after issue of his long-running zine, *Murder Can Be Fun,* on a trusty manual typewriter. MCBF meticulously details his favorite crimes, disasters, and other "abnormal" behavior. Send $2.00 for a sample issue to John Marr, MCBF, P.O. Box 640111, San Francisco, CA 94164.

LYNN PERIL's zine, *Mystery Date: One Gal's Guide to the Good Stuff,* unearths the lost meanings of thrifted board games, beauty guides, and home economics textbooks. Send $2.00 for a sample issue to Mystery Date, P.O. Box 641592, San Francisco, CA 94164-1592.

Comments, complaints, and tales of "Best Thing Ever Thrifted" can be sent to Al Hoff at P.O. Box 90282, Pittsburgh, PA 15224 or by e-mail to hoffo@drycas.club.cc.cmu.edu. Sample copies of *Thrift SCORE: The Zine About Thriftin'* can be obtained from the above address. Please include a buck and a first-class stamp.